Redeeming the Time

Redeeming the Time

*An historical and theological study
of the Church's rule of prayer
and the regular services of the Church.*

Byron David Stuhlman

THE CHURCH HYMNAL CORPORATION, NEW YORK

The Church Hymnal Corporation
800 Second Avenue
New York, NY 10017

5   4   3   2   1

Contents

Tables in the Text

Author's Preface

I owe the basic insights developed in this present work to two people, Alexander Schmemann and Howard Galley. It was Alexander Schmemann whose *Introduction to Liturgical Theology* first taught me the importance of what he calls "the liturgy of time." Ultimately, however, I have come to understand that liturgy differently from the way in which he understood it. My 1991 doctoral dissertation at Duke University, "An Architecture of Time: A Critical Study of Alexander Schmemann's Liturgical Theology," argues that to understand the liturgical tradition properly, we need to make connections between the temporal cycles of the day, the week, and the year, and the rites which are characteristic of those cycles—the daily office, the eucharist on the Lord's Day, and the baptismal liturgy proper to Easter, Pentecost, and Epiphany. On occasion I have included materials from that dissertation in this present book.

It was Howard Galley who first called my attention to the fact that the calendar—the rhythm of the day, the week, and the year—constitutes the *rule* of prayer which *regulates* what

American Prayer Books designate as "the *regular* services" of the church—"*Daily* Morning and Evening Prayer," and "the Holy Eucharist" as "the principal act of Christian Worship on *the Lord's Day and other major Feasts*" (*Book of Common Prayer 1979*, page 13). In this work I argue that the *Book of Common Prayer 1979*, by removing baptism from the pastoral offices and by specifying certain days as baptismal feasts, also restores baptism to its proper place as a *regular* service of the church. In our present prayer book baptism has become once again the characteristic rite of the great feasts of the annual cycle.

Anglicans have customarily argued for their rule of prayer on the basis of tradition, and they have done so very well. What we have all too often failed to do is to explore the meaning of the rule of prayer handed down to us by tradition—to articulate the theological connections between the various cycles and the rites proper to them. I have focussed my attention in this book on those connections, developing the insights of Schmemann and Galley to understand the church's liturgy as an "architecture of time" (to borrow a phrase from Abraham Heschel). This is an architecture which is articulated not only by the ancient sacramentaries and euchologies, but also by the *Book of Common Prayer 1979*. The church's rule of prayer as an architecture of time is designed to frame our lives in the context of our relationship to God, a relationship which finds its focus in the death and resurrection of Jesus. It is Christ's passover from death to life by way of the cross that finds expression in the church's celebration of light each day at sunrise and sunset, in the eucharistic service of word and table each week on the Lord's Day, and in the baptismal liturgy each year at the Great Vigil of Easter. These are the connections which we must make if we are to understand the church's rule of prayer not just in terms of tradition, but also in terms of the church's witness to Christ, whose death and resurrection are the mystery of our salvation, the tangible embodiment of the saving purposes of God as God reaches out to touch and transform our lives.

I wish to acknowledge here the guidance of Geoffrey Wainwright and Teresa Berger, who have been my mentors for the past three years in liturgical studies, and the assistance of Brent Laytham, a fellow graduate student, and Richard Bardusch, a divinity student at Duke, who as readers of the draft of this work have sought to sharpen the clarity of my argument. I have also incorporated suggestions from Marion Hatchett, Boone Porter, and Rowan Greer, who graciously read this manuscript after I submitted it to the Church Hymnal Corporation.

Byron David Stuhlman

The Feast of St. Polycarp, 1992

Introduction

Making Connections: The Church's Rule of Prayer and the Regular Services of the Church

An often-neglected clue to the meaning of Christian worship is what we might call its temporal "architecture"—the rule of prayer which determines what service is appropriate for a particular occasion according to when that occasion falls in the rhythms of the day, the week, and the year. The attentive reader of *The Book of Common Prayer* will notice how these rhythms structure the rule of prayer by which that book is organized. Similar patterns can be found in the worship of other churches as well. A frequently-unrecognized aspect of the liturgical genius of Thomas Cranmer, to whom we are indebted for the first *Book of Common Prayer*, is the skillful way in which he preserved largely intact the rule of prayer or pattern of worship which was worked out in the early centuries of the church's life.

This rule of prayer, in turn, is the church's adaptation, its messianic transformation, of Judaism's rule of prayer. Abraham Heschel has written of the Jewish liturgical tradition:

> Jewish ritual may be characterized as the art of significant forms in time, as *architecture of time*. Most of its observances . . . depend on a certain hour of the day or season of the year. It is, for example, the evening, the morning, or afternoon that brings with it the call to prayer. The main themes of faith lie in the realm of time. We remember the day of exodus from Egypt, the day when Israel stood at Sinai; and our Messianic hope is the expectation of a day, of the end of days.[1]

It is the "Messianic hope" and the belief that the "day" has come and the "the end of days" is upon us that differentiate Christianity from Judaism and Christian liturgy from Jewish liturgy. For the Christian creed confesses its belief in Jesus as the Messiah who *"came* down from heaven" and *"will come* again to judge the living and the dead." The basic pattern of Christian worship is, like the Jewish pattern, an architecture of time, but it finds a new focus in the mystery of Christ, who is the Lord of time.

The prayer book pattern of worship consists of four temporal cycles, each with its distinctive rites:

1. **the daily cycle** with **worship at dawn and sunset;**
2. **the weekly cycle** which finds its focus in the celebration of the **Eucharist** on the **Lord's Day;**
3. **the annual cycle** organized around the feasts of **Easter and Pentecost** as one pole and around the feasts of **Christmas**

and Epiphany as a secondary pole, with **the baptismal vigil** on Easter, Pentecost, and (in the East and in the *Book of Common Prayer 1979*) Epiphany or the Sunday after Epiphany as its distinctive rite; and

4. **the cycle of the Christian life,** with the **pastoral offices for important moments in the lives of individuals** as its distinctive rites.

The distinctive services of the first three cycles are the *regular* services of the church—that is, the services *regulated* by the calendar as the church's *rule* of prayer. The services of the fourth cycle are *occasional* services by their very nature, for (while they may be integrated into the regular services) they are designed for *pastoral* occasions in the lives of individual Christians which no calendar can regulate. Cranmer attempted to preserve each of these cycles and the distinctive services proper to them.

Anglicans more than any other church of the Reformation worked to preserve the pattern of daily worship (daily Morning and Evening Prayer). Like Luther and Calvin, Cranmer made valiant (but largely unsuccessful) efforts to restore the Sunday eucharist with a general communion of the congregation as the distinctive form of weekly worship. These are what Episcopalians have come to call the *regular services*[2] of the church. Cranmer was less perceptive, however, in the way in which he dealt with baptism, the characteristic rite of the annual cycle of the church's liturgy. He recognized (as the introduction to baptism in the 1549 Prayer Book reveals) that baptism was the distinctive service for Easter and Pentecost,[3] although he did not think it opportune to restrict baptism to those feasts in his day, and treated it as a *pastoral or occasional office* appropriate to Sundays and feasts rather than as a *regular service* for the baptismal feasts (as the *Book of Common Prayer 1979* has done).[4] The other pastoral offices of the 1549 book show a sensitive re-appropriation of ancient forms. Confirmation was rethought as a rite of commitment after catechesis;[5] Marriage was intended to be integrated into the weekly cycle so that the newly-married couple could make communion at the Sunday eucharist the first act of their married life;[6] provision was made to communicate the sick, when possible, from elements consecrated at the parish eucharist;[7] unction, long understood as a last rite, was restored as a sacrament of healing;[8] an appropriate form was provided for the reconciliation of a penitent[9] and notice was taken of Lent as a season for public penance;[10] burial rites were integrated with the daily office and given a set of eucharistic propers.[11]

Cranmer handled tradition with great sensitivity (though some gains—like extended communion of the sick and unction—were lost in 1552). But he failed to undergird his preservation of the traditional pattern of worship with appropriate theological links between the cycles and their distinctive rites. He did not, in other words, find a way to relate services theologically to the appointed times for their celebration. The key to Morning Prayer and Evening Prayer as the early church understood them was the celebration of the resurrection of Christ as the sun rose in the morning sky and the celebration of the Christ as the light that darkness has never quenched as lamps were lit at sunset. Cranmer, however, placed his emphasis on these services as a means by which

> all the whole Bible, (or the greatest parte thereof) should be read ouer once in the yeare, intendyng thereby that the Cleargie, and specially suche as were Ministers of the congregacion, should (by often reading and meditacion of Gods worde) be stirred up to godlines themselfes, and be more able also to exhorte other by wholsome doctrine, and to confute them that were aduersaries to the trueth. And further, that the people (by daily hearyng of holy scripture

read in the Churche) should continuallye profite more and more in the knowledge of God, and bee the more inflamed with the loue of his true religion.[12]

Here the theological link of these daily services with their time of celebration has been lost sight of. The key to the celebration of the eucharist on the Lord's Day in the early centuries is found in Luke's account of the meal at Emmaus as well as in the story of the last supper: the rite is both an *anamnesis* or remembrance of Christ's death and a means of sharing the life of the Risen Lord who manifested himself in the breaking of bread. But Cranmer's eucharistic rite, in a way characteristic of most Western eucharistic theology, Catholic and Reformed, finds its exclusive focus in the sacrifice which Christ made on the cross: the congregation is assembled in God's name "to celebrate the commemoration of the most glorious death of [God's] sonne."[13] The link with Christ's resurrection, his *passover* from death to life, is forgotten. No connection is made between the Lord's Day as the weekly feast of the Lord's resurrection and the Lord's Supper as the rite which celebrates that resurrection. Similarly, in the introduction to the baptismal rite, Cranmer acknowledges the ancient practice of restricting baptism to the feasts of Easter and Pentecost. Yet he fails to make the theological link between baptism as the rite by which we die with Christ to sin that we may rise with him to new life (Romans 6) and in which we receive the gift of the Spirit and the feasts of Easter and the Day of Pentecost which celebrate those realities.

The rites characteristic of the cycles which provide the structure of the church's liturgy, when they are grounded in tradition alone, without making these theological links, can seem entirely arbitrary. There is no reason that we as Christians should worship daily at dawn and sunset if these times have no particular theological meaning; it would be equally appropriate to gather publicly at noon, or to do our private bible-reading whenever it best fits our schedule. There is no reason that it is appropriate for us to celebrate the eucharist once a week, rather than daily, or monthly, or quarterly, or annually, if the rite has no theological connection with the day on which it is celebrated. The reason set out by Cranmer for the celebration of baptism at Easter and Pentecost (in the ancient church) or on Sundays and holy days (in 1549) was to administer it

> openly in the presence of all the congregacion . . . when the most numbre of the people may come together. . . . As well for that the congregacion there present may testifie the receyuyng of them, that be newly baptyzed, into the noumbre of Christes Churche, as also because in the Baptisme of Infantes, euery manne presente maye be put in remembraunce of his owne profession made to God in his Baptisme.[14]

If this is the only reason, then the church might well baptize whenever the congregation can gather (the later abuse of baptism as a rite attended by the family rather than the congregation was not envisaged by Cranmer, who incorporated it into Morning or Evening Prayer).

Since the mid-nineteenth century, when—on the one hand—it became rubrically possible to separate the services which had formerly been combined on Sunday morning (Morning Prayer, the Litany, and Communion or Ante-communion), and—on the other hand—the eucharist was cut loose from its connection with those days when propers were provided for it (Sundays and holy days) and began to be celebrated either daily or on occasional weekdays, the church's rule of prayer, its inherited pattern of worship, has broken down. Since its defenders failed to ground it theologically, to make the connections between the cycles and their distinctive rites, they have

6

had a hard time putting the pieces back together again. As a consequence, Episcopalians have tended to follow their idiosyncratic personal preferences in their patterns of worship, rather than to adhere to the church's rule of prayer.

The purpose of this study is to re-establish those theological links between the church's rule of prayer (its architecture of time) and the "regular services" of the church which articulate the meaning of this architecture. The next three chapters will be devoted respectively to

1.   The daily cycle and the services of Morning and Evening Prayer;
2.   The weekly cycle and the eucharist; and
3.   The annual cycles which find their focus in the baptismal feasts and the baptismal liturgy.

In each part we shall look first at these cycles and their rites as they emerged in the early centuries of the church's worship, the form which they took in the late middle ages, then at the form which they took in Cranmer's liturgical revision of 1549, and finally the form which they take in *The Book of Common Prayer 1979*. The fourth cycle, that of the pastoral offices, is a separate study in its own right, and its services are not part of the *regular services* of the Church. In exploring the way in which this rule of prayer and the distinctive rites for each of its cycles are theologically related, we shall discover once again the focus of our worship in Christ, the Lord of time, who by his passover from death to life has "redeemed the time" for us. The reader may find the chapter on the first cycle the slowest going. Recent scholarship has considerably altered our understanding of the early forms of daily worship and the theology which undergirds daily worship, and I have attempted to set out the results of this scholarship for the reader and to reference the literature which sets out this new understanding. But readers should be warned that they will probably encounter more unfamiliar material here than elsewhere.

In the conclusion, I shall look at one way in which the church has tried to understand this pattern theologically—the theology of Christ as the *mysterium salutis,* the mystery of salvation. It is this theology, particularly as it found expression in the theology of Pope Leo the Great in the fifth century, that has provided the framework for a contemporary theology of the church's liturgy in terms of the paschal mystery. The church's rule of prayer and the regular services of the church are one way in which the paschal mystery shapes our lives as we follow him who is the way, the truth, and the life.

Notes to the Introduction

1. Abraham Joseph Heschel, *The Sabbath: Its Meaning for Modern Man* (NY: Ferrar, Straus, and Giroux, 1975), page 8.

2. *The Book of Common Prayer* (henceforth cited as BCP) *1979,* "Concerning the Service of the Church," page 13 ("the regular services appointed for public worship in this Church"). Cf. BCP 1928, "Concerning the Service of the Church," page vii, which uses the same language.

3. BCP 1549, page 236: "It appeareth by auncient wryters, that the Sacramente of Baptisme in the olde tyme was not commonly ministered, but at two tymes in the yeare, at Easter and whytsontyde. . . ." For the BCP 1549 and 1552, I cite henceforth from *The First and Second Prayer Books of Edward VI,* E. C. S. Gibson, editor (NY: E. P. Dutton & Co., 1910, reprinted 1957).

4. This shift in the understanding of baptism is quite clear from the fact that in the 1979 book it has been removed from the pastoral offices. This shift moves it into the *regular*

services, though that fact has not been recognized in the rubrics *Concerning the Service of the Church* on page 13.

5. See Marion Hatchett, "Thomas Cranmer and the Rites of Christian Initiation" (unpublished S. T. M. thesis, General Theological Seminary). His conclusions as regards confirmation may be found in his *Commentary on the American Prayer Book* (NY: Seabury Press, 1980), pages 257–264.

6. This is implied by the last rubric in the 1549 service (BCP 1549, page 158), directing that the newly-married couple "(the same daye of their mariage) must receiue the holy communion." See Hatchett, *Commentary*, page 429–430.

7. BCP 1549, opening rubric, page 266.

8. See the text of the form for anointing, BCP 1549, pages 264–265.

9. The form of absolution is found in the rite for the Visitation of the Sick, BCP 1549, page 264; see the reference in the exhortation at communion, page 217, which speaks of "auriculer and secret confession."

10. See the exhortation which opens the proper rite for Ash Wednesday in the BCP 1549, page 280. Here Cranmer expresses the conviction that the restoration of public penance "is muche to be wyshed."

11. Text for the burial itself, BCP 1549, pages 269–270; texts for the office, pages 270–276; eucharistic propers, pages 276–277.

12. BCP 1549, page 3.

13. BCP 1549, page 223 (eucharistic prayer).

14. BCP 1549, page 236.

Chapter One

Redeeming the Day:
The Celebration of Light
at Morning and
Evening Prayer

The Day as a Unit of Time

The fundamental unit of time in the rhythm of human life is the day, the period from one sunrise to the next. Within this unit, daylight hours are given over to activity, nighttime hours are given over to rest. The nodal points of the day (more prominent in human experience before the rhythm of life was modified by the advent of electric light) are sunrise, when the day begins and we rise from sleep, and sunset, when we retire from the day's activity. In other words, light shapes the contours of our daily existence. Sunrise presents the world to us as a new creation, and our thoughts instinctively turn to the day's activities before us; sunset prompts us to reflect on the activities of the day just past and foreshadows for us life's end.

Religious observance at the nodal points of the day frames human existence in terms of our relationship to God. In the morning, we give thanks as we receive the world afresh from the hands of the creator and consecrate the day to God. In the evening, we reflect on the day's successes and failures and on life's finitude in the face of death. Our experience is further shaped by the religious traditions which interpret for us God's dealings with us. God's redemptive approach to God's people in the biblical tradition means that Jews and Christians alike understand God as creator from the perspective of God's redemptive activity: both traditions share the conviction that the God revealed in redemptive love in their history is none other than the creator of heaven and earth.

The Day in Judaism and Early Christian Centuries

Jewish observances:[1] The Old Testament prescribes daily morning and evening sacrifices for Israel.[2] It also prescribes the recitation when we rise and when we retire, of the *Shema*—Israel's confession of faith that the Lord is one.[3] In the first century of the common era, the evening sacrifice in the temple had been moved to the later afternoon. Tradition in this era obligated the individual Jew to recite the *Shema* twice daily, as prescribed in the Old Testament, and also to pray three times daily. In Pharisaic Judaism, the times of prayer were probably morning and evening and the afternoon hour for the "evening" sacrifice in the temple. The form that prayer took in the Pharisaic tradition was the *Amida* or *Tefillah*, a set of eighteen *berakoth* that included both thanksgiving and intercession *(Shemoneh Esreh,* another name for these prayers, means "eighteen").[4] Sectarian Judaism may have prescribed different practices—the custom of the Qumran community seems to be prayer at sunrise, midday (rather than afternoon), sunset, and the middle of the night.

In this period the private prayer prescribed for the individual Jew may already have begun to take the shape of communal observance in the local synagogue. Evidence does not permit us any certainty in this matter and tells us even less about the content of these communal services, although in the morning and the evening they undoubtedly included the *Shema* and all three Pharisaic services probably included the *Tefillah.* Our evidence for Jewish practice, unfortunately, comes not from this period but from the Pharisaic Judaism of the next century. The *berakoth* in which the *Shema* was set probably date from this period, however. The most important of these for our purposes is the *berakah* known as the *Yotzer.* This acknowledges God as the one who "forms the light and creates the darkness"; it links the recitation of the *Shema* to the times prescribed for its recitation.[5]

The core of the communal observance at sunrise and sunset in the synagogue was thus praise and prayer. The morning service on sabbaths and festivals appended readings from the torah and the prophetic books to the daily elements, and the torah portion was repeated on the weekly fasts of Monday and Thursday. What other elements were included in the daily

12

service we have no way of ascertaining. The "verses of song" from the end of the psalter may already have been a part of the Jewish morning devotions (though they are not attested till later); if so, they may lie at the origin of the later Christian custom of concluding the morning psalmody with the psalms of praise (the Latin *laudes* and the Greek *ainoi*, Psalms 148–150).[6]

Christian Observances: Christians took over the Jewish tradition of prayer at sunrise and sunset (and often at a third time during the day, as we see in the *Didache*).[7] Prayer in the middle of the night was also frequently prescribed[8]—a fact which may suggest that Christian usage followed the sectarian rather than the Pharisaic pattern.[9] In Hippolytus and Tertullian[10] we find a fivefold pattern for the daytime hours—morning, evening, and at the third, sixth, and ninth hours. Morning and evening prayer (which Tertullian calls *legitimae orationes*) have a certain priority; prayer at the other hours is recommended. The first hint which we have of the content of the observances is the prescription in the *Didache* that Christians recite the Lord's Prayer three times a day (the hours are not specified).[11]

When the church acquired freedom of cult in the fourth century, the communal observance of the morning and evening hours rapidly became universal;[12] what other hours might be observed varied widely from region to region. The fourth-century *Apostolic Constitutions* prescribe Psalm 63 as the morning psalm and Psalm 141 as the evening psalm.[13] Other elements of praise were also frequently included. In the morning these might include Psalm 51[14] as an alternative or addition to Psalm 63 and Psalms 148–150 to conclude the psalmody;[15] in the evening other psalms might be added to Psalm 141. Old Testament (and later New Testament) canticles eventually became part of the morning office. Similar materials of Christian composition (known as *psalmoi idiotikoi*) were often included also, although with the rise of gnosticism most of these were ultimately rejected. The two best-known compositions in this category are the morning hymn which we know as the *Gloria in Excelsis* and the evening hymn which we know as the *Phos hilaron*.[16] The shape of the morning and evening office thus looked something like this:

Morning Office	**Evening Office**
Psalm 51 and/or 63	Psalm 141 (with or without
Old Testament canticle(s)	other psalms
Psalms 148–150	
Gloria in excelsis	*Phos hilaron*
or other hymn or canticle	or other hymn or canticle
Intercessions	Intercessions

Prayers (much like the *berakoth* in which the *Shema* was set in Jewish liturgy) might be assigned to various components of the office. The intercessions probably took much the same form as the Jewish *Tefillah* did. In the fourth-century *Apostolic Constitutions* they took the form of a litany—diaconal biddings with a response by the people and a concluding prayer by the presbyter or bishop presiding.

The further development of these services moved in two directions after the church had acquired freedom of cult in the fourth century. The popular or congregational form of the office (to which Anton Baumstark gave the somewhat misleading name of the "cathedral office") underwent further elaboration. Some offices acquired proper psalms and canticles for the days of the week in addition to the daily psalms and canticles. Various styles were used for rendering the psalms and canticles:

> **Unison** recitation might be used for well-known psalms. Basil indicates in a letter that Psalm 51 was recited in this way in his church.

Responsorial recitation called for a cantor to sing the psalm by verses, half-verses, or groups of verses after first intoning a refrain which the people would add throughout the psalm.

Antiphonal recitation originally called for the congregation to be divided into two groups, which responded alternately to the verses sung by the cantor (or by alternating cantors). In more elaborate forms of antiphonal psalmody, two different refrains might be used.

Recitation **in directum** (primarily a monastic usage) called for the cantor to sing the psalm straight through while the people listened attentively.[17]

In the popular or congregational office, responsorial recitation was probably the most common usage. As time went on, different forms of recitation were intermixed with each other, and the choir and cantors tended to take over elements of popular participation.

Another feature of the popular office was the offering of light and incense with the morning and evening thanksgivings for light. This might be associated in the morning with a hymn of light (such as the *Benedictus* of Benedictine lauds or the Byzantine refrains of light, known as *photagogika*) and in the evening with either the *Phos hilaron* or Psalm 141 (with its plea that our prayer arise before God like incense). Other ceremonial elaborations, such as processions, also became characteristic of the popular office. The various orders of ministry had clearly defined functions in the office in its popular form.

A final development of the popular office in the East was the incorporation of originally independent liturgies of the word.[18] The most notable liturgy of the word to be incorporated into the office was the Sunday vigil of the resurrection, which is an independent service in Egeria's account of worship at Jerusalem in the late fourth century, but which soon became fused with the morning office in many rites. In its original form its basic components were:

> three psalms or canticles with prayers and
> the gospel of the (passion and) resurrection with the offering of incense.

This weekly vigil was undoubtedly derived from the Easter vigil: the paschal canticles of the vigil (especially the *Benedictus Es, Domine* and the *Benedicite, omnia opera* from the Septuagint version of Daniel and *Cantemus Domino*, the song of Moses from Exodus) often formed part of the repertory of the office. Though the *Apostolic Constitutions* interpret these three (psalms or canticles with) prayers as a symbol of the three days of Christ crucified, buried, and risen, it is not clear that this interpretation was widespread. The use of incense was clearly associated with the spices which the "myrrh-bearing" women brought to the tomb, however. In many rites the gospel has been lost and only the three psalms or canticles remain.[19] In the Byzantine rite, great feasts also acquired a festal variant of the Sunday vigil. Often one or more canticles were also incorporated into the *weekday* morning office, perhaps because the church saw morning prayer as a daily celebration of the resurrection, linking it with sunrise, as Cyprian indicates.[20]

Other liturgies of the word also came to be incorporated into the office.[21] Lenten catechesis, which originally constituted a separate service, was eventually incorporated into the office in the Byzantine rite, with three lessons divided between one of the little hours and vespers. Vespers on the eves of great feasts might also serve to introduce a vigil of readings (normally from the Old Testament). The final result in the Byzantine office was a festal form of the office which included readings from the Old Testament at first vespers and a gospel at the morning office. In a similar way, the stational observances of Jerusalem led at

16

times to the incorporation of readings into the office—most notably in the form of the office now known as the "royal hours" for certain feasts.

How are we to interpret this popular office theologically?[22] Several themes which we have already noted as characteristic of morning and evening observances are woven into the Christian form of morning and evening prayer. Morning is an appropriate time to consecrate ourselves to God's service as we begin the day's activities. Prayer at sunrise includes thanksgiving for creation: we experience the world afresh as a gift from God each morning. Christian prayer at this hour takes these themes and transforms them by reference to Christ. The rising sun is experienced not only as an image of God's creation, but also as a sign of the new creation initiated by Christ's redemptive activity: in the dawn of the sun each day we see an image of the rising sun of righteousness in Christ's resurrection from the dead. Thus the celebration of light in the morning becomes a celebration of Christ's resurrection—a theme picked up by the use of paschal canticles in the morning office[23] and in the use in some rites of the Lucan canticle *Benedictus* as the sun rises in the sky.

In a similar way Christian prayer in the evening incorporated themes characteristic of religious observances at that hour—review of the day's activities in thanksgiving and penitence and approach to the day's end as an image of the end of human life. The kindling of lamps at the beginning of evening worship became for Christians a reminder that Christ is "a light to enlighten the nations" (in the words of the *Nunc Dimittis*), "the light that darkness has never quenched" (as the prologue to John's gospel reminds us), and "the pure brightness of the everliving Father in heaven" (as the *Phos hilaron* proclaims). The evening lamplighting is akin to the blessing of lights on the sabbath and festivals in Jewish homes and is frequently associated with the oblation of incense. It often has markedly eschatological overtones, with reference to the new Jerusalem where there is neither sun nor moon, since "the glory of God is its light, and its lamp is the Lamb" (Revelation 21:23).

In some rites the morning and the evening office take on a markedly penitential overtone. Penitence in the morning prepares us to receive life afresh from God each day and to consecrate the day's activities to God; penitence in the evening allows us to face the end of life with confidence, forgiven for what we have done amiss in the course of the day. Patristic interpretations of Psalms 51 and 63 for the morning and Psalm 141 for the evening often develop such themes,[24] and Syrian offices even interpret the oblation of incense in this way.[25]

A final significant theme of morning and evening worship is articulated in the intercessions, which may be understood as our exercise of the royal priesthood of Christ which we share through our baptism.[26] Both offices are concluded with extensive intercessions. In their fullest form (as found in book 8 of the *Apostolic Constitutions*),[27] these intercessions begin with prayers for those preparing for baptism (catechumens and *photizomenoi*) and for those who have lost the right to exercise their royal priesthood (public penitents and the possessed). These groups are then dismissed and the faithful exercise their priestly office through extensive intercessions for the needs of the church and the world. The transition from worship to work and witness in the world is marked by a final set of petitions in Eastern offices, the "angel of peace" petitions. These petitions might be understood as prayers for faithful discipleship in the world.[28]

What we know as the little hours in various rites are often given a Christological interpretation and related to Christ's passion. In some rites these hours include midday prayers, such as Byzantine terce-sext; in others terce, sext, and

18   CHAPTER ONE

none as hours once designated for private devotion in Hippolytus and Tertullian; in still others prime or a second morning office and compline or bedtime prayers in addition to the three hours of terce, sext, and none. The Christological scheme for the commemoration of the paschal mystery of Christ's death and resurrection is most fully developed in the Western hours of the passion.[29] The commemoration of the gift of the Holy Spirit at the third hour was a popular observance which fell outside this passion sequence. Psalmody (and hymnody in the West) are the primary components of these hours. They never acquired the extensive intercessions of morning and evening prayer.

The Daily Worship of the Desert Monks:[30] The fourth century saw the rise of the monastic movement in the church—in part a reaction to the danger of secularization of the church once it had received legal recognition under Constantine. The pre-Constantinian church had known ascetics supported by the local congregations (virgins and widows on the roll of the local church) and occasional solitaries or wandering ascetics, but in the fourth century a flood of solitaries withdrew into the desert of Egypt. Some of these solitaries lived a semi-eremetical life rather than a purely solitary one. Those who were to have the greatest influence on the liturgy gathered twice daily for common devotions and followed what Cassian called the "rule of the angel," which stipulated the recitation of twelve psalms in the nocturnal vigil before dawn and twelve in the evening. The first eleven psalms were recited in course by a reader; the community added alleluia as a refrain to the twelfth psalm. Each psalm was followed by a period of silence for meditation and prayer. To the psalmody some added a reading from the Old Testament and a reading from the new Testament (except on Saturdays and Sundays and in Easter Season, when both readings were from the New Testament).

The office of these desert monks shared the times appointed for prayer with the popular office (although the monks rose and retired somewhat earlier). But the content of the office was quite different. Psalms were read in course (that is, in their numerical sequence) as an aid to meditation, rather than selectively as an appropriate expression of praise related to the hour of the day. The lessons from scripture were also read in course as an aid to meditation. The extensive intercessions of the popular office were lacking, for the monks initially considered ordination incompatible with a monastic vocation and so had no deacons to give out the biddings and no presbyters to conclude the intercessions with prayer. In place of the intercessions, the monks joined in silent prayer as the fruit of their meditation on each psalm. The purpose here was no longer the original one of "framing" life in prayer; the monks attempted to fill all of life with prayer.

The Elaboration of Daily Worship

Early Monastic Worship Elsewhere: Elsewhere monastic communities developed their worship along different lines.[31] In Cappadocia, monastic daily worship at first filled out the horarium of the church by adding to the popular offices of daily morning and evening prayer the little hours (terce, sext, and none) and a midnight office, transforming times of private devotion into communal observances. Other hours might be added as well—a second morning office (prime) and bedtime prayers (compline). These offices were constructed largely out of appropriate psalms.

Hybrid Offices: Under the impact of these forms of monasticism, most churches eventually adopted both the expanded horarium and the custom of reciting psalms in course 1) at a midnight vigil or a vigil just before the morning office, and 2) before vespers. These hybrid rites were thus composed of elements of the popular ("cathedral") office and elements from various monastic offices. The predominant forms of daily worship of both the Byzantine rite in the East and the Roman rite in the West were hybrid rites of this sort. In the East, *two* hybrid rites were eventually fused—the *akolouthia asmatike* of the Great Church in Constantinople and the Palestinian rite of Jerusalem. Although it is customary to speak of the rite of Constantinople as a "cathedral" office and that of Jerusalem as a "monastic" office, a careful examination of the texts will reveal that both were hybrid rites which combined popular and monastic elements.[32] Eventually the Palestinian office prevailed, though it incorporated elements from the *akolouthia asmatike.* In the West, the two predominant forms of daily worship were the Roman office and the Benedictine office. They are very similar, for Benedict modified the old Roman office and the Roman office in turn later incorporated Benedictine elements. It was once common to speak of the Roman office as secular and the Benedictine office as monastic, but here too we are in fact dealing with two hybrid rites, each incorporating popular and monastic elements. Let us look at the predominant rites of Byzantium and Rome—the present Byzantine office and the classic Benedictine office. Both have had their impact on the office in the *Book of Common Prayer 1979.*

The Byzantine Office: Byzantine daily worship is a very complex series of services. The forms of the morning office *(orthros)* and the evening office *(hesperinos)* may be conveniently found in Orthodox prayer books such as Isabel Hapgood's *Service Book of the Holy Orthodox-Catholic Apostolic Church* or in Kallistos Ware and Mother Mary's *Festal Menaion*. The services seem baffling at first, but repay careful study because the core of these services preserves the basic pattern of early Christian worship better than Western rites. The reader is encouraged to use one of these books to follow the services in the following analysis. The basic structure of the present Byzantine office may be outlined as follows. The early components are here set out in boldfaced type, the parochial components in capitals.

Byzantine Vespers *(Hesperinos)*

COMPONENTS FROM JERUSALEM	COMPONENTS FROM CONSTANTINOPLE

1. Monastic Psalmody

Fixed Invitatory
   Initial blessing and verses
      from Psalm 95
   Introductory Psalm: Psalm
      104
   Great *Synapte* (litany)

Seven "Lamplighting Prayers" (once distributed through the office)

Kathisma of Psalms in Course
   Little litany

2. Congregational Vespers

PSALMS 141/142/130/117
   with intercalated *troparia*
   (stichera)
Censing and Entrance

Prayer of Entrance

PHOS HILARON
Responsory *(prokeimenon)*
[Readings for vigils and Lent]

INTERCESSIONS
  Augmented Litany
    [originally, **GREAT**
    SYNAPTE]
  Kataxioson
  DISMISSAL LITANY

                              Prayer of Inclination (blessing)

3. Appended Devotions

Troparia with selected psalm verses *(aposticha)*
Procession with intercessions on feasts *(lite)*
Nunc Dimittis, Trisagion, Lord's Prayer
troparion (apolytikion)
Blessing of Bread, Wine, Oil

The Byzantine Morning Office *(Orthros)* for Sundays and Major Feasts

COMPONENTS FROM JERUSALEM	COMPONENTS FROM CONSTANTINOPLE

1. Monastic Vigil

Fixed Invitatory
  Blessing
  **Luke 2:14a (3x),
    Psalm 51:16 (2x)**
  Psalms 3/38/63
  Psalms 83/103/143   Twelve "dawn prayers"
  Great *Synapte*   (once distributed
                                          through the office)

Responsory from Psalm 118 (originally from **Isaiah 26**) *Troparia* with *doxa* (*Gloria Patri*)	
Monastic Psalmody	
First Section *(kathisma)* Little litany, *troparion* (*kathisma*) Reading of ascetical literature	
Second Section (like the first)	
Third Section (like others on ordinary days)	Third Section (Sundays and major feasts) Psalm 119 or Psalms 135/136 Incensation and Procession to Ambo *Eulogitaria*
Little litany, *troparion*	Elements from *Pannychis* antiphons from the gradual psalms variable *prokeimenon* fixed *prokeimenon* (from Psalm 150) Little litany Gospel of the resurrection *Troparion* after the gospel
Psalm 51, with *troparia* on the *doxa* Intercession	

2. The Palestinian Vigil of the Resurrection

Odes 1/2/3 of the poetic canon
  Little litany, *troparion (kathisma* or *hypakoe)*
Odes 4/5/6 of the poetic canon
  Little litany, *kontakion*
  Reading from the *synaxarion* (martyrology)

ODES 7/8/9 of the poetic canon
  Responsory on Sundays from Psalm 99
  [GOSPEL OF THE RESURRECTION, now displaced]
  Sunday *exaposteilaria*

3. The Palestinian Morning Office

[PSALM 51, now displaced]

Photagogika or *Exaposteilaria*

PSALMS 148/149/150 *(ainoi)* with intercalated *troparia (stichera)*
Sunday Responsory from Psalms 9/10

GLORIA IN EXCELSIS (festal), *KATAXIOSON* (ferial), *trisagion
troparion (apolytikion)* (Sundays and feasts only)

INTERCESSIONS
  Augmented Litany [originally, GREAT *SYNAPTE*]
  DISMISSAL LITANY

                              Prayer of Inclination
                              (blessing)

4. Appended Devotions

Troparia, with selected psalm verses *(aposticha)*
  (omitted on Sundays)
Trisagion and Lord's Prayer
Troparion and concluding devotions

The core of these offices is the congregational office, consisting in the evening of Psalms 141/142/130/117, the *Phos hilaron,* and the intercessions, and in the morning of Psalms 51 and 149/149/150, the *Gloria in excelsis* (for Sundays and the feasts) or *Kataxioson* (a cento of scriptural verses for the ferial office), and the intercessions. Prefaced to these daily are a vigil of monastic psalmody in the morning (with a fixed invitatory and units of psalmody in course) and an opening section of psalmody in the evening (with a fixed invitatory and units of psalmody in course). On Sundays and major feasts, a popular vigil (whose primary components were three canticles and the gospel reading) originally followed the monastic vigil and preceded the congregational morning office.

The developments which the office underwent when various forms were fused are very complex. The first important witness to the office in Jerusalem is Egeria at the end of the fourth century. In her day, the popular and monastic elements had already been brought together. But the office as she describes it is an office in which both the local church and the religious take part. When the office was used in monastic communities for their own worship, it was modified in several ways. Psalms and canticles, which were recited responsorially or antiphonally in Egeria's account, were recited without refrain by a reader in monastic communities. In the rite as Egeria describes it, appropriate prayers were associated with each of the major components of the office. Monastic communities without ordained members omitted these prayers altogether. For the same reason the intercessions with which the office concluded were omitted. The only prayer used by monks was the Lord's Prayer. In place of the litanic intercessions of the deacon they substituted multiple repetitions of the response to the litany, "Lord have mercy." They also omitted all but the most ancient of the hymnodic elements (retaining only the *Phos hilaron* and the *Gloria in excelsis*).

Monastic communities did not remain exclusively lay in character, and the hybrid monastic office eventually reincorporated both elements proper to deacons and presbyters (litanies and prayers) and hymnody. The standard litanies did not vary greatly in Eastern rites, and it was relatively easy to reincorporate them. Some changes occurred, nonetheless. The original form of the concluding intercessions may be seen in the *akolouthia asmatike* of Constantinople:

> Litany for the catechumens
>> Prayer for the catechumens recited aloud to conclude the litany
>
> Great litany *(synapte)* of the faithful
>> Prayer for the faithful recited silently by officiant during litany
>>
>> Prayer for the faithful recited aloud to conclude the litany
>
> Dismissal litany ("angel of peace" petitions)
>> Dismissal prayer *(apolysis)* recited aloud to conclude these petitions
>
> Diaconal bidding to bow the head
>> Prayer of blessing recited aloud with bowed heads *(kephaloklisia)*
>
> Diaconal dismissal[33]

When the intercessions were restored, however, the great litany migrated to the beginning of the office, and it was replaced in the concluding intercessions by a penitential litany (to which intercessory petitions were added)—known as the augmented litany or the litany of fervent supplication. Litanies for other groups of people were not reintroduced, except for the litany of the catechumens in Lenten vespers and the litany for the *photizomenoi* in vespers for the latter part of Lent. In addition, simple biddings before prayers took on the more elaborate form of "little litanies."

The prayers once proper to the rite of Jerusalem were apparently lost. When prayers were restored, the prayers used were those proper to the rite of Constantinople. Because the structure of that office was not the same as that of Jerusalem, the prayers could only be distributed through the office with difficulty. Various ways of distributing them were tried, but in the end most of the prayers came to be recited silently at the beginning of the office during the introductory psalmody. It has now become customary for the officiant to recite most prayers secretly, singing aloud only their final doxology (the *ekphonesis*);[34] as a consequence, the officiant now concluded the litanies with doxologies detached from the prayers of which they had once been the conclusion.[35]

Hymnodic elements also re-entered the office in a bewildering variety of ways. The predominant form was a short composition in rhythmic prose whose generic name is *troparion*. It acquired specific names according to the elements with which it was associated—*doxastikon, theotokion, eulogitaria, kathisma, stichera, heirmos, katabasia, photagogika, apolytikion*, and so on. Perhaps its original use in this rite was as a refrain for the *doxa (Gloria patri)* at the conclusion of psalms and canticles *(doxastikon)*. A Marian *troparion* might be attached to the *doxa* also (the *theotokion*). But its use soon expanded in a variety of ways: additional *troparia* might be interpolated into the last verses of psalms *(stichera)* and canticles (whose model *troparion* is the *heirmos* and whose final *troparion* is the *katabasia*). The *troparia* might become detached from the psalm and sung with the *doxa* (and perhaps with a few verses of the psalm) as an element in its own right (as with the *eulogitaria* once attached to Psalm 119). The *troparia* themselves might be the major element and the *doxa* or detached psalm verses might be used to facilitate the recitation of the *troparia* in their customary fashion (the *photagogika* or *exaposteilaria* and the *aposticha*). Some *troparia* are sung independently *(the apolytikion* and the *troparia* appointed for the *lite,* the procession after vespers).

Another ancient hymnodic element was the *kontakion*. In its original form, it consisted of an introductory stanza *(proiemion)* and a series of other stanzas *(oikoi)* which ended with a common refrain and which formed a meditation or dramatic dialogue. This is a genre borrowed from the Syrian compositions of the deacon Ephrem of Edessa, who won the epithet "harp of the Holy Spirit." He died in 373 and is commemorated in the calendar of the Book of Common Prayer on June 10. The early Greek master of the genre was Romanos the Melodist, who died sometime in the course of the sixth century. He is said to have written over a thousand hymns. Only eighty survive today, and in the current rite only the introductory stanza and the first *oikos* are used. The *kontakion* originally seems to have served as a meditative interlude between the monastic vigil and the morning office. As other forms of hymnody came to predominate, the *kontakia* were eventually reduced to the *proiemion* and a single *oikos* (only the *kontakion* for the burial of a priest still preserves the full form in the present office).

The growth of *troparia* led to the abbreviation or even the suppression of many of the original elements of the office. Except for Psalm 51, the original psalms of the congregational office are customarily sung in abbreviated form today. The canticles which were once a part of the Sunday vigil have entirely disappeared today, replaced by canons made up of *troparia* once interpolated into them as their refrains, *troparia* now sung with a short refrain of their own. Only the *Magnificat* has escaped suppression in the course of this development (it is now customarily sung in addition to the ode made up of *troparia* once attached to it).

A final development which has further obscured the original shape of the office is the incorporation on Sundays and major feasts of two elements from *asmatikos orthros* of Constantinople: 1) Psalm 119, divided into three antiphons, as the third section of monastic psalmody on Sundays, or Psalms 135/136 as the third section on feasts (and as a replacement for Psalm 119 on Sundays in some uses); and 2) elements from the service known as *pannychis* (the refrains once sung with gradual psalms and a gospel—perhaps this was the form that the resurrection vigil took in Constantinople). The incorporation of *pannychis* seems to have led to the suppression of the original gospel of the vigil for Sundays and major feasts in Jerusalem usage and the incorporation of the canticles into the morning office (after Psalm 51).

The use of scriptural canticles itself is a complex and obscure development. The original usage would seem to have been the recitation of three paschal canticles *(Benedictus Es, Domine*; *Benedicite, omnia opera*; and *Cantemus Domino)* with a gospel of the resurrection in the Sunday vigil. In the monastic all-night vigil, however, monks recited all 150 psalms between vespers and the morning office and expanded the three paschal canticles to nine, with eight Old Testament canticles and a New Testament canticle made up of the *Benedictus* and the *Magnificat*. Since the festal cycle eventually expanded to include almost every day of the year, canons of *troparia* for all nine odes were composed for almost every day of the year. The earlier monastic usage for ferias, however, is probably revealed by the Armenian office, which concludes the canon of psalmody for the monastic vigil with a variable canticle and uses the two canticles from Daniel as a kind of prelude to the congregational morning office. Evidence of this usage in the Byzantine rite (in a later and somewhat different form) can be found in the daily ferial canticles for which Lenten *troparia* are appointed. Except in Lent, the second canticle (from Deuteronomy) dropped out of ordinary use because of its markedly penitential character (so that it seemed inappropriate in canons of festal *troparia*).

The result of this extraordinarily complex development is an office whose shape and rationale today reveals itself only to patient historical detective work (and tentative hypothetical reconstruction). But whatever the exact course of development, the original components and their rationale are reasonably evident to us.

The Roman Benedictine Office: In the West, the daily office originally took a wide variety of forms. But what eventually prevailed was the hybrid rite of Roman monasticism in two variants—the so-called "secular office" (which is in fact the monastic office of the Roman basilicas) and the adaptation of that office which Benedict appointed in his rule. This office (in both forms) consisted of a vigil during the period just before dawn, lauds and vespers as the principal daytime hours, the little hours of prime, terce, sext, and none, and the additional evening hour known as compline. We shall look at the Benedictine form of the vigil (now customarily known as matins, though Benedict does not use that name) and the principal hours known as lauds *(laudes matutinae* or matins in Benedict's rule) and vespers.[36] Their shape may be seen in the following outlines. The elements of the vigil, lauds, and vespers which ultimately derive from popular, non-monastic usage are printed in boldfaced type.

The Benedictine Vigil

1. Invitatory

Psalm 51:16 (3x)
Psalm 3 *in directum*
Psalm 95 with refrain
Metrical Hymn

2. First Section *(nocturn)*

6 psalms in course with refrains
Versicle
Blessing by the abbot
Lessons with responsories (3 in winter, 1 in summer, 4 on Sundays)

3. Second Section *(nocturn)*

6 psalms in course with refrains
Versicle
Blessing by the abbot
Lesson from epistles with responsory (four readings with
    responsories on Sundays)
Kyrie eleison (perhaps without petitions: "supplicatio litaniae, id
    est Kyrie eleison")
    (the rule does not indicate the *Kyrie* for Sundays)

4. Third Section *(nocturn)* on Sundays

3 canticles with alleluia
Versicle
Blessing by the abbot
4 New Testament lessons with responsories
Te Deum Laudamus
Gospel (perhaps originally of the resurrection)
Te decet laus
Blessing

Benedictine Lauds

1. Psalmody

Versicle: Psalm 70:1 with *Gloria Patri* and perhaps alleluia
    (in later forms of the office; not mentioned in the rule)
Psalm 67 *in directum*
Psalm 51 with refrain (alleluia on Sundays)
2 variable psalms (selected psalms rather than psalms in course)
    with refrains

Sunday	Psalm 118	Psalm 63
Monday	Psalm 5	Psalm 36
Tuesday	Psalm 43	Psalm 57
Wednesday	Psalm 64	Psalm 65
Thursday	Psalm 88	Psalm 90
Friday	Psalm 76	Psalm 92
Saturday	Psalm 143	First part of Saturday Canticle

Variable canticle (***Benedicite*** on Sundays) with refrain
Psalms 148/149/150 under a single refrain

2. Liturgy of the Word

Lesson from the Epistles (Revelation on Sundays)
Responsory
Hymn
Versicle
Benedictus Dominus Deus Israel **with refrain**

3. Concluding Intercession ("missa")

Litanic intercession *(litania)*
Lord's Prayer recited aloud by abbot
Dismissal

Benedictine Vespers

1. Psalmody

Versicle: Psalm 70:1 with *Gloria Patri* and perhaps alleluia
(in later forms of the office; not mentioned in the rule)
4 psalms in course with refrains

2. Liturgy of the Word

Lesson
Responsory
Hymn
Versicle
***Magnificat* with refrain**

3. Concluding Intercession

Litanic intercession ("missa")
Lord's Prayer recited aloud by abbot
Dismissal

In considering the Benedictine office, we should first note the essentially popular character of lauds. Psalm 51 and Psalms 148/149/150 are the ancient psalmody for this hour. Other psalms appointed are also popular in character, for they are selected as appropriate to the hour of the day rather than simply following the sequential course of the psalter in monastic fashion. The canticle *Benedictus Dominus Deus Israel* was not in Benedict's Roman prototype; he may have borrowed it from the *Rule of the Master*, a somewhat earlier Italian monastic rule. Like the psalms, it is appropriate to the hour (with its reference to Christ as the dawn or dayspring), and in festive forms of the office it is sung while incense is offered. The intercessions too are part of the original core of the office. Although they are now reduced to the *Kyrie eleison,* Benedict probably intended a full litany. They were concluded by the Lord's Prayer in Benedict's office because Roman tradition reserved collects for the bishop. Subsequently collects were added to the conclusion of the office in ordinary usage. The hymn is borrowed from the Ambrosian usage of Milan. The lesson (a short reading recited from memory) represents an Egyptian monastic usage. The responsory and versicle are probably remnants of a responsorial psalm borrowed from the Roman office and now separated by the hymn. The third portion of Benedict's vigil also incorporates elements of the popular vigil of the resurrection—three canticles and a gospel, now interspersed with other elements of monastic provenance.

Benedictine vespers, on the other hand, has lost almost all of its popular characteristics (even though its current structure looks analogous to lauds). The psalmody is not popular in character, but a sequential course recitation. The evening psalmody has apparently disappeared entirely; and there is no celebration of the evening light. A possible remnant of the popular usage is the frequent use of a verse from Psalm 141 as the versicle; it is perhaps an indication of the original responsorial recitation of that psalm. The offering of incense now associated with the *Magnificat* (perhaps borrowed from the *Rule of the Master)* may at one time have been associated with this psalm in the antecedents of the Roman office.[37] The intercessory conclusion to the office does retain (as at lauds) its ancient character.

Like the Byzantine office, the Benedictine office restricts the course recitation of psalmody to the vigil and vespers (sections of Psalm 119 and other appropriate psalms are used for the little hours; the psalms of compline are fixed and selected for their nighttime themes). Benedict envisages the recitation of the psalms and canticles with refrains when the size of the community permits, with the exception of Psalm 3 at the vigil and Psalm 67 at lauds, which are to be recited without refrain. He probably intended a responsorial recitation; although he calls the refrains "antiphons," we have no indication that he intended antiphonal recitation in the original Byzantine sense. Today in the West antiphonal recitation means that two parts of the choir sing the verses alternately, with the refrain sung only at the beginning and end of the psalm, but this is probably an abbreviation of the original mode of recitation.

Like the desert monks of Egypt of whom Cassian writes, Western monks did their course reading of the scriptures during the vigil (the Byzantine office never adopted the custom at all). Another Egyptian custom was the recitation from memory of a portion of scripture: this is probably the origin of the lessons at lauds, vespers, and the little hours, as well as the lesson at the second nocturn of the vigil (and also the first in the summer). Patristic commentaries on the scriptures were also read during the vigil. Benedict does not always clearly specify whether scriptures or patristic commentaries are to be read during the various nocturns; subsequent usage followed various patterns in this regard.

In the course of the middle ages, the daily office grew increasingly complicated. The principal factor here was the way in which the calendar was filled out with almost daily commemorations of the saints. In the Byzantine office, this did not affect the weekly cursus of psalms, but it did add an enormous amount of proper hymnological material. The original Western custom was to recite both the daily office and the festive office on major feast days (the original "double office"). Later, the material for the feast (psalms, refrains, lessons, hymns, and collects) displaced the ferial provisions in differing proportions, depending on the importance of the feast. In addition, offices of devotion (the hours of the cross, of the Virgin, of the Holy Spirit, of the dead, and so forth) might be appended to the public office and might also serve as a substitute for the office in private recitation by the laity. In some monasteries at some periods, the greater part of the day was thus spent in recitation of this expanded office. The major disadvantage suffered by the Roman rite, which the Byzantine rite did not share, was that its liturgical language was no longer accessible to most of the people. Latin was the language of the learned in the Middle Ages, not a vernacular. The daily office then was dysfunctional in meeting the devotional needs of the people, and para-liturgical devotions, such as the recitation of the rosary, became the popular form of prayer.

Cranmer's Reforms and the Prayer Book Tradition

By the time of the Reformation, the need for the reform of daily worship was apparent. Thomas Cranmer, drawing on the reforms proposed by Cardinal Quiñones (who had published an extraordinarily popular simplification of the Roman office in 1535) and Lutheran projects as well as the variants of the Roman office current in England, sought to restore public daily worship to its rightful place in the life of the church. He rightly perceived that the morning and evening services of lauds and vespers, popularly known as mattins and evensong in England, were the principal offices for daily worship; and he composed new forms for these, drawing on the Roman vigil, lauds and prime for his service of morning prayer and on Roman vespers and compline for his service of evening prayer.[38]

The tradition of daily worship was so heavily monasticized in the West, however, that the principles for daily worship on which he based his new services were not derived from the congregational offices of the early church, as he believed, but from monastic customs. In his prefaces to these services in 1549 he declares that:

> There was neuer any thing by the wit of man so well deuised, or so surely established, which (in the continuance of time) hath not been corrupted; as (among other thinges) it may plainly appere by the common prayers in the Churche, commonlye called diuine seruice: the firste originall and grounde whereof, if a manne would searche out by the auncient fathers, he shall finde that the same was not ordeyned, but of a good purpose, and for a great aduauncement of godlines: For they so ordred the matter, that all the whole Bible (or the greatest parte thereof) should be read ouer once in the year. . . .
>
> . . . the auncient fathers had deuided the psalms into seuen porcions [to be read successively on the seven days of the week]. . . .[39]

However admirable the goals of reading the Scriptures through once each year (or the Old Testament once and the New Testament thrice in Cranmer's new scheme) and reciting the psalter once a week (or once a month in Cranmer's new scheme), they are *monastic* goals and quite unrelated to the way in which the "ancient fathers" organized the course of daily *public* worship. Cranmer nonetheless did a remarkable job in devising forms for morning and evening worship by rearranging the traditional elements according to these principles. The following outlines set out the services which he drafted in 1549.[40]

CHAPTER ONE

Mattins
in The Book of Common Prayer 1549

Lord's Prayer

1. The Invitatory and the Psalter

Psalm 51:16 as versicle and response
Psalm 70:1 as versicle and response
Gloria Patri
Alleluia

Psalm 95, *Venite*, (without refrain) (after 1552, Christ our Passover
   as Easter invitatory)
One of sixty portions of the psalter read in sequence

2. The Word of God

Lesson from the Old Testament
Te Deum or (In Lent) *Benedicite*
   (after 1552 an alternative at any time)

Lesson from the New Testament
Benedictus Dominus Deus Israel (Psalm 100, *Jubilate Deo*,
   as alternative after 1552)

3. The Prayers

Threefold *Kyrie eleison*
Apostles' Creed (*Quicunque vult* on appointed feasts)
Lord's Prayer (directly preceded by Salutation and *Kyrie
   eleison* after 1552)

Suffrages (psalm verses used as intercessory versicles and responses)
Salutation and response (moved in 1552)

Collect of the day
Collect for peace
Collect for grace

Evensong

in The Book of Common Prayer 1549

Lord's Prayer

1. The Invitatory and the Psalter

Psalm 51:16 as versicle and response (added in 1552)
Psalm 70:1 as versicle and response
Gloria Patri
Alleluia

One of sixty portions of the psalter read in sequence

2. The Word of God

Lesson from the Old Testament
Magnificat (Psalm 98, *Cantate Domino*, as alternative
    after 1552)

Lesson from the New Testament
Nunc Dimittis (Psalm 67, *Deus Misereatur*, as alternative
    after 1552)

3. The Prayers

Threefold *Kyrie eleison*
Apostles' Creed
Lord's Prayer (directly preceded by Salutation and
    Kyrie eleison after 1552)

Suffrages (psalm verses used as intercessory versicles and responses)
Salutation and response (moved in 1552)

Collect of the day
Collect for peace
Collect for aid against all perils

Cranmer, working on the basis of the mediaeval forms of the office as he knew it, treated morning and evening prayer as liturgies of the word which aim at edification. He did a remarkably good job at this, though it is important to remember that the original offices were *not* liturgies of the word at all, but services of praise and prayer appropriate to the hour of the day. The course recitation of the psalter, however, makes any relation of the psalms to the time of the day coincidental. The canticles are employed by Cranmer not as independent elements of praise but as responses to readings. What he devised was a remarkably effective form of worship, but its purpose was not that of the original morning and evening offices at all; its purpose resembled much more closely the edificatory goals of the daily worship of the desert monks!

The structure of the Anglican offices of matins and evensong has remained remarkably stable since 1549.[41] In 1552 a penitential introduction with a sentence, an exhortation, a confession, and an absolution was prefaced to both morning and evening prayer. The Creed was moved at that time so that it followed immediately after the second canticle. Psalms were provided as alternatives to the *Benedictus Dominus Deus Israel* in the morning and to both the *Magnificat* and the *Nunc Dimittis* in the evening in this same revision; later revisions have provided a variety of additional alternative canticles. Revisions from 1662 on have appointed various prayers for use after the third collect, and permission has been granted to sing a hymn or anthem before these prayers. Various revisions have been made of the lectionary (generally relating it to the liturgical year), and some revisions have permitted a distribution of psalms over a longer period of time (with attention to the appropriateness of psalms for morning or evening). The *shape* of the office has remained largely unchanged, however.

Morning and Evening Prayer have been recited in a

variety of ways: cathedrals and collegiate churches, with bodies of resident choristers, adapted traditional music, so that (except for the introduction and the concluding prayers) the entire office was sung; parochial usage was much simpler. Most of the great choral music for Anglican worship was written for these offices. The purpose of the office in Anglican tradition is well-phrased in the exhortation which Cranmer drafted in 1552 to introduce the confession before the invitatory of matins and evensong: we gather

> to set foorth [God's] moste worthye praise,
> to hear his most holy word, and
> to aske those things which be requisite and necessarye. . . .[42]

The canon law of the Church of England and the rubrics of its Book of Common Prayer have always required its clergy to recite the office daily, and its clergy with parochial cures to do so in their parish churches. Choral evensong is still the principal form of daily worship in English cathedrals (though daily choral matins has long since disappeared in most places). In parish churches daily worship was surprisingly well-attended until the 1830s;[43] the radical changes in life wrought by the industrial revolution have made it increasingly difficult for people to continue the pattern since that time, and the daily pattern (while far from unknown) has never been so prevalent in the Episcopal Church in the United States. Private or family prayers became an increasingly common substitute for daily public worship; forms for these have been bound up with every edition of the American Book of Common Prayer. In addition, the growing frequency with which the eucharist has been celebrated on weekdays since the Oxford Movement has worked to the detriment of the maintenance of the office as the normative form of *daily* worship.

CHAPTER ONE

The Daily Office in
the Book of Common Prayer 1979

In the late 1960s, the Episcopal Church in the United States began the task of revising *The Book of Common Prayer*—a task which was completed in 1976 (when the present book received its first legislative reading in General Convention). Although (as we shall see) the calendar, the baptismal and initiatory rites, the eucharist, the pastoral offices, and the episcopal services were all revised extensively, the daily office retained its classical Anglican shape (with suitable provisions for both flexibility and enrichment). When this revision was being undertaken, scholarship still tended to understand morning and evening prayer as liturgies of the word; as such, the classic structures of matins and evensong had stood the test of time and could hardly be improved. Only since that time have we come to realize that these services were not in their origin liturgies of the word, but services of praise and prayer which were closely related to their time of celebration, with an early focus on the celebration of the light of Christ at sunrise and lamplighting. From this perspective, the classic forms of matins and evensong are considerably less satisfactory. The task of appropriate revision is far from finished (though the Order of Worship for the Evening recaptures the focus of evening prayer). The following outlines for Daily Morning and Evening Prayer and the Order of Worship for the Evening[44] reveal both the continuity of the 1979 offices and their expanded flexibility.

Redeeming the Day

Daily Morning Prayer
in *The Book of Common Prayer 1979*

Optional Introduction

Morning Sentences or Seasonal Sentences
Bidding to Confession
Confession
Absolution

1. The Invitatory and the Psalter

Psalm 51:16 as versicle and response
Gloria Patri
Alleluia

Venite (partial or full psalm), *Jubilate*, or (in Easter Season)
  Christ our Passover
Appointed psalm(s)

2. The Word of God

One, two, or three lessons
Variable canticle after the first (and second) lesson

*A sermon or reading from Christian literature may
  follow the readings.*

Apostles' Creed (may be omitted at one office during the day)

3. The Prayers

Salutation and response
Lord's Prayer

Suffrages (two alternatives)
  a. Revision of traditional suffrages
  b. Suffrages once attached to the end of the *Te Deum*

One or more of the following collects:
  a. Collect of the day
  b. Seven morning collects (proper collects for Sundays, Fridays, and Saturdays)
One of three prayers for the mission and ministry of the church

Optional Concluding Elements

Hymn or Anthem
Sermon
Authorized intercessions and thanksgivings
The General Thanksgiving
A Prayer of St. Chrysostom
Dismissal and response ("Let us bless the Lord")
One of three concluding sentences

Daily Evening Prayer
in *The Book of Common Prayer 1979*

Optional Introduction

Evening Sentences or Seasonal Sentences
Bidding to Confession
Confession
Absolution

1. The Invitatory and the Psalter

Psalm 70:1 as versicle and response
Gloria Patri
Alleluia

Phos hilaron or another suitable hymn or one of the morning
  invitatories (optional)
Appointed psalm(s)

2. The Word of God

One, two, or three lessons
Variable canticle after the first (and second) lesson
   (*Magnificat* & *Nunc Dimittis* printed)
A sermon or reading from Christian literature may follow the readings.

Apostles' Creed (may be omitted at one office during the day)

3. The Prayers

Salutation and response
Lord's Prayer

Suffrages (two alternatives)
   a. Revision of traditional suffrages
   b. An evening form of the Byzantine dismissal litany
      ("angel of peace" petitions)

One or more of the following collects:
   a. Collect of the day
   b. Seven evening collects (proper collects for
      Sundays, Fridays, and Saturdays)
One of three prayers for the mission and ministry of the church

Optional Concluding Elements

Hymn or Anthem
Sermon
Authorized intercessions and thanksgivings
The General Thanksgiving
A Prayer of St. Chrysostom
Dismissal and response ("Let us bless the Lord")
One of three concluding sentences

An Order of Worship for the Evening

Celebration of Light

Greeting and Response (proper forms for the seasons of Easter and Lent)

Short lesson with reference to light (various options)
The lesson may be omitted when a biblical reading follows later.

Prayer for Light (various options)

Appropriate psalm or anthem (optional) while lamps are lit
The Book of Occasional Services provides proper anthems.
These anthems are responsories followed by a verse and response.

Phos hilaron or other appropriate hymn
Incense may be offered during this hymn.

The service may continue with the Order for Daily Evening Prayer, beginning with the psalms. It may also continue with the Eucharist, a meal or other activity. When it is used as an independent office, it continues as follows:

Other Components of the Evening Office

Selection from the Psalter (a psalm collect may follow the psalm)

Bible Reading
Sermon or Reading from Christian literature (optional)

Canticle (*Magnificat* or another canticle or hymn of praise)
In this form of the office this is an independent element.

Prayers
A litany or other suitable intercession
The Lord's prayer
A suitable collect

Hymn (optional)

Blessing and/or Dismissal

The Peace (optional)

Morning and Evening Prayer are the "regular services appointed for public worship" in the Episcopal Church each day.[45] We shall therefore look at them in their 1979 form in some detail.[46] We should first of all look at the appointed psalms and lessons in this book. While the divisions for a monthly recitation of the psalter in course are still indicated, the normative use of the psalter is that appointed in the Daily Office Lectionary. There the psalms are arranged in a seven-week course ("except in the weeks from 4 Advent to 1 Epiphany and Palm Sunday to 2 Easter"[47] and on major feasts with their own propers). While this provides a semi-sequential recitation of the entire psalter, care has been taken to assign appropriate psalms not only to morning and evening, but also to Fridays (penitential and passion psalms), to Wednesdays (sections of Psalm 119 at one of the offices), and Saturdays and Sundays (psalms of creation and of paschal deliverance). Provision is made to omit certain psalms or verses of psalms because of their imprecatory nature.[48] This is probably as skillful a distribution of the psalter as can be made so long as one attempts its integral recitation over a fixed period of time. Nonetheless, we might well ask whether it would be more desirable *not* to require an integral recitation, and to allow the use on a regular basis of the psalms traditionally assigned to morning (Psalms 51, 63, and 148–150) and the traditional evening psalm (Psalm 141).

A rubric provides that an appropriate refrain may be used with psalms.[49] Various modes of recitation are suggested. Besides the plainsong tones and various harmonized chants (traditional Anglican chants, simplified Anglican chants, and new compositions) in the Accompaniment edition of *The Hymnal 1982*, the Church Hymnal Corporation has published an Anglican Chant Psalter (with a congregational and a choir setting for each psalm) and a Plainsong Psalter (which gives refrains for each psalm from Howard Galley's *Prayer Book*

Office). In both offices an invitatory precedes the psalmody. The *Jubilate* (Psalm 100) has been provided as an alternative to the *Venite* as an invitatory to the morning psalms, while *Christ our Passover* may serve as the invitatory throughout Easter Season. Refrains for the invitatory psalms are provided for optional use on any day. In the evening, the *Phos hilaron* or an appropriate hymn serves as an optional invitatory (or one of the morning provisions may be used).

The lectionary provides a two-year course of three lessons each day (one from the Old Testament, one from the gospels, and one from the other New Testament literature), as well as lessons for major feasts. Two lessons may be read in the morning (one from each testament) and one in the evening if both offices are read daily; an Old Testament lesson may be borrowed from the alternative year if two lessons are desired in the evening; or all three lessons may be read at one office, if the office is read only once a day. In this manner the major part of the Old Testament is read every two years, while the major part of the New Testament is read once a year. The readings are distributed so that appropriate books are read during certain seasons of the year. In order to avoid breaking the sequence of readings from a book, the rubrics allow the redistribution of lessons before or after a major feast which interrupts that sequence.[50] The permission for the use of an additional reading from non-biblical Christian literature is an enrichment of the office.[51]

The repertoire of canticles for this prayer book has been greatly expanded. Seven canticles from the Old Testament and Apocrypha are now provided; the three gospel canticles are retained; there are two new canticles from the Book of Revelation; and the *Gloria in Excelsis* (the ancient morning hymn in Eastern usage) has joined the *Te Deum* as a canticle of ecclesiastical composition. The last portion of the *Te Deum* has been detached and restored to its original use as a set of suffrages (Suffrages B for Morning Prayer). Refrains may be used with any canticle except the two ecclesiastical compositions,[52] and many settings of the canticles in *The Hymnal 1982* provide for the use of refrains (principally from Howard Galley's *Prayer Book Office*). The canticles may be distributed in any appropriate way; a table on pages 144–145 of the *Book of Common Prayer* suggests an appropriate distribution. The inclusion of the Apostles' Creed as the final element in the section of the office devoted to the Word of God makes its use here analogous to the use of the Nicene Creed at the eucharist: it represents our response of faith to the word read. It may be omitted at one office if both offices are read daily.[53]

The prayers at Morning and Evening Prayer begin with the salutation and the Lord's Prayer (the *Kyrie* having fallen out of usage in the American office). The traditional suffrages (form A) have been carefully revised to secure a more inclusive scope of intercession; the suffrages once attached to the *Te Deum* (and to the *Gloria in Excelsis* in some rites) serve as alternative suffrages in the morning (form B), while a version of the Byzantine dismissal litany (the "angel of peace" petitions) serves as the evening alternative (form B). Considerable latitude is given in the use of collects: the selection includes the collect of the day and the seven printed in each office. One or more is to be used. Besides the two traditional office collects, there are collects for Sundays, Fridays, and Saturdays and two additional new collects for each office—a total of seven. This makes it possible to assign a collect to each day of the week if that is desired. The collect(s) must be followed by one of three new prayers for the mission and ministry of the church printed in each office.

The optional introductory and concluding sections of the offices offer provisions similar to those of past prayer books;

a new feature is the permission to use the traditional Western dismissal ("Let us bless the Lord"). Other rubrics specify how Morning or Evening Prayer is to be adapted when used as the liturgy of the word at the eucharist; this combination (which is useful for certain situations) is not one of the *regular* services of the church and will not concern us here.

The Order of Worship for the Evening might be used to provide a festal introduction to the evening office for the first and/or second evensong of Sundays and major feasts; or a festal office might be constructed for these occasions from the outline provided. When used to introduce evensong, this order allows the recovery of the evening oblation of light and incense which is the core of the ancient office; when used as an independent office, it provides an alternative which follows ancient models much more closely than the traditional Anglican form of Evening Prayer. The standard opening greeting for this office is adapted from Mozarabic usage. The prayer for light restores an ancient emphasis and can be seasonally varied. The *lucernaria* provided by the *Book of Occasional Services* are likewise a Mozarabic adaptation. The provision for psalter collects when the order is used as a full office restores another ancient practice. The requirement for a biblical reading adjusts this form of evening worship to standard Anglican practice (readings are not necessarily a component of the ancient form of evening prayer). The canticle is an independent element here, rather than a response to the lesson as in Anglican usage. The prayers conclude the office in the traditional way. It would be possible, as I have suggested in *Prayer Book Rubrics Expanded*, to adapt this service as an anticipated vigil of the resurrection on the eve of Sundays.

While the twofold daily office remains the norm, the *Book of Common Prayer 1979* also makes optional provision for two other offices in the course of the day: adaptations of traditional services for midday and compline. The Order of Service for Noonday follows the traditional pattern of the Roman little hours and conforms to the normative Anglican shape of psalms, readings, and prayers. Any appropriate psalmody may be used. The suggested hymns, lessons, and collects allow the service to be adapted to forenoon, noon, and afternoon (terce, sext, and none) While it is intended as a single midday service, it could in fact be used to provide offices for all of these traditional hours. Compline follows the traditional Western pattern. It provides fixed psalms proper to the evening. Any of the traditional compline hymns may be used; several appropriate short readings are provided as alternatives; and the *Nunc Dimittis* highlights the eschatological theme traditional to compline.

In addition to these public offices, the *Book of Common Prayer 1979* also provides flexible alternatives as Daily Devotions for Individuals and Families in the morning, at noon, in the early evening, and at the close of day (the fourfold pattern of the public offices). Each of these devotions consists of brief elements of praise, reading, and prayer and so conforms to the shape of the public offices in Anglican tradition. They also give expression to the concern of contemporary Episcopalians to make every suitable provision for the restoration of the discipline of daily prayer.

How successful are the provisions for daily worship in the *Book of Common Prayer 1979*? Without doubt they represent a genuine enrichment of what has proved the most viable tradition of daily public worship in the West since the era of the Reformation. Great care has been taken to adapt the office in such a way that due emphasis is given to the themes of traditional weekday commemorations on Sunday, Friday, and Saturday in the canticles and the office collects and that appropriate psalms are assigned to these days. But except for the restoration of the *Phos hilaron* for permissive use and the optional provision for an oblation of light and incense in the evening, the elements which link Morning and Evening Prayer to the traditional themes of sunrise and sunset and their Christological interpretation have *not* received due emphasis. *None* of the traditional psalms for these two offices has been restored as a fixed element in the rite. It is possible to use either the *Benedictus* or the *Gloria in Excelsis* as one of the canticles at Morning Prayer each day, but this is not required, and, because canticles are used at Morning Prayer as responses to the lessons rather than as independent elements which represent the Christological climax of the office at dawn, even the use of one of these canticles does not necessarily make the connection of dawn and Christ's resurrection for a congregation. Moreover, the two canticles of paschal deliverance which are traditional options for morning prayer (the *Benedicite* and the *Benedictus Es, Domine*) have entirely lost their paschal associations for Anglicans and are customarily understood as songs of creation. If we are to restore the theological connection between our daily rule of prayer and the services which articulate its meaning and focus it on Christ as the risen sun of righteousness and the light which knows no setting, then we will need to make the Order of Worship for the Evening the normative form of Evening Prayer and to construct an analogous form of worship for the morning. In addition, we will need to de-emphasize the office as a context for the reading of scripture in course. Such a reading is appropriate for a community which can gather daily; it makes little sense in the context of parochial life where much of the congregation will of necessity change from day to day.[54] However successful the traditional Anglican services of matins and evensong have been (and we should not underestimate their success), we shall find it necessary to adapt them radically if we are to make the appropriate links between our daily rule of prayer and the services which articulate their most authentic meaning.

Notes to Chapter One

1. For a careful contemporary study of Jewish observances in the early centuries of the common era, see Paul F. Bradshaw, *Daily Prayer in the Early Church* (NY: Oxford University Press, 1982), chapter 1. It is largely him whom I am following in the description which I give of Jewish practices.

2. See Exodus 29:38–41 and 30:7–8; Numbers 28:3–8. In the fourth century, John Chrysostom will cite the Old Testament prescription as a warrant for Christian times of prayer *(Exposition of Psalm 140:3)*, and this is probably what lies behind the term *legitimae orationes* in Tertullian (cited below).

3. The customary texts are Deuteronomy 6:49 and 11:13–21 and Numbers 15:37–41. In the first century this seems to be the liturgical agenda of what Tzvee Zahany calls the "scribal brotherhoods." See his article, "The Politics of Piety," in Paul F. Bradshaw and Lawrence A. Hoffmann, editors, *The Making of Jewish and Christian Worship* (Notre Dame, IN: University of Notre Dame Press, 1991), pages 22–41.

4. On the *berakah* (plural, *berakoth)* as a genre of Jewish prayer, see Bradshaw, *Daily Prayer in the Early Church*, pages 11–15. For our earliest texts of these *berakoth* see Lucien Deiss, *Springtime of the Liturgy: Liturgical Texts of the First Four Centuries*, translated by Matthew J. O'Connell (Collegeville, MN: Liturgical Press, 1979), pages 9–14. In the article cited above Tzvee Zahavy links these *berakoth* to the liturgical agenda of what he calls the priestly aristocracy. He argues that the liturgical agenda of this group and that of the scribal brotherhoods were united in a period of consolidation about the middle of the second century.

5. The text of the *berakoth* that has come down to us may be found in Deiss, *Springtime of the Liturgy*, pages 15–16.

6. Anton Baumstark in the first part of this century considered it an established fact that the Christian use of Psalm 148–150 derived from Jewish usage. Subsequent discussion disputed this claim. The most recent discussion, which inclines once again to accept this claim as historically probable, is found in W. Jardine Grisbrooke, "The Laudate Psalms: A Footnote," in *Studia Liturgica* 19:2, pages 162–184.

7. See *Didache* 8:2–3, which prescribes the recitation of the Lord's Prayer three times a day.

8. See for example, chapter 41 of the *Apostolic Tradition* of Hippolytus, which includes midnight in the cursus of recommended hours of prayer; also Clement of Alexandria, *Paedagogus* 2:9.

9. On all of this see Bradshaw, *Daily Prayer in the Early Church*, chapters 2 and 3. Liturgical scholars have had a tendency to read later practice back onto early evidence (reading references to three times for prayer as references to prayer at the third, sixth, and ninth hours, for example). Bradshaw is inclined to see a threefold pattern of daily prayer (morning, midday, and evening) as well established in the early centuries, but obscured by two factors: 1) the later dominance of morning and evening prayer, and 2) the development of terce, sext, and none as hours of the passion.

10. Hippolytus, *Apostolic Tradition*, chapter 41 (the longer and probably later form of the daily cursus in this work); Tertullian, *On Prayer*, chapter 25; *On Fasting*, chapter 9.

11. *Didache* 8:2–3.

12. See the claim of Eusebius, *Commentary on Psalm 64:10*, as cited in Bradshaw, *Prayer in the Early Church*, page 72: "throughout the whole world in the churches of God in the morning at sunrise and in the evening hymns and praises and truly divine pleasures are established to God. The pleasures of God are the hymns which everywhere in the whole world are offered in his Church are at morning and evening time." Note that patristic citations of psalms follow the Septuagint and Vulgate numbering; in this book I have used the Hebrew numbering in my text and in translating other texts.

13. *Apostolic Constitutions* 2:59:2.

14. See, for example, Basil of Caesarea, *Letter 207*. The practice described does *not* seem to be a purely monastic one.

15. On these psalms see most recently, W. Jardine Grisbrooke, "The Laudate Psalms: A Footnote," in *Studia Liturgica* 19:2, pages 162–184.

16. The *Gloria in Excelsis* is given as the morning hymn in the *Apostolic Constitutions* 7:47–48, along with an evening cento which includes the *Nunc Dimittis*. For an early reference to the *Phos hilaron*, see Basil of Caesarea, *On the Holy Spirit* 29:73, which refers to this hymn as a long standing usage.

17. For a careful discussion of the genres of recitation for psalmody, see Joseph Gelineau, *Voices and Instruments in Christian Worship: Principles, Laws, and Applications*, translated by Clifford Howell (Collegeville, MN: Liturgical Press, 1964), chapter 7. For Byzantine usage, see Juan Mateos, *La célébration de la parole dans la liturgie byzantine: Étude historique*, Orientalia Christiana Analecta 191 (Rome: Pont. Institutum Orientalium Studiorum, 1971), pages 7–26, "La psalmodie: ses genres."

18. The classic study here is Rolf Zerfass, *Die Schriftlesung im Kathedraloffizium Jerusa-lems*, Liturgiewissenschaftliche Quellen und Forschungen 48 (Münster, Westfallen: Aschendorffsche Verlagsbuchhandlung, 1968).

19. The classic study of this service is Juan Mateos, "La vigile cathédrale chez Egérie," *Orientalia Christiana Periodica* 27 (1961), pages 281–312. Mateos's conclusions need to be modified in some instances, I think. See my discussion in "The Morning Offices of the Byzantine Rite: Mateos Revisited," in *Studia Liturgica* 19 (1989), pages 162–178, and the bibliography cited there.

20. Cyprian, *On the Lord's Prayer* 35.

21. Zerfass reviews this whole process in *Die Schriftlesung im Kathedraloffizium Jerusa-lems*.

22. Thoughtful discussions of the theology of daily worship are found in Robert Taft, *The Liturgy of the Hours in East and West: The Origins of the Office and Its Meaning for Today* (Collegeville, MN: Liturgical Press, 1985), especially chapters 21 and 22, and in two articles of Juan Mateos, "The Morning and Evening Office," *Worship* 42 (1968), pages 31–47, and "The Origins of the Divine Office," *Worship* 41 (1967), pages 477–485.

23. It is important to note that the *Benedicite* came into the morning office not as a canticle of creation (as it is customarily understood in the morning office of Anglicanism) but as a canticle of redemption.,

24. See Mateos, "The Origins of the Divine Office," pages 34–35 and 44–46.

25. See the discussion in Gabriele Winkler, "Über die Kathedralvesper in den verschiedenen Riten des Ostens und Westens," *Archiv für Liturgiewissenschaft* 16 (1974), pages 53–102, here pages 63–64 (in a discussion of Theodoret).

26. See Robert Taft, *The Liturgy of the Hours in East and West*, pages 359–361.

27. The full form is found in the order for the eucharist; the form for the office only sketches the outline of the diaconal biddings for the litany and gives concluding prayers. For a good brief analysis of the genre, see Robert Taft, *Beyond East and West: Essays in Liturgical Understanding* (Washington, DC: Pastoral Press, 1984), pages 154–156.

28. See the discussion of these petitions in Robert Taft, *The Great Entrance: A History of the Transfer of Gifts and Other Preanaphoral Rites of the Liturgy of St. John Chrysos-tom*, second edition, Orientalia Christiana Analecta 200 (Rome: Pont., Institutum Studi-orum Orientalium, 1978), chapter 9, and Juan Mateos, *La célébration de la parole dans la liturgie byzantine*, pages 158–159.

29. Cf. the hymn cited by Massey Shepherd, *The Paschal Liturgy and the Apocalypse*, Ecumenical Studies in Worship 6 (Richmond, VA: John Knox Press, 1960), page 74:

> At *Mattins* bound, at *Prime* reviled,
>   Condemned to death at *Tierce*,
> Nailed to the Cross at *Sext*, at *Nones*
>   His blessed side they pierced.

> They take him down at *Vesper-tide*,
>   In grave at *Compline* lay,
> Who thenceforth bids his Church observe
>   her sevenfold hours alway.

Note that the morning celebration of the resurrection has fallen out of this sequence.

30. On this, see Robert Taft, *The Liturgy of the Hours in East and West*, chapter 4.

31. See Gabriele Winkler, "Das Offizium am Ende des 4. Jahrhunderts und das heutige chaldäische Offizium: Ihre strukturellen Zusammenhänge," *Ostkirchliche Studien* 19 (1976), pages 289–311, here 289–301.

32. See my article, "The Morning Offices of the Byzantine Rite: Mateos Revisited."

33. See the analysis by Miguel Arranz in "L'office de l'Asmatikos Hesperinos ('vêpres chantées') de l'ancien euchologe byzantin," *Orientalia Christiana Periodica* 44 (1978), pages 107–130, here 117–118. See also Taft, *Beyond East and West*, pages 154–156.

34. This represents a clericalization of the cult under the impact of "mysteriological piety," which will be dealt with in the next chapter.

35. For a study of these prayers and the way in which they were distributed in both the *akolouthia asmatike* and the Palestinian office, see Miguel Arranz, "Les prières presbytérales des matines byzantines," *Orientalia Christiana Periodica* 37 (1971), pages 406–436, 38 (1972), pages 64–115; and "Les prières sacerdotales des vêpres byzantines," *Orientalia Christiana Periodica* 37 (1971), pages 85–124.

36. See the edition of the rule in Timothy Fry, editor, *RB 1980: The Rule of St. Benedict in Latin and English with Notes* (Collegeville, MN: Liturgical Press, 1981), and Nathan Mitchell's article, "The Liturgical Code in the Rule of Benedict," which is printed as Appendix 3 in that edition; also Robert Taft, *The Liturgy of the Hours in East and West*, chapter 7. The outlines are adapted from Taft.

37. On this see Gabriele Winkler, "Über die Kathedralvesper in den verschiedenen Rites des Ostens und Westens," pages 100–101.

38. See the discussion in Marion Hatchett, *Commentary on the American Prayer Book*, pages 89–97, with comparative charts on pages 100–101.

Redeeming the Day   57

39. BCP 1549, page 3.

40. In constructing these outlines, I have used headings and subheadings from the BCP 1979.

41. The development of the offices in various editions of the BCP from 1662 can be traced in Paul V. Marshall, editor, *Prayer Book Parallels: The public services of the Church arranged for comparative study*, Anglican Liturgy in America 1 (NY: Church Hymnal Corporation, 1989), pages 86 ff. For details of the earlier history of the daily office in the *Book of Common Prayer*, see Marion J. Hatchett, *Commentary on the American Prayer Book*, pages 89–97 (general history), 97 ff. (various components).

42. BCP 1552, page 348. I owe this reference to Howard Galley.

43. See George Guiver, *Company of Voices: Daily Prayer and the People of God* (NY: Pueblo, 1988), chapter 16, for a study of parochial practice in England after the Reformation.

44. I have constructed these outlines on the basis of the headings and subheadings in the services.

45. BCP 1979, page 13.

46. These two offices are provided in traditional and contemporary language. New canticles are found only in contemporary forms, as are the order for Noonday Prayer, the Order of Worship for the Evening, and the Daily Devotions.

47. BCP 1979, page 934.

48. BCP 1979, page 935.

49. BCP 1979, 141; also page 935.

50. BCP 1979, page 934.

51. BCP 1979, page 142. A sermon may also be preached at this point in the service.

52. BCP 1979, page 141; also page 935.

53. BCP 1979, page 142.

54. Optional course readings might be provided for use in communities which gather daily for worship; appropriate readings might be provided for feasts and Sundays. Otherwise

readings might be omitted from the office as a service of praise and prayer. The Old Testament canticle at Morning Prayer would then conclude the psalmody, while the *Benedictus*, the *Gloria in Excelsis*, and the *Te Deum* might be left as alternate canticles before the prayers which form a climax to the morning praise. In the evening one of the two gospel canticles might likewise serve as an independent element which would form the climax to the evening praise.

Chapter Two

Redeeming the Week:
The Lord's Day and
the Eucharist

The Week as a Unit of Time

The rhythm of the week is so much a part of our lives
that it comes as something of a shock to realize that the week
is not a "natural" unit of time (like the day, which corresponds
to the earth's rotation, or the month and the year, which corre-
spond roughly to the moon's orbit around the earth and the
earth's orbit around the sun), but a human convention. As a
conventional unit, it has tended to eclipse the importance of the

month as an intermediate unit between the day and the year. Most societies seem to have found the month too long a unit for convenience and to have introduced a shorter unit to organize the rhythms of their life. The week as such a unit of time seems to have its origins in ancient near-Eastern civilizations. It reached the Greco-Roman civilization (to which we are heirs) in two forms in the early centuries of the common era. The first, "mythologized" form, which has left its imprint to the present day on our English names for the days of the week, seems to have rooted the week in the nature of things by relating the days of the week astrologically to the seven principal heavenly bodies of ancient astronomy (the sun, the moon, and five of the planets) and bringing each day under the influence of one of these bodies.[1] The second, "demythologized" form is the Judaeo-Christian one whose aetiological myth we find in Genesis 1:1–2:4. This account roots the week in the nature of things by relating it to the seven days of creation. It explicitly demythologizes the heavenly bodies by designating them as creations of God on the fourth day (Gen. 1:14–19); so concerned is it to desacralize these heavenly bodies that it refuses even to give them their customary names, since these were the names of deities: they are simply called the "lights" in the heavens, and the sun and the moon are described only as the greater lights, one to rule the day and the other the night. God creates them "to separate the day from the night" and "for signs and for seasons and for days and years" (Genesis 1:14).[2] These are the two ancient explanations of why the week as a conventional unit of time is a "natural" unit. We have no non-theological evidence for the origin of the convention itself. It seems most likely that the week represents a regularization of the rough calculation of the quarters of the lunar month achieved by discarding the fraction of a day and cutting the cycle of the week free from the lunar cycle of the month.[3]

Redeeming the Week

The principal nodal point of the week as a unit of time is the day which demarcates one week from the next—a function which the first or the last day of the week serves best. For the Jews the nodal point was the last day of the week, the sabbath, reckoned as beginning at sunset on Friday and concluding at sunset on Saturday. The account of Genesis 1:1–2:4 is the aetiological myth for the sabbath as well as for the week.[4] On the seventh day God brought the work of creation to a conclusion and rejoiced in its goodness. The observance prescribed for the sabbath therefore entails cessation of all labor, so that we may enter into the joy of God's sabbath. As the nodal point of the week it is the weekly feast of Judaism.

We designate the important occasions in our communal life as "feasts." The very name indicates the ordinary way by which we observe these occasions—by eating and drinking. The meal is both a fundamental social institution and a fundamental religious institution. The Christian Bible opens in Genesis with a meal (eating the "forbidden fruit") and closes in Revelation with a meal (the wedding feast of the Lamb). Alexander Schmemann writes eloquently of the ineradicable religious significance of the meal:

> Man is a hungry being. But he is hungry for God. All desire is finally a desire for Him. To be sure, man is not the only hungry being. All that exists lives by "eating." The whole creation depends on food. But the unique position of man in the universe is that he alone is to *bless* God for the food and the life he receives from him. He alone is to respond to God's blessing with his blessing. . . .
>
> Men understand all this instinctively if not rationally. Centuries of secularism have failed to transform eating into something strictly utilitarian. Food is still treated with reverence. A meal is still a rite—the last "natural sacrament" of family and friendship, of life that is more than

"eating" and "drinking." To eat is still something more than to maintain bodily functions. People may not understand what that "something more" is, but they nonetheless desire to celebrate it. They are still hungry and thirsty for sacramental life.[5]

The day which marks the nodal point of the week is our weekly feast day, and it is generally marked by a meal (a "feast") as its significant rite.[6]

The Week, the Sabbath, and Sabbath Rites in Judaism

The Week in Judaism: Since the week as we know it is of Jewish origin, what was said above already sets the context for the Jewish observance of the week. The Jewish sabbath gives the key to the Jewish understanding of the week: the observance of the sabbath is a temporal "refraction" of Israel's faith in Yahweh its Redeemer as the creator of heaven and earth. Through its observance Israel enters into the joy of the sabbath rest of its Lord, acknowledging the goodness of the divine work of creation. Judaism in the first century of the common era prescribed special sacrifices in the temple for the sabbath, but these were not the observances which impacted most directly on the lives of Jews. The restriction of the sacrificial cultus to the temple in Jerusalem meant that sacrifice could not be the characteristic sabbath observance for ordinary Jews. Sabbath observances found their focus, rather, in the home and the local community. In the home, the primary observance was the meal which marked the beginning of the sabbath on Friday evening. In the local community, the primary observances were the gatherings for prayer on the eve of the sabbath, on the morning of the sabbath, and on the evening with which the sabbath closed, and the readings from the torah and the prophets (including what we think of as the historical books of the Old Testament) added to the service on the morning of the sabbath.

The Sabbath Meal in the Home: In one sense, of course, the sabbath meal *is* a sacrifice in the most basic sense of the word. The English word "sacrifice" covers a variety of ritual acts for which there are distinct terms in the language of the Old Testament. When we use the word in a cultic sense, we are usually referring to animal sacrifices—which Judaism restricted to the temple in Jerusalem. But from another perspective, every meal is a communion sacrifice. Louis Bouyer writes:

> a sacrifice remains essentially a meeting with God in a sacred meal. To repeat, it is originally a meal in which man recognizes that in every meal he meets God. He meets Him there because it is God who provides him with food, who is present there with him, who is at once his fellow sharer in the meal and his provisioner.[7]

> The primitive view of sacrifice, and this is something more permanent than a temporary phase preceding the later developments, is the meeting par excellence of God and man. It is an act that is inseparably social and individual. Each man feels that he is personally engaged in what is basically a common celebration. It is at the same time a full realization of God's interest in mankind. All this comes from the fact that a common meal makes men appreciate their relation with the cosmos which provides the natural resources for their life. Eating in common is the human act par excellence, where society is built up as from within, while each man perfects himself by integrating himself with the universe. It is moreover the first and supreme act in which man apprehends himself in his living relationship with God. Man undoubtedly comes to the meal to secure this relationship, and, in a way, to secure everything, since

he there receives nourishment for his life. But he also goes there to give, to give himself. In other words, he realizes, not in thought, but in a decisive act, that his life is not his own, that it depends upon God alone. And thus, at last, in sacrifice the life of man comes, or comes again, to participate in the life of God.[8]

This is very much in line with Schmemann's perspective, as cited above.

Every meal for the pious Jew had something of this meaning, articulated in the *berakoth* which served as table graces, but on the sabbath (and on festivals) this meaning was brought to focus in the concluding grace of the meal, the *birkat ha-mazon*.

Lucien Deiss describes the *birkat ha-mazon* in the following way:

> The *Birkat ha-mazon* . . . contains four parts: the *Birkat ha-zan*, which blesses the Creator; the *Birkat ha-aretz*, which gives thanks for the land, the covenant, and the law, and is thus a memorial of the history of salvation; the *Birkat-Ierushalayim*, which is a prayer of intercession for Jerusalem and the house of David; and the *Birkat ha-tob we-ha-metib*, which is a general blessing at the closing.[9]

Deiss goes on to give L. Finkelstein's reconstruction of the primitive text:

> You are blessed, Lord our God
>   King of the universe
> you who nourish the entire world
> with goodness, tender love, and mercy.
>   You are blessed, O Lord,
> you who nourish the universe.
>
> We will give you thanks, Lord our God,
> for you have given us a desirable land for our inheritance,

[that we may eat of its fruits
and be filled with its goodness].
You are blessed, Lord our God
for the land and the food.

Lord our God, take pity,
on Israel your people and Jerusalem your city,
on Zion, the place where your glory dwells,
on your altar and your sanctuary.
You are blessed, Lord our God
   King of the universe,
(you who are) good and filled with kindness!

You are blessed, Lord our God
   King of the universe,
(you who are) good and filled with kindness![10]

On sabbaths and feasts, the meal opens with the *Kiddush,* a
berakah over a first cup of wine which "sanctifies" the day by
remembering the reason for its holiness. This blessing at the
beginning of the meal and the *birkat ha-mazon* at its end thus
frame the meal as a religious observance. The text of the *Kiddush* for sabbaths is as follows:

You are blessed, Lord our God
   King of the universe.
You have given us as an inheritance the Sabbath of
your holiness,
   out of love and good will,
as a memorial of the works of your creation (Lev. 23:3).
This day is the first of your holy convocations.
It is the memorial of the exodus from Egypt.
You have chosen us among all peoples,
you have sanctified us,
you have given us as an inheritance the Sabbath of your
holiness,
   out of love and good will.
You are blessed, O Lord, who sanctify the Sabbath.[11]

CHAPTER TWO

We should note here the twofold focus of the blessing: the sabbath is the "memorial of the Exodus from Egypt" as well as "a memorial of the works of [God's] creation." The sabbath meal acknowledges Israel's faith that the Lord who redeemed Israel from Egypt is the creator of heaven and earth. The weekly sabbath is the key to Judaism's "architecture of time," and the key to the meaning of the sabbath is found in this acknowledgment that the Lord who brought Israel out of Egypt is the creator who built the sabbath observance into the order of creation itself.

The Synagogue Service on the Morning of the Sabbath: At the morning service on the sabbath a liturgy of the word was appended to the customary order of praise and prayer. This appended liturgy consisted of a reading from the torah, to which a reading from the prophetic literature *(Haftarah)* had been added by the first century of the common era. Judaism in the first century of the common era divided the torah into portions to be read over the course of one year or three years (the Babylonian and Palestinian usages respectively). The prophetic portions may not yet have been organized so systematically, but read *ad libitum.* Feasts and special sabbaths would have their own readings which were independent of this sequence. Psalmody may have been interspersed between the readings. A homily might follow the readings. The components of this service for the morning of the sabbath would then be:

1. **Morning praise and prayers**
   perhaps the "verses of song," the *Shema* with its *berakoth,* the *Tefillah*

2. **The Liturgy of the Word**
   torah portion, reading from the prophetic literature, sermon

Our sources for the synagogue liturgy, unfortunately, come from later centuries of the common era, so that we cannot be more precise about either the components of the service in the first century or their sequence. As regards the *Tefillah* we should note that Jewish usage omitted the intercessory *berakoth* on the sabbath and feasts, while Christian usage retained them.

The Weekly Fasts: In the first century of the common era, pious Jews observed the market days—Monday and Thursday—as fast days, abstaining from food until the evening meal. This was understood as an intensive form of prayer for the redemption of Israel. By the first century, it was customary to mark these days (when people would have come to towns for the markets) with a liturgy of the word at the morning service of praise and prayer in the synagogues where the sabbath portion from the torah was repeated.

The Week in Sectarian Judaism: Until recent decades, we generally understood first-century Judaism largely in terms of the Pharisaic Judaism which became normative after the fall of Jerusalem. But in reality first-century Judaism was a much more varied phenomenon, and other forms of Jewish thought and practice (which we think of as "sectarian" today) would seem to have had a much greater impact on the early church than has generally been realized. We noted in chapter 1 that many early Christians may have followed sectarian rather than Pharisaic practice in the times fixed for daily prayers. Sectarian Judaism likewise seems to have influenced the way in which Christians observed the week. Liturgical scholars stand indebted to Annie Jaubert for her careful work with this material,[12] even though it is unwise to accept all her conclusions as established historical facts.[13]

The calendar with which Jaubert works is described by Roland de Vaux in the following way:

The calendar . . . is entirely governed by the week. It is found most clearly in the apocryphal week of Jubilees: fifty-two weeks make a year and 364 days, divided into quarters of thirteen weeks, that is, of of ninety-one days; seven years make a week of years (as in Daniel), seven weeks of years form a jubilee. This same calendar is found in a part of the Apocrypha ascribed to Henoch [Enoch], and in the Qumran literature. The purpose of this reckoning is to make the same feasts fall every year on the same days of the week. **The liturgical days are the first, fourth and sixth days of the week; the sabbath is the day of rest.**[14]

We shall have occasion in the next chapter to work out the consequences for the liturgical year (it results in a fixed date for Passover, and hence for Easter, which will always fall on the first day of the week). What we need to note at present is that this calendar provides for liturgical assemblies on Sundays, Wednesdays, and Fridays, while the sabbath remains a day of rest. This is exactly the way that the church structured its week.

The Week, the Lord's Day, and the Eucharist in the Early Christian Centuries

The Lord's Day, the Sabbath, and the Station Days

The Lord's Day: With the resurrection of Jesus on the first day of the week, the architecture of time was transformed for Christians. The nodal point of the week for Judaism had been the sabbath, whose observance was an acknowledgement that the God who had redeemed Israel from bondage was the creator. For the followers of Jesus, however, the resurrection of Jesus from the dead was the new focus for their experience of God's redemption, and the day of the resurrection displaced the sabbath as the day around which the week was organized. The creation of light on the first day of the week was refracted for them in the rising of the "sun of righteousness" on that same day. Justin Martyr in the second century explains the Christian observance of the first day of the week in this way:

> It is on Sunday that we all assemble, because Sunday is the first day: the day on which God transformed darkness and matter and created the world, and the day on which Jesus Christ our Savior rose from the dead. He was crucified on the eve of Saturn's day, and on the day after, that is, on the day of the sun, he appeared to his apostles and disciples and taught them what we have now offered for your examination.[15]

Already in the New Testament there are references to the Lord's Day, the κυριακε 'ημερα or *dies Dominica*. Almost certainly the expression is a reference to the first day of the week as the day on which the risen Jesus was manifested as both Lord and Christ. There is also perhaps an implicit allusion here to the day of the Lord in the literature of the Old Testament, that eschatological moment when God will make good the promises of redemption and bring the world to judgment.

This aspect of the theology of the Lord's day is what lies behind the reference to the day in early Christian literature as the "eighth day": it is the day after the work of creation has been brought to its conclusion, the first day of the new creation. Justin Martyr also refers to this name, but our earliest reference is the *Letter of Barnabas*:

CHAPTER TWO

Furthermore [the Lord] says to them: *I will not abide your new moons and your Sabbaths* (Isa. 1:13). You see what He means: the present Sabbaths are not acceptable to me, but that Sabbath which I have made, in which, after giving rest to all things, I will make the beginning of the eighth day, that is, the beginning of another world. Therefore we also celebrate the joy of the eighth day on which Jesus rose from the dead, was made manifest, and ascended into heaven.[16]

The typological symbolism of the eighth day, so arcane to us, enjoyed great popularity in the early Christian centuries. What the name tries to articulate is the conviction that the resurrection of Christ makes us proleptic participants in a new age. We are participants because of the gift of Christ's Spirit to us—a gift bestowed either on the day of Christ's resurrection itself (John 20:19) or on the day of Pentecost—a "week of weeks" later (Acts 2).[17] The Lord's Day is also the day of the eschatological gift of the Spirit.

It is crucial that we be mindful of the origin of the Christian observance of the Lord's Day if we are to understand why we observe it and how we might observe it appropriately. It is *not* the sabbath, which Judaism observes by refraining from work. Ordinary Christians undoubtedly were forced in most circumstances in early centuries to schedule their Christian assembly on the Lord's Day at a very early hour, for Sunday would have been a working day in both Jewish and pagan communities. It was only when the legislation of the fourth century made Sunday a day of rest to allow Christians leisure for their liturgical observances that Christians began to confuse it with the sabbath—a confusion which is compounded when we call Sunday the sabbath and base our observance of it on the prescriptions of the ten commandments.

Christian Observance of the Sabbath: The sabbath, as we have seen, is the point of reference for establishing when the Lord's Day occurs: the Lord's Day is "the first day after the sabbath," the μια των σαββατων (John 20:1; cf. Mark 16:2; Matthew 28:1). But Christian attitudes to the observance of the sabbath, once the Lord's Day had become the focus of the week for them, varied widely. No doubt until they were expelled from the synagogue, many Jewish Christians continued to observe the sabbath in much the same way that their fellow Jews did. Gentile Christians would have had no reason to observe the sabbath, though sabbath observance like other Jewish practices had a certain attraction for many of them. In the second and third centuries most Christian authors show a marked hostility toward any kind of sabbath observance. Ignatius of Antioch's attitude is typical of the majority of second-century Christian authors:

> Do not be led astray by wrong views or by outmoded fables that count for nothing. For if we go on observing Jewish rites we admit that we never received grace. The divine prophets themselves lived Christ Jesus' way. That is why they were persecuted, for they were inspired by His grace to convince unbelievers that God is one, and that He has revealed Himself in His son Jesus Christ, who is His Word proceeding from silence and who was pleasing in all things to Him who sent Him.

> Those, then, who lived by ancient practices arrived at a new hope. They ceased to keep the Sabbath but lived by the Lord's Day, on which our life as well as theirs shone forth, thanks to Him and His death, though some deny this. . . . It is out of place to talk Jesus Christ and to practice Judaism.[18]

Christians are those "who live by the Lord's Day," not by the sabbath.

A true sabbath rest for Christians is not the intermittent cessation of work, but a constant cessation from sin, as Origen argues:

CHAPTER TWO

He who abstains from the works of the world and frees himself *for* spiritual things, he it is who celebrates the feast of the Sabbath. He bears no burden on the journey. For the burden is any sin, as the Prophet says: They weigh on me like a heavy burden. On the sabbath day, every one stays seated in his own place. What is the spiritual place of the soul? Justice is its place, and truth, wisdom, holiness, and everything that Christ is, this is the true place for the soul. And it is from this place that it should not go out if it is to keep true Sabbaths: "He who dwells in me, I also will dwell in him" (John 15:5).[19]

The dominant approach to the sabbath was not to observe it at all, but to interpret it typologically as a reference to a perpetual sabbath from sin, or to the sabbath rest which God has prepared for us in heaven (Hebrews 4:1–11) and which we find in Christ.

Later, the church's approach to the sabbath would diverge between the Latin- speaking West and the Greek-speaking East. In the West, the sabbath was treated as a fast day, a weekly analogue of the church's yearly fast on the great sabbath when Christ, taken from us, rested in the tomb. The Byzantine church, on the other hand, and some others in the East, came to observe the sabbath as a second eucharistic feast day in the week. This is still the approach found in the Byzantine euchologies, which treat the sabbath as a feast of creation. We do not know what caused this change of attitude in the East. Perhaps it was a concern to affirm liturgically the goodness of creation in opposition to gnostic, Marcionite, and Manichean denial of that goodness.

Wednesdays and Fridays as Weekly Station Days: Already in the *Didache* we find an obligation set out for Christians to fast on Wednesday and Friday each week—a practice set in contrast to the Jewish fasts on Mondays and Thursdays. The sectarian calendar which we noted above surely lies at the origin of the observance of these days. They are liturgical days in that calendar, however; here they are fast days, like the Pharisaic observance of Monday and Thursday.[20] They are perhaps best understood as days of preparation by fasting as a form of intensive prayer for the weekly feast on Sunday. By the time of the *Didascalia* in the third century, however, these weekly observances have been "historicized." They are understood as the weekly remembrance of the betrayal of Jesus (Wednesday) and his crucifixion (Friday), just as the Lord's Day is the weekly remembrance of his resurrection.[21] Although the Wednesday fast fell out of use in most places over the course of time, Western catholic usage has continued to observe the Friday fast in commemoration of the crucifixion.[22]

The Eucharist as the Characteristic Rite for the Lord's Day

The Origin of the Eucharist: Judaism's characteristic rites for the sabbath were the family meal which opened the sabbath on Friday evening and the liturgy of the word as the rite for the morning of the sabbath. Early Christians continued to worship in the synagogue, but interpreted the law and the prophets as finding their fulfilment in Jesus as the Messiah. The climax of the week for them, however, was the community meal on the Lord's Day, when the risen Christ made himself known to them in the breaking of the bread, as he had manifested himself to the disciples at Emmaus on the evening after his resurrection. The liturgy of the word and the Lord's supper thus became the characteristic rites in the Christian observance of the week. When Christians were expelled from the synagogues, they continued to observe a liturgy of the word in their own communities. They also gathered for a weekly community meal on the day when the Lord had first made himself known to them in the breaking of bread, using *berakoth* for this meal which gave it a Christological interpretation. The prayers of the *Didache*, known to us in the metrical paraphrase, "Father, we thank thee who hast planted," are early Christian *berakoth* of just this sort.

Practical considerations soon made it expedient for Christians to gather, not for a full meal each week, but for a sacramental meal which consisted of that food and drink to which Jesus had given a new meaning at the last supper. The key components of this weekly sacramental meal, then, were 1) taking bread, 2) giving thanks, 3) breaking the bread, and 4) sharing the bread , as Jesus had at the beginning of the last supper; and 5) taking the cup of wine, 6) giving thanks, and 7) sharing of the cup, as Jesus had at the end of the supper. When the "main course" of the meal fell out of use, this sevenfold shape was generally telescoped into a fourfold one: 1) taking bread and wine, 2) giving thanks over them, 3) breaking the bread, and 4) sharing the bread and the cup. Once Christians began to observe their own liturgy of the word and also began to separate their sacramental meal from a full community meal, it was natural that they should combine these two observances. We have little evidence of just how this all happened, but it had taken place by the time that Justin Martyr described the weekly worship of the Christian community about 150 CE. The full meal may already have fallen out of use in the New Testament period: "after supper" has fallen out of the cup words in all of the New Testament accounts except that of the long version of Luke.

In Justin's description we can discern the clear outline of the Christian eucharist as we know it. The basic structure has remained remarkably constant down to the present, and recent revisions have served to re-emphasize this basic structure:

The Liturgy of the Word

On the day named after the sun, all who live in city or countryside assemble.

The memoirs of the apostles or the writings of the prophets are read for as long as time allows. When the lector has finished, the president addresses us and exhorts us to imitate the splendid things we have heard.

Then we all stand and pray. *We offer prayers in common for ourselves . . . and for all men everywhere. It is our desire, now that we have come to know the truth, to be found worthy of doing good deeds and obeying the commandments, and thus to obtain eternal salvation.*

When we finish praying, we greet one another with a kiss.

The Liturgy of the Table

The bread and a cup of wine mixed with water are brought to him who presides over the brethren.

The president then prays and gives thanks according to his ability, *glorifying the Father of the universe through the name of the Son and of the Holy Spirit, and he utters a lengthy eucharist,* and the people give their assent with an "Amen."

Next, the gifts over which the thanksgiving has been spoken are distributed, and everyone shares in these, while they are also sent via the deacons to the absent brethren.[23]

From this description of Justin Martyr and from later evidence, such as that of the *Apostolic Tradition* of Hippolytus early in the next century, we can sketch out the basic components of the eucharist as the Sunday worship of the Christian Church. The basic early components are in bold-faced type. Justin's was a narrative description. He touches lightly on the act of assembling and says nothing of the act of dismissal. These are, however, the actions which frame the eucharist, and they have their own theological significance, as we shall see. Other functional actions are also passed over in silence here. The fraction or breaking of the bread, for example, was a practical necessity, but Justin saw no need to make special mention of it. The outline is constructed

76   CHAPTER TWO

from the perspective of later developments, and I have included early additions to the original outline in ordinary typeface.[24]

The Shape of the Eucharist

The Assembly of the Church *(synaxis of the ekklesia)*
 Entrance psalm (antiphonal)
 Entrance prayer
  (before the psalm in the Byzantine rite; after the greeting at Rome)
 Greeting by the presiding minister

The Proclamation of the Word of God
 Reading(s) from the Old Testament (later lost in most rites)
 Responsorial psalmody
  After the loss of the Old Testament reading, the Roman gradual was shifted to a position before the Alleluia; the Greek prokeimenon remained in place before the epistle.
 New Testament Reading from the Epistles, Acts, or Revelation
 Alleluia responsory
 Gospel Reading
 Homily

The Prayers of the People
 Common Prayers
  Eastern usage: litanies with diaconal biddings, people's response, prayer
  Roman usage: series of biddings, silences, collects (later lost)
 Exchange of the Peace
  Eastern shift of position: during preparation of gifts
  Roman shift of position: after the Lord's Prayer

The Celebration of the Holy Communion
 Preparation of the Table with psalmody
  Byzantine custom: the Great Entrance is the diaconal transfer of the gifts which have been presented by people before the service. At first done in silence, this entrance acquired as a chant verses from Psalm 24 with alleluia as a refrain. Later alleluia was replaced by a troparion.

Roman custom: the people came forward in procession to present their offerings of bread and wine to the clergy just before the Great Thanksgiving. The deacons then selected what was necessary for the service and prepared the table. This procession was accompanied by an antiphonal psalm which was concluded with a prayer.

The Great Thanksgiving (Roman Canon Actionis, Byzantine Anaphora)

The Fraction (Breaking of the Bread)

The Communion
Lord's Prayer (sometimes before the fraction)
Administration of communion
Communion psalm (antiphonal; perhaps once responsorial)
Prayer after communion

The Dismissal of the Church (by the deacon)

The Gathering and the Dismissal: In outlining the rite, I have framed it by two liturgical actions whose profound significance is often overlooked: the assembly and the dismissal. The eucharist is the heart of the church's life, toward which Christian existence moves in *systole* and from which it flows in *diastole*, as Jean-Jacques von Allmen reminds us.[25] It is, as he also says, the "epiphany of the church," the place where the church is most truly revealed.[26] Alexander Schmemann calls the eucharist the "sacrament of assembly," for the eucharist is the *synaxis*, the "gathering," of the *ekklesia*— the people whom God has "called out" from the world in Jesus Christ on a pilgrimage to God's kingdom.[27] The gathering of the community is the liturgical act in which the very meaning of the church as God's *ekklesia* is embodied. The eucharist exists for the upbuilding of this *ekklesia* that it may be the body of Christ. Because the eucharist is the sacrament of assembly, it is properly celebrated only when the church can gather. It is inappropriate as an act of special devotion for small groups apart from the ecclesial assembly.

In the fourth century, what was an informal action took on formal characteristics as the assembly took the shape of an entrance rite. Originally, the presiding minister had begun the eucharist by calling the church to order with his opening greeting. When the local churches developed into large assemblies, however, what was essentially an informal rite of necessity took on a more structured shape. In the Byzantine rite it would seem that all gathered outside the church and entered the church together, the clergy processing down the central aisle into the apse, the laity flowing into the nave. Sometimes the people and clergy might gather in one place and move in procession to the church where the eucharist was to be celebrated. Such an entrance required very complicated orchestration, however, and eventually the Byzantine custom conformed to the ordinary practice in Rome, where the laity assembled in the church and awaited the clergy, who entered in formal procession.[28] In the East this entrance procession was eventually opened by a prayer of entrance and accompanied by an antiphonal psalm. Selected verses from Psalm 95 with a refrain were the ordinary introit; a special psalm and refrain might be appointed for the most important feasts; and on penitential occasions verses from Psalm 80 might be sung, with the *trisagion* as the refrain. In Rome the procession was accompanied by a variable antiphonal psalm with a refrain, which was concluded with a collect after the greeting. Everywhere the danger was that the entrance might change the liturgical act from one which manifested the church as the sacrament of assembly to one which served principally to display ecclesiastical (and even secular) power. Moreover, the expansion of the entrance rite over the course of the centuries would result in the abbreviation of the liturgy of the word which followed.

The eucharist ends with the dismissal, which has given the rite its most popular name in Roman Catholic usage, *missa* or the mass. A *missa* is a sending forth, a com*miss*ioning, of God's people to bear witness to God and to carry out God's work of reconciliation in the world. The church does not exist for its own sake, but for the sake of the world to whom Christ was sent and for whom he gave his life. An ancient hymn from the rite of the Church of Malabar catches all of this very well:

> Strengthen for service, Lord, the hands
> that holy things have taken;
> let ears that now have heard thy songs
> to clamor never waken.

> Lord, may the tongues which "holy" sang"
> keep free from all deceiving;
> the eyes which saw thy love be bright,
> thy blessed hope perceiving.

> The feet that tread thy hallowed courts
> from light do thou not banish;
> the bodies by thy body fed
> with thy new life replenish.[29]

The liturgical actions which frame the eucharist, the assembly and the dismissal, define the church as the people called out by God and sent forth on God's mission. The eucharist is the visible manifestation of that call and that commissioning.

The Proclamation of the Word of God: The dual foci of the Christian eucharist are the pulpit and the table. At the pulpit Christ is manifest as the Word of God; at the table he is revealed as the Bread of life; or, put differently, Christ is the Proclaimed Word and the Word Made Flesh. Alexander Schmemann aptly describes the first part of the eucharist as the sacrament of the word. In Judaism the liturgy of the word which was appended to the morning synagogue service consisted of the reading of the law and the prophets. The law (or torah) held pride of place as the first reading. Our earliest relatively complete account of the Christian eucharist, that of Justin Martyr, reports that "the memoirs of the apostles or the writings of the prophets are read for as long as time allows." This is not meant to be a precise description, and probably we should understand it simply as a witness that readings from both the Old Testament and the apostolic literature (which was just beginning to acquire the status of "scripture" in the church) were included in the eucharistic liturgy by this time. At first, of course, Christians read from the Old Testament as the Jewish synagogue had done, but interpreted it as a prophecy of Christ. Readings from the New Testament appeared when the church developed its own canon of scripture. Probably the liturgy of the word in its fully-developed form in the early centuries consisted of readings from the law, the prophets, the "epistles" (including Acts and Revelation), and the gospels. The reading from the gospel was the climax of the Christian liturgy of the word. This is the series of lessons appointed in the *Apostolic Constitutions*. Soon the Old Testament was restricted to a single reading in most rites, and then, with the increasing complexity of the entrance rite, it disappeared altogether. Lessons before the gospel would be interspersed with responsorial psalmody, known as the gradual (since it was sung from the step—*gradus*—of the gospel pulpit) in the Roman rite and the *prokeimenon* (from the verse "placed before" it as a refrain) in the Byzantine rite. An alleluia responsory preceded the gospel. The function of the homily or sermon by the presiding minister was to "break open" the scriptural word so that it became the living Word, God's word to the present congregation. We might also say that it served to enable the church to make Christ's story its own, to allow Christ's work of reconciliation to shape and define the character of the church's own life.

Systems of readings were slow in developing. Initially they must have been largely at the discretion of the the presiding minister. The controlling lesson was, in most cases, the gospel. Other readings might be selected to complement the gospel chosen for a service. Important feasts and festal seasons undoubtedly were the first days to acquire fixed lessons in the various traditions. Easter Season (from pascha to the day of Pentecost) and the season of baptismal catechesis acquired carefully constructed series of lessons in most ritual families, as we shall see in the next chapter. Apart from that, a selective sequential reading of gospels and epistles was probably the most common way of organizing the New Testament readings. Initially the major patriarchal sees probably used their characteristic gospels for the eucharist: Matthew's gospel was characteristic of the see of Antioch (Syria and Palestine); Mark's gospel was characteristic of the sees of Rome and Alexandria; John's gospel was characteristic of the churches of Asia Minor. Later, as the four gospels were accepted as part of the New Testament canon, churches drew on all of them. The further development of the lectionary system is a part of the story of the annual cycle.

What is the function of the liturgy of the word as a part of the eucharistic liturgy? Alexander Schmemann puts it very well:

> . . . in the liturgical and spiritual tradition of the Church, the Church's essence as the incarnation of the Word, as the fulfilment in time and space of the divine incarnation, is realized precisely in the unbreakable link between the word and the sacrament. . . . In the sacrament we partake of him who comes and abides with us in the word, and the mission of the word presupposes the sacrament as its fulfilment, for in the sacrament Christ the Word becomes our life. The Word assembles the church for his incarnation in her. In

CHAPTER TWO

separation from the word the sacrament is in danger of being perceived as magic, and without the sacrament the word is in danger of being "reduced" to "doctrine." And finally, it is precisely through the sacrament that the word is interpreted, for the interpretation of the word is always witness to the fact that the Word has become our life. . . . The sacrament is his witness, and therefore in it lies the source, the beginning and the foundation of the exposition and comprehension of the word, the source and criterion of theology. Only in this unbreakable unity of word and sacrament can we really understand the meaning of the affirmation that the Church alone preserves the true meaning of scripture. That is why the necessary *beginning* of the eucharistic ceremony is the first part of the liturgy—the *sacrament of the word,* which finds its fulfilment and completion in the offering, consecration, and distribution to the faithful of the eucharistic gifts.[30]

The prophetic word of the Old Testament became flesh in Jesus Christ. The word of the church's scriptural witness to Christ becomes the living word of the church's testimony in the homily in order that it may then be written in flesh and blood in the Church as the body of Christ. In the eucharist Christ is proclaimed as the Word of life in order that he may be received as the Bread of life for the church which is his embodied presence in the world.

The Prayers of the People: The church's first response to the proclamation of the word is intercession. By baptism Christ has incorporated the church into his royal priesthood, and in the prayers of the people we exercise this royal priesthood in the eucharistic assembly, sharing in Christ's priestly ministry of intercessory prayer. In this way the church is manifest as the New Israel. In Exodus God declares to the people of Israel:

> Now therefore, if you obey my voice and keep my covenant, you shall be my treasured possession out of all the peoples.

> Indeed, the whole earth is mine, but you shall be for me a priestly kingdom and a holy nation (Exodus 19:6).

This promise is fulfilled in Christ, in whom God has made a new covenant with us, into which we are incorporated by baptism. The author of 1 Peter therefore bids us:

> Come to [Christ], a living stone, though rejected by mortals yet chosen and precious in God's sight, and like living stones, let yourself be built into a spiritual house, to be a holy priesthood, to offer spiritual sacrifices acceptable to God through Jesus Christ (1 Peter 2:4–5).

> . . . you are a chosen race, a royal priesthood, a holy nation, God's own people, in order that you may proclaim the mighty acts of him who called you out of darkness into his marvelous light.

> Once you were not a people
> but now you are God's people,
> once you had not received mercy,
> but now you have received mercy (1 Peter 2:9–10).

In the liturgy of the word, this priestly vocation is exercised in intercessory prayer. In the early centuries, this prayer took a variety of forms, coordinating the "liturgies" of the presiding minister (bishop or presbyter), deacon, and congregation. In the East this generally took the form of a series of diaconal biddings to which the people added a response; the presiding minister then concluded the intercessions with a presidential prayer. In the *Book of Common Prayer 1979,* this is the shape which these prayers take in Forms 1 and 5 of the Prayers of the People in the eucharistic liturgy. The classic shape of eucharistic intercessions in the West is that which was retained in the Good Friday liturgy as the solemn collects. It took the form of a series of biddings for particular concerns, silent intercession by the congregation after each bidding, and prayers by the presiding minister to conclude each bidding. On Sundays and in Easter Season Christians prayed standing, for they had been *raised* with Christ to share in his royal priesthood. The canons of the Council of Nicaea go so far as to prescribe disciplinary measures against any of the faithful who kneel for prayers at these times.

The Exchange of the Peace: Peace was Christ's Easter gift to his church (John 14:27; cf. 20:21). It is the concrete expression of the reconciliation between God and humanity and between one human and another when the gospel has taken root in our lives; it is the precondition for presenting ourselves and our gifts before God in the eucharistic meal, for that meal embodies the unity of the God's people in the one bread and the one cup. It is therefore the hinge between the liturgy of the word and the liturgy of the meal, the result of one and the precondition for the other. In the catecheses which Cyril delivered to the newly baptized, he sees the exchange of the peace as the church's obedience to Jesus' injunction to his followers in Matthew's gospel:

> So when you are offering your gift at the altar, if you remember that your brother or sister has something against you, leave your gift there before the altar and go; first be reconciled to your brother or sister, and then come and offer your gift (Matthew 6:23–24).

The exchange of the peace is the concrete expression of the eucharist as the sacrament of unity, for as Aquinas says,

> In a sacrament we may consider the sacrament itself, that is, the sign, and the reality *(res)* there. The reality *(res)* in the Eucharist is the unity of Christ's mystical body. . . .[31]

Eventually in the Roman rite, the peace was shifted to a position after the eucharistic prayer and the Lord's Prayer, probably as a concrete expression there that we have indeed "forgiven those who trespass against us."

The Celebration of the Holy Communion 1: The Preparation of the Table: The first action of the church's eucharistic meal is the "taking" of bread and wine, the preparation of the food and drink for the meal. In origin this is a purely functional act. Within the first centuries of the common era, it became customary for the congregation to provide the bread and wine for the meal, bringing to the eucharistic assembly the food and drink which would be necessary. Different churches organized this procedure in different ways. The custom which prevailed in the East was for the faithful to present their gifts in the sacristy before the beginning of the liturgy of the word. The deacons then prepared the gifts, selecting what would be necessary, and at the conclusion of the liturgy of the word went out to the sacristy, transferred the gifts to the altar, and prepared the table. As Theodore of Mopsuestia describes this transfer of the gifts (in the rite of Antioch), it is a solemn action which is performed in silence. Soon it acquired a psalm as an accompaniment, however—probably verses from Psalm 24 with alleluia as a refrain. Later, the refrain was expanded into a *troparion* which concluded with alleluia. After the initial singing of the *troparion* and its repetition, the alleluia was sung after each of the psalm verses. The *troparion* was repeated again at the end of the psalm. Meanwhile the presiding clergy prepared themselves to preside at the meal with a ritual washing of the hands, a dialogue between the concelebrants, and a prayer of preparation. When the preparation of gifts and celebrants was complete, the Great Thanksgiving began.[32]

In the West, this procedure was organized differently. Here the faithful brought their gifts to the liturgy of the word. At its conclusion, the clergy came to the apse railing and the faithful came forward in procession to present their gifts, which the deacons then prepared for the eucharistic meal. This procedure was accompanied by an antiphonal psalm ("the offertory") and concluded by a prayer over the gifts (the *super oblata*).[33] As the custom of weekly communion declined in the West, however, the custom of the people's offering began to decline as well; when the Western church mandated the use of unleavened bread for the eucharist, it disappeared almost altogether on ordinary occasions, for this was not something which the faithful could readily provide.

Just as they organized the preparation of the table differently, so East and West interpreted it differently. The solemn transfer of gifts in the East was understood as a preparatory action for the eucharistic meal to follow. The *troparion* interprets the action for us: the church prepares itself to "lay aside all worldly care to receive the King of All" who in this procession is "escorted unseen by the angelic host." The danger here is that the people will offer to the unconsecrated gifts understood in this way the reverence properly due only to the consecrated gifts which have become the means of Christ's sacramental presence. In the West, the procedure was interpreted not in terms of preparation, but as a movement of offering. Properly this offering is fulfilled in the Great Thanksgiving, but the prayers over the gifts give proleptic expression to the church's offering of the gifts presented. In coming centuries, this proleptic expression would lead to a theologically dangerous separation between the offering of the church and the sacrificial offering of Christ. To understand this offering of the gifts properly, we need to understand it as the priestly offering of God's church which Christ incorporates in his own self-offering to the Father. In the eucharist we are caught up as the body of Christ into Christ's one perfect sacrifice for the life of the world.

The Celebration of the Holy Communion 2: The Great Thanksgiving: At the last supper, Christ gave thanks over the bread and over the cup. A proper theological understanding of the function of the Great Thanksgiving is grounded in the theology of the Jewish *berakoth* which are its prototype. The author of 1 Timothy articulates this theology very well when he writes:

> . . . everything created by God is good, and nothing is to be rejected, provided it is received with thanksgiving; for it is sanctified by God's word and by prayer (1 Timothy 4:4).

In giving thanks to God over God's gifts, we acknowledge the purpose for which God created them (usually by incorporating an appropriate citation of God's word in scripture into the thanksgiving) and so restore them to their created purpose, which we have short-circuited by sin. Food and drink were created by God as a means of communion, as links of life and love between God and us, so that we might share in God's own eternal life. God is the giver of life, and food and drink are the means by which God intended that we should share the life which God bestows. When we seek life not from God but from the world, God's purposes are short-circuited and our eating and drinking becomes a communion with death in a dying world. This meal is restored to the purpose for which God intended every meal because Christ has made it the *anamnesis* of his work of reconciling the world to God and so restoring it as a link of life and love between God and humanity.[34]

As we have already noted, the originally separate *berakoth* over the bread and the cup were eventually joined and the church gave thanks over both together. The church gave a variety of names to this series of *berakoth*. Perhaps the earliest is *eucharistia*, a name which *The Book of Common Prayer 1979* appropriately renders in English as "the Great Thanksgiving." In the Byzantine rite, the most common name for the prayer is the *anaphora* ("offering"), for this is the prayer in which the bread and wine are offered to God. A variety of names developed in the West. *Praefatio*—a name which we now give to the section of the prayer between the opening dialogue and the *Sanctus*—probably originally was understood as the "solemn proclamation" of God's mighty acts and was applied to the whole prayer. The prayer was also known as the *prex sacerdotalis*, the "priestly prayer" which was the proper liturgy of the presiding minister of the rite in his ministerial priesthood. The most common name in Western usage was *canon actionis*, which we should perhaps understand as *canon gratiarum actionis*, the "rule" or "prescribed form" for "giving thanks."

Justin says in the passages that we cited above that the person who presides at the eucharist "gives thanks according to his ability, *glorifying the Father of the universe through the name of the Son and of the Holy Spirit.*" At first the Great Thanksgiving was improvised by the president on the basis of a general thematic outline. But the liberty to improvise the church's thanksgiving is a dangerous one, as Christians discovered in their struggle with heretical distortions of the gospel in the early centuries, and local churches soon adopted standard forms of the eucharistic prayer (although appropriate interpolations might adapt the thanksgiving to the occasion, as in the Roman proper preface or the Gallican post-sanctus and post-pridie). The eucharistic prayers of the great patriarchal sees came more and more to set the texts for whole regions of the church. Sometimes the result was a carefully-crafted single prayer; at other times the result can be better understood as a sequence of inter-related prayers like the series of *berakoth* that make up the *birkat ha-mazon*. Although very early prayers (like that of the *Didache*) probably did not include either the *Sanctus* (which is still missing in the text in the *Apostolic Tradition* of Hippolytus) or the narrative of the last supper (lacking in the East Syrian prayer of Addai and Mari), these soon came to be standard parts of the eucharistic prayer. The expansion of the intercessions in eucharistic prayers disrupted the thematic sequence more seriously in some cases The Byzantine anaphoras attributed to Basil of Caesarea, John Chrysostom, and James are examples of a single, unified prayer; the East Syrian prayers (like that of Addai and Mari) and the Roman canon (with its numerous intermediate terminations) are examples of a eucharistic prayer composed of a series of loosely-related petitions.

Byzantine anaphoras developed an explicitly trinitarian form, so that we might think of them almost as a creed in the form of a thanksgiving. They begin with *eucharistia*, the church's *thanksgiving* to God in which it joins with all creation in the praise of the creator. This thanksgiving comes to its climax in the *Sanctus*, undoubtedly derived from the liturgy of the synagogue, during which the whole congregation joins with the heavenly host in creation's hymn of thanksgiving to its creator. This articulates the church's understanding of the rite as a eucharistic sacrifice, that is, a sacrifice of praise and thanksgiving. Under the impact of the gnostic denial of the goodness of material creation, the church came to understand this eucharistic sacrifice as finding tangible form in the offering of bread and wine as the first-fruits of creation. After the *Sanctus*, the anaphoras move into the *anamnesis* of the mighty acts by which Christ effected our salvation. What follows the *Sanctus* in these prayers leads into the narrative of the last supper with its command to "do this as my *anamnesis*" ("remembrance"), and that in turn leads into words which articulate the church's understanding of the eucharist as its offering of bread and wine in obedient response to this command. This introduces the people's response in the form of the memorial acclamation. Finally, the prayers continue with the *epiklesis*, which *invokes* the Spirit on the church and its gifts, so that the gifts, themselves transformed, may in turn transform the church into the body of Christ. It is the Spirit which manifests the bread and wine as Christ's body and blood and also the Spirit which manifests the church itself

CHAPTER TWO

as the body of Christ. This invocation then modulates into supplication for the needs of the church. The prayer concludes, in Jewish fashion, with a final doxology, whose Christian formulation is trinitarian. The congregation affirms its assent to the prayer with its Amen.

The Roman canon is less tightly and coherently structured. The theme of sacrifice and offering is the predominant element here, and the thanksgiving series with which the prayer opens is greatly abbreviated. After the *Sanctus* a series of petitions of intercession and pleas for the acceptance of the church's offering lead into the narrative of the last supper. As in the Byzantine anaphoras, this narrative is followed by a carefully-structured petition which identifies the eucharist as the church's offering made in remembrance of Christ. Then the canon continues with another series of pleas that God would accept the church's offering, further intercessions, the remnant of a petition for the blessing of other offerings, and a concluding doxology. In this tradition there is no invocation of the Spirit; the pleas for God's acceptance of the church's offering serve in its stead.[35]

The Celebration of the Holy Communion 3: The Fraction: At the last supper, the breaking of the bread and the libation of the wine were understood as an acted parable which foreshadowed Christ's coming death and interpreted that death in sacrificial terms. Perhaps surprisingly, when the church reflected on the meaning of its own breaking of bread, this was not the line of interpretation which prevailed. Instead, the one loaf broken that all might share was understood as a sign that we, though many, are one body in Christ, for we all share the one loaf (1 Corinthians 10:17). Only when the church at Rome adopted the *Agnus Dei* as a fraction anthem did the sacrificial interpretation of this practical action come into prominence. But this was not a part of the rite which underwent ritual elaboration in the early centuries.

The Celebration of the Holy Communion 4: The Communion: The Great Thanksgiving is clearly the verbal focus of the Celebration of the Holy Communion. It is the principal prayer of the rite and it interprets the meaning of the rite. The ritual climax of the rite, however, is the act of communion, the reception of the gifts. The eucharistic prayer manifests the bread and wine as the tangible presence of Christ to his church in order that his church, united with him by the reception of these gifts, might become the body of Christ and manifest his redemptive presence to the world.

It was taken for granted in the church's first centuries that all the faithful who were present would receive communion. Communion was understood not in terms of the sanctification of the individual Christian but in terms of the "edification," the building up, of the body of Christ. Only with the disruption brought by the dilemma of how to deal with the lapsed after the persecutions and by the dilemma of how to safeguard the holiness of the church when crowds of the half-converted flooded into it after the conversion of Constantine did it become thinkable for a Christian not to receive communion at the church's celebration of the eucharist. This shift in the understanding of the meaning of communion has had disastrous consequences in the theological self-understanding of the church from that time forward. By the middle ages, it was necessary to mandate the annual reception of communion at Easter. A disastrous gap had arisen between the meaning of the celebration of the eucharist and the meaning of receiving communion. It has only been in recent decades that this gap has begun to close once more, so that the communion of the congregation is once again understood as the proper climax of the eucharistic meal.

Most churches incorporated the Lord's Prayer, with its petition for daily bread, into the rite between the conclusion of the eucharistic prayer and the reception of communion (either before or after the fraction). Here it served as an act of preparation for communion. An antiphonal psalm was used to accompany the procession of the people for the reception of communion, and a postcommunion prayer brought the service to a close. Then, as we have seen, the diaconal dismissal sent the church forth into the world once more as witnesses to Christ and as instruments of his peace.

Issues in Understanding the Eucharist

The Meals in the Gospel as the Context for Establishing Eucharistic Theology: To understand the meaning of the church's eucharistic meal, we need to try to understand the meaning which meals had in Judaism. As we noted above, the meal is at its most basic level a communion sacrifice, in which God shares life with humanity through the food and drink which the worshiper acknowledges as God's gifts. The basic meaning of the eucharistic meal is perhaps best understood if we think of it in terms of both the last supper and the meal at Emmaus: it is both the *anamnesis* of Christ's sacrificial death on the cross and the means by which he manifests his risen presence in our midst. We should also remember the meals which Jesus shared with sinners in his day: his willingness to share with them at table was a concrete, tangible expression of God's acceptance of them and mediated to them God's forgiveness of their sins. Finally, we should remember the feeding of the multitudes, which we should surely understand as a proleptic foretaste of the wondrous bounty of the messianic banquet.

The Eucharistic Sacrifice: At least as early as the *Didache*, the church understood the eucharist as a sacrifice. But it is critically important to define our terms very carefully here. The eucharist is not to be understood in terms of the mediatorial sacrificial cult of Judaism. That sacrificial system, which was intended to overcome the estrangement between God and us which is the result of our sin, is both ended and fulfilled in Christ's self-offering on the cross. Christ, the priest for ever after the order of Melchisedek, has made the offering which we could not make and has closed the gap which our sins opened up between God and us. That self-offering is the sole sufficient sacrifice for the sins of the whole world. In a similar way, God's presence to us is no longer mediated by the temple where sacrifice was offered; Christ's own body is the true temple, in which heaven and earth are joined once more and we are reunited to God. In another sense, Christ has incorporated us into his priesthood and made of the whole church a royal priesthood through the waters of baptism. He has likewise incorporated us into his self-offering to God for the life of the world. And he has also made of us the temple of the Holy Spirit, the physical concrete embodiment of the Spirit's presence in the world.

How does the eucharist relate to the sacrifice of Christ understood in this way, as a sacrifice for sin? The church's answer has been that it is the effective *anamnesis* of that sacrifice, the way in which the church appropriates the benefits of that sacrifice and seals them to believers. Such an *anamnesis* is not a mere act of remembrance. It is the effective re-presentation before the assembled church and before God, not of the events themselves, but of their saving power. The church can make this *anamnesis* because Christ renders himself tangibly present in the words and acts by which the church fulfills his command to do this for his *anamnesis*. It is the presence of the living Christ to his Church which makes the sacrifice of Christ a present reality for us. Traditionally, the church has based this understanding of the eucharist on the theology of the letter to the Hebrews: the church's eucharistic liturgy renders present and efficacious for us the sacrifice which Christ pleads in the heavenly sanctuary before the Father.

The rite is also a eucharistic sacrifice, a sacrifice of praise and thanksgiving, a thank-offering which is our response to what God has done for us in Christ. Early in the Christian era the church tended to understand the eucharistic offering as its "holy and living sacrifice" and "reasonable act of worship"— θυσια ζωσα 'αγια and λογικη λατρεια (Romans 21:1) or as its "spiritual sacrifice"—πνευματικη θυσια (1 Peter 2:5). That is to say, it understood it as an act of prayer and not as a material oblation. However, the gnostic denial of the goodness of creation led the church to think of the bread and wine of the eucharist as an offering of the first-fruits of creation which gave tangible expression to its offering of thanks. Thus already in the mid-second century Justin Martyr was writing:—

> . . . the offering of fine flours . . . was a type of the bread of the Thanksgiving, which Jesus Christ our Lord commanded us to make in remembrance of the Passion which he suffered for those of mankind who purify their souls from all unrighteousness; so that at the same time we might also give thanks to God both for having created the world with everything in it for the sake of man, and for having delivered us from the evil in which we were born, and having destroyed the principalities and powers, through him, who became subject according to his counsel. . . . [God says that] "in every place incense will be offered unto my name, and a pure offering [Malachi 1:11]. He at that time foretells concerning us those sacrifices which are offered to him in every place by us Gentiles, that is the bread of the Thanksgiving and the cup likewise of the Thanksgiving. . . ."[36]

Irenaeus in his controversy with gnosticism echoes later in the century this same train of thought:

> . . . And likewise the cup, which is part of that creation which exists for our benefit, he acknowledged to be his blood and he taught it as the new oblation of the New Covenant. Receiving this from the apostles, the church offers it

throughout the whole world to God, to him who furnishes food to us, as the first fruits of his gifts in the New Covenant. Concerning this Malachi, among the twelve prophets, foretold thus: ". . . from the rising of the sun," etc.[37]

For as bread from the earth, by receiving the invocation of God, is no longer common bread but is Eucharist, consisting of two elements, an earthly and an heavenly; thus also our bodies, by receiving the Eucharist, are no longer corruptible, having the hope of the resurrection unto eternity. For we offer him, not as though he was in need, but as giving thanks for his gift and as sanctifying his creation. For God, who is in need of nothing, takes up our good works unto himself for this purpose: that he may give us a means of recompensing his blessing.[38]

It is this understanding of sacrifice, I believe, that is embodied in the paragraph within the Roman canon which asks God to accept our sacrifice:

Graciously look upon [our offering from "the gifts you have bestowed upon us"—*de tuis donis ac datis*] with mercy and favor, and accept them as you graciously accepted the gifts of your righteous servant Abel, the sacrifice of our patriarch Abraham, and what your high priest Melchisedek offered to you . . .[39]

Iconographically, this understanding may be seen worked out in the mosaics of San Vitale in Ravenna, where the very scenes to which this paragraph alludes (Abel's offering, the scene in which Abraham spreads a meal before his three heavenly visitors and that in which he is ready to offer his only son Isaac in sacrifice, and finally the scene in which Melchisedek offers bread and wine to God) adorn the walls about the altar. Here the artist has portrayed the Old Testament figures of what is being enacted liturgically in the eucharist, and that in turn is understood as the type of Christ's perfect oblation in heaven.

The eucharist may thus be understood as our effectual

CHAPTER TWO

anamnesis of Christ's sacrifice, which seals to us the benefits of that sacrifice and incorporates us into his self-offering to God; it is likewise a communion sacrifice, in which Christ has restored our food and drink as the means of our communion with God; it is finally a sacrifice of praise and thanksgiving for God's creation and redemption, a thank-offering which finds tangible expression in the bread and wine which we present as the firstfruits of creation.

The Eucharist as Sacrament and Mystery: In the concluding chapter of this book, I shall have occasion to turn to the theme of Christ as the *mysterium salutis*, the mystery of God's saving purposes which took tangible form in his flesh. In a carefully worked out sequence of theological thought, the church linked Christ as the tangible embodiment of God's saving purposes, the mighty acts by which those purposes were achieved, the church as Christ's body in which those purposes are achieved, and the church's rites in which that salvation becomes tangibly present. For the present, we need to note that the point of this theology is the tangibility of God's saving presence in our midst when we gather as the church for worship. The eucharist is the preeminent sacramental act of the church in this sense: it is where our tangible response to God's tangible approach to us finds its focus. And what makes this all possible is Christ's covenanted presence with the church in this rite. It is the mystery of this presence which makes the eucharist the effectual *anamnesis* of Christ and his sacrifice, for he is present in our midst as the Lord who has risen from the dead and who will come again to make all things new, that God may be all in all. He is present as the one who has come and who will come: in him, past, present and future meet. On the Lord's Day the church encounters its risen Lord in the breaking of bread at the Lord's supper and passes over with him from the death of sin to the new life of righteousness.

Redeeming the Week

The Christian Observance of the Station Days

From an early time, as we have noted, Christians observed Wednesdays and Fridays as fast days, known in liturgical language as "stations." This observance articulates the basic rhythm of the Christian life, holding in tension the fact that in Christ salvation has *already* drawn near to us and the fact that Christ's saving work has *not yet* achieved its final consummation. In a way this is the tension between Christ's absence and his presence, between the fact that the church is "not of this world" but lives out its life "in this world." In the course of the week this tension is articulated by the rhythm of fast, because the bridegroom has been taken from us, and feast, because in the eucharist on the Lord's Day we are granted a proleptic foretaste of his coming presence.[40]

The Sunday feast is of necessity a corporate observance. Fasting cannot by nature take on the same kind of corporate character, except in its conclusion. The station days might simply be kept by refraining from food until the evening meal. If a corporate observance was desired, it might take the form of a liturgy of the word, much as a liturgy of the word was added to the service of the synagogue on the Monday and Thursday fasts (though Christians used this liturgy to conclude the fast and so celebrated it in the late afternoon or early evening). Fasting finds its fulfilment in the breaking of the fast. Christians frequently found the reception of communion an appropriate way to conclude the fast. The most ancient form which communion took on fast days was the reception of gifts consecrated at the eucharist on the Lord's Day. Daily communion in this manner was in many places a pious observance: Christians took home from the eucharist on the previous Lord's Day sufficient bread to receive the bread of life as the first food each day of the coming week. If a corporate reception of the sacrament was desired on fast days, they might receive communion from gifts reserved in the church for this purpose at the conclusion of the liturgy of the word. This liturgy of the presanctified might either be held as a separate late afternoon service (after none in the daily cursus) or be incorporated into vespers. Such is the form that communion on fast days still takes in the Byzantine rite. In the West, the sole remainder of this custom is the communion from the reserved sacrament at the afternoon liturgy of the word on Good Friday, although in earlier times perhaps communion was received in this way on all the station days during Lent. Here the concern is to avoid the celebration of the eucharist as the ritual expression of a feast which is inappropriate on a fast. Eventually, however, a late afternoon or evening celebration of the eucharist became acceptable to most of the church, and it became the customary way to observe a fast in the Roman rite (where it was appointed for celebration after none, the ninth hour of the day). Eventually a daily celebration of the eucharist became customary in the West. This has never been the case in the Byzantine rite, where only the Lord's Day or another feast warrants the celebration of the eucharist.

The Elaboration and Disintegration of the Weekly Cycle and the Eucharist

The Weekly Cycle

Sunday has always retained a privileged place within the weekly cycle of Christian worship. But the church's consciousness of the theological significance of the day faded over the centuries. The fully-developed theology of the Lord's Day makes it a trinitarian celebration. But when the concreteness of its observance as the day of light, the day of the Lord's resurrection, the day of the Spirit's bestowal, and the first day of the new creation was reduced in theological shorthand so that it became, as it did in the West, a weekly feast of the Trinity, then its unique character became too abstract to grasp. When this happened, the links between the Lord's Day as the church's weekly observance of its Lord's resurrection and the eucharist as the feast which gives concrete expression to that observance faded from the popular consciousness of the church. The Western tendency to focus on the eucharist as an *anamnesis* of the cross and to forget the equal truth that it is a means of sharing in Christ's risen life exacerbated this tendency. The eucharist as it was popularly understood in the West in the Middle Ages was a rite more appropriate to Friday than to Sunday!

As time went on, every day of the week acquired a "votive" character, a special meaning.[41] This further undercut the primary significance of Sunday and the rhythm between Sunday as a feast day and the station days as fast days. The luxuriant growth of saints' days in the course of the Middle Ages eventually completely swamped the weekly cycle and gave every day a quasi-festal character. In effect, the annual cycle of commemorations almost completely displaced the weekly cycle, and within the annual cycle the sanctoral commemorations threatened to displace the seasonal observances. The Christological character of the church's worship stood in danger of being obscured in the popular consciousness by this overgrowth of sanctoral commemorations. Theoretically, distinctions were maintained by the elaborate system of "grading" feasts (solemnities, greater doubles, doubles, semi-doubles, simple commemorations, and so forth) and by the time appointed for the celebration of the eucharist on these various days (calibrated so that the length of the eucharistic fast corresponded to the importance of the day). In reality, the system was so complicated that it escaped most people's understanding and was often ignored.

The Eucharist

Liturgical Changes: By the beginning of the Middle Ages, the shape of the eucharist in major rites had acquired its basic form, but changes in succeeding centuries would have an impact on it that obscured, distorted, and even altered its original proportions. One of these changes was the custom, apparently under the impact of what Alexander Schmemann calls "mysteriological piety,"[42] of reciting the officiant's prayers silently (μυστικως, as the rubrics of Byzantine euchologies say). Only when the people's response needed to be signalled did the officiant recite words aloud. This affected Eastern rites first and went farther there than it ever did in the West.[43] As a result, in most prayers of the Byzantine rite, the officiant recites only the concluding doxology aloud. In the eucharistic prayer, he also recites phrases which lead into the people's parts—e.g., the words leading into the *Sanctus* and the memorial acclamation. In the Roman rite, this trend affected primarily the eucharistic prayer, in which the only portion recited aloud after the *Sanctus* was the concluding doxology. Originally, the whole prayer had been recited in the preface tone, for it was the church's *praefatio*, its "solemn proclamation," of God's praise. This silent recitation of prayers is one aspect of a mysteriological piety which "sacralizes" the cult by clericalizing it: the clergy are set apart from the laity as cultic figures. The congregation is increasingly segregated from them in worship—a segregation which is articulated in restricting access to the part of the church where the clergy are seated (not merely demarcating it by railings, *cancelli*, as had long been customary, but eventually screening it by a solid partition), in restricting access to communion, by distinctions in dress, and in this withdrawal of the officiant into a whispered silence during the most important prayers of the church's worship.

The decline in the communion of the congregation is another aspect of this piety. In an earlier era, it was unthinkable that any but the those under the discipline of public penance would fail to receive communion at the church's eucharist on the Lord's Day and major feasts. The transformation of the church into the body of Christ by the reception of the body of Christ was the goal of the celebration as the "sacrament of assembly." But when half-converted crowds flooded the church's worship after the fourth century, fear of profaning the sacrament led the church to emphasize the awesome, fear-inspiring nature of the act of communion—not to discourage the congregation from receiving communion, but to encourage worthy communion. The "worthiness" they demanded, however, meant that in the end people approached the sacrament with such fear that in the West it was necessary to adopt canonical legislation (at the Lateran Council of 1215) in order to ensure that people would communicate at least *once a year!* When the solemn proclamation of the church's *eucharistia* had fallen silent and the congregation had ceased to receive communion, the eucharist had lost what we earlier described as its "verbal focus" and its ritual climax.

Other major changes occurred at what Robert Taft identifies as the "soft points" of the rite—those places in the early outline of the eucharist which entailed significant movements or actions of the officiants or the congregation but which originally had no fixed text. He identifies three major soft points in the rite:

1. the entrance procession;
2. the preparation of the table (the offertory procession in the West, the great entrance in the East), along with the prayers of the people and exchange of the peace which preceded it;
3. the communion (including preparatory devotions) and the dismissal.

Each of these processions acquired an accompanying chant (an antiphonal psalm, though in some rites some of these chants were probably originally responsorial) and its own prayer (proper in the Roman rite; part of the ordinary in the Byzantine rite). Eventually they acquired masses of other material as well— the remnant of an entrance litany from stational liturgies and the *Gloria in excelsis* (in the Roman rite),[44] acclamations (like the Roman *laudes regiae* or *Gallicanae* and the Byzantine *polychronion*),[45] fraction anthems such as the Roman *Agnus Dei*, private devotional material (like the prayers at the foot of the altar and the devotional *apologiae* of the celebrant at the offertory and before communion in the Roman rite before Vatican II), and ritual elaboration (like the commixture after the fraction). The ultimate result was that secondary elements of the rite overshadowed the primitive elements and often led to their abbreviation or suppression. In this way the Old Testament reading(s) disappeared from most rites; the original prayers of the people were drastically abbreviated (as in the Byzantine rite) or disappeared altogether (as in the Roman rite); and the peace was reduced to a verbal exchange.

Theological Changes: The theological shifts in the way the eucharist was understood and experienced were no less significant than the liturgical changes in the rite. One major shift came in the way in which people understood the nature of

Christ's presence. For Christians of late antiquity, Christ was present in the world under many modalities. In the eclectic Platonism of their world view, the world was an intricately inter-related symbolical system. From such a perspective, articulated in various ways, the symbol revealed the presence of what it symbolized and made its presence tangible and accessible. It did not represent what was absent, but revealed what was present. It was a means of participation and communion. The epiphany of that presence in its many modalities was the eucharist: Christ was present in the church; his presence was brought to a focus in its members, in its ministers, in the word proclaimed, and in the food and drink which were offered and received in communion.[46]

As the church entered the middle ages, however, per-spectives shifted. Now a *real* presence was contrasted to a *symbolic* presence. The language of figure and type and symbol which had articulated Christ's real presence to the early church now seemed inadequate: symbols and types represented what was *absent*. The eucharistic controversies in the West put the *real* presence of Christ over against a *merely symbolic* presence in a way that would have been unthinkable for the early church. This transition in understanding came quite early in the West. We can see it in the change in wording between the text of the the paragraph before the narrative of the last supper *(Quam oblationem)* in the canon as given by Ambrose in the fourth century and that given by Pope Innocent in the next century:

> **Ambrose:** Grant that this offering may be . . . acceptable, *because it is the figure of* the body and blood of our Lord Jesus Christ.
>
> **Innocent:** Grant, O God, that this offering may be in every respect . . . acceptable, *so that it may become for us* the body and blood of your beloved Son, our Lord.Jesus Christ.[47]

Note the different in the italicized words. It no longer seemed adequate to speak of the bread and wine as *figures* of the body and blood of Christ; it now seemed necessary to pray that they *might become* the body and blood of Christ.

A further factor in all of this was the decline of regular communion on the part of most of the laity. Christ is present in the eucharistic elements for the purpose of communion; the bread is transformed into his body in order that the church as the eucharistic assembly may be transformed into his body. When people ceased to communicate, however, the forms of piety shifted. In the East, two schools of liturgical commentary developed. For one, the "typological" tradition which ultimately derives from Antiochene exegesis, the purpose of the eucharist becomes the symbolic representation of the life of Christ. For early Christians, the eucharist was the *anamnesis* of Christ because he covenanted to be with us when we share this meal as his *anamnesis*. It was not in any sense a *reenactment* of his death. But this school of Byzantine interpretation eventually made it a symbolic reenactment not only of his death but of the whole "economy" (οικονομια) of his saving deeds. The symbolism was no longer *intrinsic*; it became very *extrinsic* indeed. The second tradition of interpretation derives from the Alexandrian school of exegesis and makes of the eucharist a means of anagogic ascent from the world to God in contemplation. The first major eucharistic commentary of this sort is the *Ecclesiastical Hierarchy* of Pseudo-Dionysius, who was probably a monophysite of the school of Severus of Antioch. Eventually both strands of interpretation were interwoven in Byzantine commentaries. Typological or anagogic contemplation *(theoria)* has become a substitute for communion.[48]

In the West this kind of commentary was not unknown, and it did affect to some extent the ceremonial of the rite, but the eucharistic piety which came to prevail was one which understood the eucharistic presence of Christ as a focus for adoration. The sacrament which the church had almost from the beginning reserved for the communion of the sick now became the focus of devotion in the West in a way that would have been unthinkable in the early church (and remains alien even today to the Christian East). Western theologians such as Aquinas carefully nuanced the Western doctrine of the real presence (and of transubstantiation as the means by which that presence is effected),[49] but such distinctions were ignored in popular piety. Christ was understood to be present in his *natural* body and blood under the *species* of bread and wine, and the transformed character of his natural body after the resurrection was forgotten. This led to a radical shift in the liturgical climax of the eucharist, which was no longer the reception of communion by the assembled church, but the adoration of the eucharistic species immediately after their consecration by an otherwise passive congregation. The theology of a *moment* of consecration would have seemed strange to the early church: the church consecrates the bread and wine by offering them to God with thanksgiving, according to a eucharistic theology in touch with its Jewish roots. Now consecration was understood to occur when the celebrant *in persona Christi* recited the words of Christ over the elements (words which were lacking in early prayers like that of the *Didache* and which in the New Testament are words of *administration,* not words of *consecration*). Now the eucharistic prayer became merely the setting for the true operative words: "this is my body; this is my blood."

In the West, the theology of the eucharistic sacrifice also underwent substantial shifts. We have already noted that the Roman canon focusses more heavily on the theme of sacrifice than most other traditions. By the late Middle Ages, this emphasis had been exacerbated in a variety of ways. On a popular level, the eucharistic sacrifice began to be understood not in terms of participation in Christ's sacrifice, but as an independent work. It became traditional in the West to offer the eucharist *for* particular intentions in a way that never became customary elsewhere. The early church had understood the eucharist as the action of the gathered church, the *synaxis* of the *ekklesia*. But from a relatively early period in the West, the eucharist came to be understood in such a way that it could be celebrated as a votive offering for a particular intention by the celebrant. Eastern anaphoras offer the eucharist *for* the concerns of the congregation when it gathers, concerns which are articulated in the intercessions of the anaphora, but they never treat the eucharist as a sacrifice which can be *applied* to a particular intention in the way that became characteristic in the West—particularly in votive masses for the repose of the departed, which were understood to assist the departed in purgatory. Chantries were endowed for this sole purpose in the West; the East, on the other hand, generally ceased to celebrate the eucharist for the departed even at funerals, because the eucharist *required* the assembly of the parish community in a way that was not ordinarily possible at funerals. The doctrine of such theologians as Thomas Aquinas about the eucharistic sacrifice is generally carefully nuanced. But for popular piety, priests not only *made* Christ by consecrating the elements at the eucharist, they also *sacrificed* Christ by offering the consecrated elements to God.[50] Eucharistic piety had moved very far indeed from the theology of the early church.[51]

Since the corporate communion of the congregation was no longer understood as the climax of the eucharist, the meaning of communion shifted radically also. Its purpose had once been understood in terms of building up the body of Christ, as realizing the unity of the church. Now it was understood in terms of individual sanctification as a means of grace. Once it had followed the rhythm of the church's rule of prayer: when the community gathered for the eucharist, all but the unbaptized and the public penitents received. Now it followed rhythms of individual piety.

Of course, the early church would not have denied that the reception of communion was a means of individual sanctification, but it set that meaning in the context of the wider purposes of the sanctification of the community. Now that context was forgotten. The link between communion as sharing the life of the risen Christ and the Lord's Day as the feast of the resurrection also fell into the background.

The meaning of fasting also changed. It had been an expression of the eschatological tension of Christian existence in the early church, of the fact that we live in the world but are no longer of the world. The weekly fasts of Wednesday and Friday had reached their fulfilment in the eucharistic feast on Sunday. Now fasting was no longer understood as a corporate expression of our hunger for God, which is satisfied in our foretaste of the messianic banquet on Sundays, but as a work of penance, a way of atoning for sin. The architecture of the weekly rhythm had faded from Christian consciousness.[52]

Cranmer's Reforms and the Prayer Book Tradition

Thomas Cranmer's patristic learning and liturgical sensitivity led him to draft for the *Book of Common Prayer 1549* provisions which, had they been implemented in their integrity, would have restored the shape of the week as the early church celebrated it. For Sundays (as well as major holy days in the course of the year) that book mandates the celebration of "The Supper of the Lord and the Holy Communion, commonly called the Masse." Cranmer intended a celebration of the eucharist with a general communion of the congregation for every day for which he provided a set of propers. Like all the reformers, he insisted that there should be members of the congregation who would receive communion with the priest whenever the eucharist was celebrated. This was a radical shift in eucharistic piety, since annual communion at Easter had been set as the minimum norm in the thirteenth century, and Cranmer realized that extraordinary measures would be required to secure a weekly celebration. The rubrics of the 1549 rite attempt to establish a way of doing this:

> *Also, that the receiuing of the Sacrament of the blessed body and bloud of Christ, may be most agreeable to the institucion thereof, and to the usage of the primitive Churche: In all Cathedrall and Collegiate Churches, there shal alwaies some Communicate with the Prieste that ministreth. And that the same may bee also obserued every where abroade in the countrey: Some one at the least of that house in euery Parishe to whome by course after the ordinaunce herein made, it apperteyneth to offer for the charges of the Communion, or some other whom they shall prouide to offer for them, shall receiue with the Prieste. . . . And with hym or them who offre the charges of the Communion; all other, who be then Godly disposed thereunto, shall lykewyse receiue the Communion. And by this meanes the Minister hauying alwaies some to communicate with him, maie accordingly solempnise so high and holy misteries. . . .*[53]

On Wednesdays and Fridays, the ancient station days, the 1549 Prayer Book also provides for appropriate liturgical observance—the litany and the eucharist or, if there are none to communicate with the celebrant, the litany and the liturgy of the word:

> *Upon wednesdaies and frydaies the English Letany shalbe said or song in all places. . . . And thoughe there be none to communicate with the Prieste, yet these dayes (after the Litany*

ended) the Priest shall . . . say al thinges at the Altar (appoynted to be sayed at the celebracyon of the lordes supper), untill after the offertory. And then shall adde one or two of the Collectes aforewritten, as occasion shall serue his discrecion. And then turning him to the people shall let them depart with the accustomed blessing.[54]

The eucharistic rite he designed was an extraordinarily skillful English paraphrase of the older portions of the Roman rite, theologically reworked. The following outline reveals its shape. I have used my own headings. For the eucharistic prayer, I have given in the first column the Roman canon with summary titles or Latin incipits for its component sections, and in the second column summary titles for the sections of Cranmer's prayer.

The Eucharist
in *The Book of Common Prayer 1549*

The Assembly of the Church

Full Sung Introit Psalm, while the Priest says the Lord's Prayer
    and Collect for Purity
Sung or Said Ninefold Kyrie
Sung Gloria in Excelsis
Collect for the Day and One of Two Collects for the King

The Proclamation of the Word of God

Epistle for the Day
Gospel for the Day
Nicene Creed
Sermon or Homily
Exhortation to Communion

The Celebration of the Holy Communion

The Preparation of the Table

Selection of Fixed Offertory Sentences during offering and preparation of table

> *[S]o manye as are disposed, shall offer unto the poore mennes boxe euery one accordynge as to his habilitie and charitable mynde. . . . Then so manye as shalbe partakers of the holy Communione, shall tary still in the quire, or in some conuenient place nigh the quire, the men on the one side, and the women on the other syde.*

The Great Thanksgiving

Roman Canon	1549
Dialogue	Dialogue
Preface	Preface
Sanctus/Benedictus	Sanctus/Benedictus
Commemorations A	Prayer for the Whole State of Christ's Church
1. Te igitur	1. the Church, government, clergy
2. Memento, Domine	2. those in need and those present
3. Communicantes	3. commemoration of saints
	4. the departed
Hanc igitur	Post-sanctus
Quam oblationem	Invocation of word and Spirit
Supper Narrative	Supper Narrative
Unde et memores	Memorial
Supra quae	Petition for Acceptance of Oblation
	Act of Self-Oblation
Supplices te rogamus	
Commemorations B	
4. Memento etiam	
5. Nobis quoque (=3)	("And although we be unworthy")
Per quem haec omnia	
Doxology and Amen	Doxology and Amen
Introduction and Lord's Prayer	Introduction and Lord's Prayer

The Fraction

Verbal Exchange of the Peace
"Christ our Paschal Lamb"
Breaking of each of the breads before distribution
> . . . *it is mete that the breade prepared for the Communion bee made . . . unleauened and rounde, and somethyng thicker than it was, so that it may be aptly deuided in diuers pieces: and euery one shall be deuided in two pieces, at the leaste, or more, by the discrecion of the minister, and so distributed.*

The Communion

Communion Devotions
    Bidding, Confession, Absolution, Comfortable Words
    Prayer of Humble Access
    Agnus Dei (displaced from fraction)
Selection of fixed communion sentences
Postcommunion Prayer
Dismissal with Blessing

Structurally, Cranmer has come very close to restoring the classic shape of the eucharist of the Roman rite by removing secondary elements and extraneous devotions that had obscured or distorted that shape. When we compare this rite with the outline given earlier in this chapter for the classical shape of the eucharist, only the following differences emerge:

1. The rite of gathering or the entrance rite still is "overloaded." Besides the psalm and the collect which were the original components of the entrance rite, Cranmer has retained elements of the celebrant's private preparation (the Lord's Prayer and collect for purity), the *Kyrie* (remnant of the entrance litany of the old stational eucharists), and the festive addition of the morning hymn, *Gloria in excelsis.*

2. The Old Testament reading has not been restored, and the responsorial psalmody between the readings has not been restored to its original shape, but omitted.
3. The Nicene Creed *precedes* the sermon—a dislocation that occurred in many Western usages when preaching fell out of use on most occasions, and then returned as part of a vernacular interpolation in the eucharist before the offertory.
4. The Prayers of the People have not been restored to their original place. However, in 1549 usage, extensive intercession did take place in the litany before the eucharist and within the eucharistic prayer (as prayer "for the whole state of Christ's church").
5. The peace remains in its Roman position and continues to be a merely verbal exchange.
6. The offertory procession, which had never entirely died out in the West is restored as an offering of alms in the poor men's box; after making their offerings, communicants assemble in the choir for the celebration of the holy communion.
7. A fixed selection of sentences is provided in place of the variable antiphonal psalms provided at an earlier age for the offertory and communion processions. The prayer which concluded the offertory procession is omitted; a fixed (rather than variable) prayer is provided to conclude the communion.

This is a remarkable achievement. No less remarkable is Cranmer's reworking of the eucharistic prayer.

In that prayer he has reshaped the somewhat miscellaneous components of the Roman canon into a logically ordered whole. The intercessory portions of that prayer he has gathered in the prayer "for the whole state of Christ's church" which follows the *Sanctus/Benedictus* and precedes the connecting link that I have labelled the post-Sanctus. The rest he has carefully reworked to articulate his own doctrines of eucharistic presence and eucharistic sacrifice. This represents a greater change than is first apparent. Neither the presence nor the sacrifice were explicitly linked to the bread and the wine in Cranmer's theology. W. Jardine Grisbrooke summarizes this subtle shift very well:

> Briefly, to Cranmer whatever presence of the Body and Blood of our Lord there may be in the Lord's Supper, it is in no wise *specifically* connected with the bread and wine therein taken, distributed, and consumed; and whatever there may be of sacrifice in the rite is in no way connected either with the bread and wine, or with the Body and Blood of our Lord.[55]

Cranmer's doctrine of the eucharistic presence would appear to be Reformed in character, as can be seen by the rubric inserted into the Prayer Book of 1552:

> *Lest yet the same kneeling [to receive communion] myght be thought or taken otherwyse, we dooe declare that it is not ment thereby, that any adoration is doone, or oughte to bee doone, eyther unto the Sacramentall bread or wyne there bodily re-ceyued, or unto anye* **real and essential** *presence there beeyng of Christ's* **naturall** *flesh and bloude. For as concernynge the Sacramentall bread and wyne, they remayne styll in theyr very naturall substaunces and therefore may not be adored, for that were Idolatrye to be abhorred of all faythfull christians. And as concernynge the* **naturall** *body and blood of our savior Christ, they are in heaven and not here. For it is agaynst the truth of Christes true* **natural** *bodye, to be in moe places then in one, at one tyme.*[56]

Like the Swiss reformers, Cranmer here seeks to deny what appears to him to be the theological incoherence of affirming that Christ's natural body and blood can be present on earth in the eucharistic elements once he had ascended bodily into heaven. Zwingli, Calvin and Cranmer were clear here about the modality of presence they were rejecting; none of them found language, however, to articulate clearly the modality of presence which they wanted to affirm. All wished to deny that it was a presence analogous to the physical presence of a human being (as indeed did Thomas Aquinas). All of them, for philosophical reasons, tended to dissociate it from the bread and wine and to locate it in the faithful recipient of the eucharistic elements. Zwingli and Cranmer made the dissociation so strong that their doctrine tended itself to become incoherent; Calvin's doctrine of the eucharistic presence is on the whole more satisfactory.[57]

Such a doctrine of the eucharistic presence tends to shift the meaning of the eucharistic prayer as a prayer of consecration. It no longer manifests the presence of Christ under the forms of bread and wine (as it did in early eucharistic theology and as the recitation of the words of Christ did for Luther, who understood consecration as occurring by the recitation of these words rather than by the recitation of the church's thanksgiving); it now sets them apart for the purposes of communion. Cranmer puts it thus:

> Consecration is the separation of any thing from a profane and worldly use unto a spiritual and godly use. . . .Even so when common bread and wine be taken and severed from other bread and wine to the use of the holy communion, that portion of bread and wine, although it be of the same substance that the other is from the which it is severed, yet it is now called "consecrated" or "holy" bread and wine. . . . Not that the bread and wine can be partakers of any holiness or godliness or can be the Body and Blood of Christ; but that they *represent* the very Body and Blood of Christ, and the holy food and nourishment we have by Him. And so they be called by the names of the Body and

> Blood of Christ, as the *sign, token and figure is called by the name of the very thing which it showeth and signifieth.*[58]

As regards the doctrine of eucharistic sacrifice, for Cranmer the eucharist is

1. "the Church's commemoration of Christ's oblation on the cross;"[59] and
2. "a sacrifice of praise for the benefits of the passion" which is articulated as "the offering of the faithful of themselves in response to Christ."[60]

Since Justin Martyr, the church had given the sacrifice of praise concrete shape in the bread and wine offered as the firstfruits of creation, but Cranmer dissociates this sacrifice of praise from the bread and wine and associates it instead with the offering of alms.[61] The bread and wine are, according to his eucharistic prayer, God's "holy gifts" with which we make "the memorial which [God's] son hath willed us to make" of his "full, perfect, and sufficient sacrifice, oblation, and satisfaction, for the sins of the whole world." But they are not, as in classical liturgies, our offering as well as God's gifts. They do not represent a link which unites Christ's sacrifice and the church's sacrifice. The language of offering and sacrifice as it applies to us is found 1) in the rubric regarding offerings made in the poor man's box, and 2) in the verbal reference in the eucharistic prayer to our offering and presenting "ourselves, our souls and bodies, to be a reasonable, holy, and lively sacrifice" to God. This understanding of sacrifice as a moral act of self-oblation draws on Romans 12:1 and on the way that Augustine used that text to speak of the eucharist as the church's sacrifice.[62] This moral act of self-oblation, which finds expression in the offering of alms in the poor man's box, not in the offering of bread and wine, is "our sacrifice of praise and thanksgiving" in response to Christ's sacrifice.

CHAPTER TWO

What we need to note in regard to Cranmer's eucharistic theology above all else, however, is that, however adequate or inadequate we may judge his articulation of the eucharistic presence and sacrifice and of the consecratory function of the eucharistic prayer, *no link is made between the eucharist and the resurrection.* The eucharist is not linked to Easter at all, except briefly in the anamnesis. In typical Western fashion, the predominant emphasis is on the cross. The interrelation between the Lord's Day as the weekly feast of Christ's resurrection and the eucharist as the rite which articulates the meaning of the Lord's Day has entirely been forgotten. The tradition of the weekly celebration of the eucharist on the Lord's Day has been strongly reaffirmed; its rationale is never articulated.

Both Cranmer's catholicizing opponents and his Reformed colleagues tended to read the 1549 rite as patient of being understood to express the very doctrines of eucharistic presence and sacrifice which he wished to avoid, and so in 1552 he issued a revised rite which unambiguously repudiated those doctrines. In so doing, however, he mutilated the traditional shape to which the 1549 rite had given such eloquent expression. Even in 1552, however, he sought to maintain the weekly eucharistic rhythm set out in 1549. For our purposes here, it will suffice to set out the appropriate shape of the eucharistic prayer and the theology of the rite as John Johnson, rector of Cranbrook in Kent in the early eighteenth century, understood it and the concrete form that Johnson's views found in the eucharistic prayer of the Scottish Episcopal Church, for that is the strand of tradition which has found expression in the *Book of Common Prayer 1979* with which we will be concerned next.

In John Johnson's works, *The Unbloody Sacrifice, The Primitive Communicant, and The Propitiatory Oblation,* classic high Anglican eucharistic doctrine found eloquent expression. Here high Calvinist sacramental doctrine, which emphasizes the role of the Holy Spirit in the eucharistic action, fused with the patristic scholarship of the Caroline divines and resulted in a theology which largely transcended the philosophical deadlock which left most of the sixteenth-century reformers without adequate language to articulate their eucharistic theology.

Johnson's doctrine of the eucharistic presence has been described as "dynamic virtualism." What this means is that Christ's presence in the eucharistic elements as the instrumental means of his presence for the faithful recipient is effected by the power *(virtue)* of the Holy Spirit who in the eucharistic prayer is invoked upon the Church and its gifts in Cranmer's 1549 rite. Johnson defines the modality of Christ's presence as follows:

> I shall only, before I pass to another Head of Discourse, observe, that the propositions hitherto laid down, concerning the Nature of the Eucharist, are fairly consistent with each other; and to this end, I will again place them all together in the Reader's View:
>
> 1. The Body and Blood in the Sacrament are the Bread and Wine.
>
> 2. The Body and Blood in the Sacrament, or the Consecrated Bread and Wine, are types of the Natural body and Blood of Christ.
>
> 3. But they are not such cold and imperfect Types as those before and under the Law.
>
> 4. Nay, they are the very Body and Blood, tho' not in Substance, yet in Spirit, Power, and Effect.[63]

This affirms a real presence in the sense of a true presence, but not in the narrow scholastic sense (which understands *realis* in terms of *res* and understands the *res* to be the *natural substance* of the body and blood of Christ). The difference between the meaning of *real* in ordinary discourse and its meaning in technical philosophical and theological discourse has often made it difficult for modern readers to understand what is being affirmed or denied in post-Reformation discussions of the *real* presence.

In Johnson's theology, consecration has a different significance than it did in the theology of Cranmer, where it was simply "the separation of any thing from a profane and worldly use unto a spiritual and godly use." Johnson describes the consecration of the eucharistic elements in this way:

> . . . the Holy Ghost was, by the Vote of Antiquity, the principal immediate cause of the Bread and Wine's becoming the Body and Blood. It now remains only that I shew, that the Subordinate or Mediate Cause of it is, 1. The Reciting of the Words of Institution. 2. The Oblation of the Symbols. 3. The Prayer of Invocation. All of these three did, in the Ancient Liturgies, immediately follow each other, in the order that I have mentioned them; and each of them was believed to contribute toward the consecration of the Elements into the Body and Blood.[64]

Johnson believed that these components were properly set in a prayer which began with the placement of the bread and wine on the altar while the priest articulated the church's thanksgiving in the Preface and the *Sanctus*.[65]

Johnson's doctrine of the eucharistic sacrifice is equally carefully crafted. He describes Christ's sacrifice and the church's sacrifice in this way:

> The sum of what these Fathers teach us is, that Christ entered upon his Priestly Office in the Eucharist; that there he began the One Oblation; there he offered himself in a spiritual mystical manner, as he afterwards did corporally upon the Cross. . . . These two parts of the Oblation were but one continued Solemnity; nay, we may add, that the Ascension of Christ into Heaven many days after, was but

the finishing of this One Oblation: The distinguishing the Oblation in the Eucharist, from that on the Cross, and that afterwards in Heaven, is really a clouding or obscuring the whole Mystery, and rendring it perplext and intricate.[66]

But that which renders the *Eucharist* the most excellent and valuable Sacrifice that was ever offer'd, except the Personal Sacrifice of Christ, is this, that the Bread and Wine then offer'd, are in Mystery and inward Power, tho' not in Substance, the Body and Blood of Christ: This raises the Dignity of the Christian Sacrifice above those of the Law of *Moses*, and all that were ever offer'd by meer Men: As it is Natural Bread and Wine, 'tis the Sacrifice of *Melchisedek*, and of the most ancient Philosophers: As it is the Sacrifice of the Body and Blood of Christ, it is the most sublime and divine Sacrifice that Men or angels can offer.[67]

Johnson also associated the offering with the church's intercession. The movement of oblation which began with the placement of gifts on the altar and was articulated in the Great Thanksgiving led into intercession in the presence of the consecrated gifts, when early Christians

did properly pray in the name of *Christ,* when they put up their Petitions at the Throne of Grace, with the Sacramental Body and Blood of Christ placed before God upon the Altar.[68]

Johnson develops his doctrine of eucharistic sacrifice in the context of the theology of Hebrews, which also underlies part of the 1549 text of Cranmer. But this association of intercession with consecrated gifts goes far beyond what Cranmer would have found acceptable. Indeed, in 1552 Cranmer took the intercessions out of the eucharistic prayer altogether and associated them with the offering of alms.

Even the eucharistic rite of 1549 does not fit the eucharistic theology which Johnson developed. In that rite both the intercessions and the invocation are in the wrong place, even if other components are construed in the way that Johnson wishes. After 1552 the rite was even harder to construe as Johnson wanted, for the invocation was changed into a prayer for fruitful communion and the anamnesis was detached from the eucharistic prayer and made an alternative postcommunion prayer.[69] Grisbrooke aptly comments,

> Johnson, himself, it is true, reconciled his teaching with the liturgy of 1662, but nowhere does he vouchsafe an answer to the pertinent query how he did so.[70]

The one Anglican liturgy which did embody this theology of eucharistic presence, consecration, and sacrifice was the rearrangement made by Scottish Episcopalians in 1764 of the abortive Scottish liturgy of 1637. By the early eighteenth century, Scottish Episcopalians had begun to use the 1637 liturgy once again, but freely transposed the components of the eucharistic prayer. By 1735 one printer published it with the customary transpositions, somewhat ambiguously signalled by the notice, *"All the parts of this Office are ranked in the natural order."* By 1762 or 1763 the church authorized revision in this manner, and the result was the Scottish Communion Office of 1764.

In that office,[71] whose printed form began with the Celebration of the Holy Communion, the eucharistic prayer has the following shape in comparison with the 1549 text:

The Great Thanksgiving

1764	1549
Dialogue	Dialogue
Preface	Preface
Sanctus/Benedictus	Sanctus/Benedictus
	Prayer for the Whole State of Christ's Church
	1. the Church, government, clergy

2. those in need and
   those present
3. the departed
4. commemoration of saints

"Prayer of Consecration:"
Post-sanctus   Post-sanctus
            Invocation of word and Spirit
Supper Narrative   Supper Narrative
"The Oblation"   Memorial
"The Invocation"
Petition for Acceptance   Petition for Acceptance
 of Oblation   of Oblation
Act of Self-Oblation   Act of Self-Oblation
Doxology and Amen   Doxology and Amen
Prayer for the Whole State
 of Christ's Church
Introduction and Lord's   Introduction and Lord's
 Prayer   Prayer

The italicized portions are those whose position has been transposed to conform to the eucharistic theology articulated by Johnson and used by the Scots as the basis of their work. They added the subheadings which I have placed in quotation marks. They also made the following changes in wording to conform to the theology of Johnson and his followers:

1. In the post-Sanctus, they made a link with the Sanctus by beginning, "All glory be to thee;" they changed "one sacrifice" to "own sacrifice" to conform to the idea that Christ's sacrifice was offered at the last supper and consummated on the cross; and for the words "perpetual memory of that his precious death" they read "perpetual memorial of that his precious death and sacrifice," articulating their understanding of the relation of the church's sacrifice to Christ's sacrifice.

2. In the "Oblation" they added to Cranmer' words

"these thy holy gifts" the words "WHICH WE NOW
OFFER UNTO THEE" (in upper case letters), thus
explicitly making this an oblation of the gifts.

3. In the "Invocation" they changed the words "be unto us
the bodye and bloude of thy moste derely beloved sonne
Jesus Christ" to "become the body and blood of thy
most dearly beloved Son," thus excluding a receptionist
interpretation.

Ceremonially the new interpretation was articulated by the
placement of the bread and wine on the altar before the Great
Thanksgiving[72] and by the lifting of the elements in the oblation which became customary during the words printed in
upper case letters. With these developments classical Anglicanism had acquired a more adequate eucharistic theology and a
rite which gave expression to that theology. It had not yet made
the theological link between the Lord's Day and the Lord's
Supper, however.

The Week and the Eucharist in the Book of Common Prayer 1979

The Week: The liturgical structure of the week did not
long retain the shape which Cranmer intended, largely because
his best efforts did not avail to secure communicants for a
weekly celebration anywhere other than in cathedral churches
(and not always there). The distinctive rite of Sunday became,
therefore Ante-communion, though the normative character of
the full eucharist as the proper rite for Sunday never entirely
disappeared from the church's memory and periodic efforts

were made at various periods to restore it. The Wesleys are notable for their efforts in this regard, and Bishop Samuel Seabury made a weekly celebration a goal of his Connecticut churchmanship, but it was not until the Oxford Movement that any significant portion of the church began to achieve this goal. Because the tractarians emphasized in a partisan way the *catholic* character of the weekly eucharist, in the end they retarded its acceptance by evangelicals in the church, even though a weekly eucharist is as characteristic of the agenda of such Reformers as Luther and Calvin as it is of distinctively *catholic* theology. Only with the liturgical movement of the twentieth century and the prayer book revision that led to the *Book of Common Prayer 1979* has the goal of the celebration of the eucharist as the principal service of the Lord's Day become a goal that transcends theological partisanship within Anglicanism and seems within reach of achievement.

Cranmer in 1549 had prescribed the observance of the ancient station days with the litany and ante-communion; after 1552 only the litany was required in addition to the daily office. Wednesdays and Fridays remained relatively popular days for weekday services over the course of the centuries, and from the nineteenth century they often became days for weekday celebrations of the eucharist (even in parishes whose principal service most Sundays of the year was Morning Prayer). In 1928 the rubric requiring the litany on Wednesdays and Fridays was dropped from the American rite. The station days thus retained a special character in the week, but their meaning had fallen out of consciousness. The custom of the Wednesday fast had fallen into desuetude long before the Reformation; the Friday fast remained, but was interpreted as a commemoration of the crucifixion. The increasing frequency of a daily celebration after the Oxford Movement also served to flatten the contours of the week.

The meaning of the Lord's Day was not entirely forgotten: liturgical and devotional commentaries and works such as the *Whole Duty of Man* made reference to its connection with the resurrection, as did some hymns of authors like Isaac Watts and Charles Wesley. Anglicans strove to uphold its festive character over against Puritan sabbatarianism. But in popular piety Sunday lost its paschal character almost entirely, and it found little explicit liturgical articulation. A collect by William Bright, which was published in 1862 and entered the collection of miscellaneous prayers in the 1928 Prayer Book, articulated the significance of Sunday as a remembrance of the resurrection. The 1928 book also included a prayer linking the risen Christ to the breaking of bread in its collect for Easter Monday, but the connection between the Lord's Day and the Lord's Supper as celebrations of the risen Christ took little root (and still is not a conscious part of the Sunday piety of most Episcopalians). The eschatological tension of the church's week had almost entirely disappeared.

The Book of Common Prayer 1979 makes the most explicit link since 1549 between the eucharist and the Lord's Day when it describes the Holy Eucharist as "the principal act of Christian worship on the Lord's Day and other major feasts."[73] It spells out the paschal character of the day in the collect for Sunday Morning Prayer and its eschatological character in the collect for Sunday Evening Prayer (and also in the Sunday prayer on page 835). In a collect for Saturday Compline, it describes Sunday worship as a celebration of the paschal mystery. The eucharistic prefaces of the Lord's Day spell out the traditional Sunday themes: creation of the light (first preface), the resurrection of Christ (second preface), recreation by water and the Holy Spirit (third preface). The Emmaus theme which links the eucharist and Sunday is explicitly stated in Eucharistic Prayer C with its acclamation, "Risen Lord, be

Redeeming the Week 125

known to us in the breaking of the Bread," and in a prayer (adapted from Mozarabic usage) on page 834, which asks that Jesus as our great High Priest be present in our midst that he might "be known to us in the breaking of the bread." The Sunday hymns (47–52) and many of the eucharistic hymns of *The Hymnal 1982* reinforce the theology of the Lord's Day in the *Book of Common Prayer 1979*.

The Friday fast is maintained as a commemoration of the cross, and the Friday collects pick up traditional themes, as do Friday psalms. The Saturday collects at Morning and Evening Prayer highlight the sabbath themes—and so guard against the confusion of Sunday with the sabbath. The commemorative shape of the week is thus recaptured in large measure. While the eschatological themes of Sunday are spelled out, however, the eschatological tension once established by the rhythm of feast and fast has not been recaptured.

The Eucharist: A distinctive feature of the Eucharist in the Book of Common Prayer 1979 is the careful use of headings and subheadings to display what it is we are doing when we celebrate the eucharist. When we put these together with the list of significant actions in the Order for Celebrating the Holy Eucharist on pages 400 and 401, we get the following outline. In this outline the bold-faced type indicates headings and subheadings; the regular type-face is taken from the order, and I have used italics for significant actions with no headings.

The Holy Eucharist:
The Liturgy for the Proclamation of the Word of God and Celebration of the Holy Communion

The Word of God

Gathering, concluding with
The Collect of the Day

The People and Priest Gather
· in the Lord's Name,

The Lessons
The Sermon
The Nicene Creed

Proclaim and Respond
to the Word of God,

The Prayers of the People

Pray for the World
and the Church,

The Confession
The Peace

Exchange the Peace,

The Holy Communion

Presentation of alms,
bread, and wine
Preparation of the table

Prepare the Table,

The Great Thanksgiving

Make Eucharist,

The Breaking of the Bread

Break the Bread,

Communion

Share the Gifts of God.

The details of the rite we can sketch in very quickly. The Eucharist is printed in traditional English (Rite I) and contemporary English (Rite II). Where the Roman rite in its classic form had antiphonal psalmody, this rite permits a hymn, psalm, or anthem—that is, at the entrance, offertory, and communion processions. The same provision is made for the place where the Roman rite had responsorial psalmody—between the lessons. Other publications provide music for responsorial psalmody at the gradual and for an alleluia responsory as well. The gathering rite is slightly less cluttered than it once was, but it still retains later expansions of the rite of gathering: 1) remnants of devotional *apologiae* (the collect for purity, optional in Rite II but still mandatory in Rite I, and the summary of the law or the commandments farced with the the *Kyrie*, both of which are retained as options in Rite I), 2) the *Kyrie eleison* or *Trisagion* in penitential seasons and ordinary time, and 3) the *Gloria in excelsis* or some other "song of praise" as a festal alternative. All of these elements intrude between an opening acclamation and the greeting and collect that once concluded the hymn, psalm, or anthem at the entrance. Three lessons are now normative for Sundays and major feasts and fasts, two for lesser feasts and fasts. The Old Testament reading has thus been restored to its rightful place. The Creed has also been restored to a place *after* the sermon, allowing the sermon to follow immediately on the gospel which it is to interpret.

In 1552 Cranmer had moved his Prayer for the Whole State of Christ's Church and confession and associated them with the offertory; the 1979 rite, by moving the offertory itself to a position just before the Great Thanksgiving, has restored a clarity of structure to the rite. In Rite I, an expanded version of Cranmer's prayer is printed in the text of the rite as the Prayers of the People. In either rite, however, any form of intercession which conforms to the range of heads of intercession listed with the six alternative forms of these prayers printed after the two rites may be used. Six forms are given, besides the one printed in the text of Rite I: two are litanies (versions of the Great Litany of the Byzantine Rite), concluded with collects or a doxology; one is a set of suffrages, concluded with a collect; two are sets of biddings (one with a standard versicle and response after each bidding and a concluding collect, the other with a silence and prayer after each bidding); and one is a list of intercessory biddings said responsively between leader and people, concluded by a confession (and absolution) or a collect. All these forms expand the scope of intercession beyond that of the form in Cranmer's rites (which was a prayer for the *church*, since other concerns were included in the litany); all carefully avoid the confusion of church and state which was characteristic of the intercessions of established churches after the Reformation. They all make provision for popular participation as well, unlike Cranmer's prayer, which was the celebrant's monologue. The confession and absolution normally follow, and this section of the service is concluded with the peace, which is generally ritually exchanged once more. Apart from their overloaded gathering rite, the 1979 provisions restore the clean lines of the primitive shape of the liturgy of the word very skillfully.

The Holy Communion moves in a logical fashion from taking the bread and wine to giving thanks and then concludes with the breaking of bread and the communion. The preparation requires that the bread and wine and other offerings be presented by representatives of the congregation, thus explicitly returning to an understanding of the eucharist as an offering of firstfruits and restoring a form of offertory procession. According to the 1979 rubrics the offerings are placed on the altar, but *not* offered up at this time. The problematic anticipation of the oblation in the eucharistic prayer is thus avoided. Except for Eucharistic Prayer C and one of the forms in the Order, all the forms of the Great Thanksgiving follow the Byzantine outline of the Scottish-American tradition in moving from *eucharistia* to *anamnesis* and oblation and finally to the invocation of the Spirit upon the church and its gifts. The two exceptions follow the Roman tradition in invoking the Spirit before the *anamnesis* in English and Roman fashion. Eucharistic Prayer D (which is a form of the anaphora of St. Basil) develops the supplication which follows the invocation into eucharistic intercession, as the Scottish church had done. All contemporary forms of the Great Thanksgiving allow for congregational response by memorial acclamations after the *anamnesis*; Prayer C has response throughout. In Eucharistic Prayer I the 1928 form is preserved intact. After the Great Amen, the Great Thanksgiving concludes with the Lord's Prayer.

Breads are then broken and chalices prepared for the distribution of communion, communion is distributed, a prayer follows, and the rite concludes with the blessing (optional in Rite II) and the dismissal (optional in Rite I), now once again detached from the blessing. The four actions of the sacramental meal follow one another in direct sequence in the clean lines of this rite.

Theologically the new eucharistic prayers articulate a theology of the real presence in its commonly-understood sense, without committing the church to any one theory about the modality of that presence. No definitive doctrine of the way the consecration is effected is expressed in the prayers, but they cohere best with the Jewish understanding of consecration by thanksgiving or the Eastern theology of consecration consummated by the invocation of the Spirit.

The imagery of the new prayers gives scope to a much broader understanding of redemption than the Anselmian doctrine enshrined in Cranmer's composition; these prayers also

130   CHAPTER TWO

expand the scope of the *anamnesis* and focus on paschal and eschatological themes much more strongly than Cranmer did. A carefully crafted doctrine of eucharistic sacrifice is found in the catechism, which picks up traditional themes yet avoids the medieval distortions that evoked the wrath of the reformers:

> [The Eucharist is called a Sacrifice because the rite], the Church's sacrifice of praise and thanksgiving, is the way by which the sacrifice of Christ is made present, and in which he unites us to his one offering of himself.[74]

The result is a eucharistic rite which restores the fulness of Sunday worship with its paschal and eschatological themes in a far more adequate way than any Western rite of the preceding millennium. The paschal and eschatological focus of the liturgical architecture of the week has been restored.

Notes to Chapter Two

1. A summary of data on the planetary week can be found in Willy Rordorf, *Sunday: The History of the Day of Rest and Worship in the Earliest Centuries of the Christian Church*, translated by A. A. K. Graham (Philadelphia: Westminster, 1968), 24–38), 24–38. It seems likely to me that Jewish observance of the sabbath throughout the empire may have contributed to the adoption of the planetary week; I am not convinced that it prompted the *development* of its Greco-Roman form, however, as Rordorf wants to argue.

2. Bernhard W. Anderson puts the point of all this succinctly in his note *ad loc.* in Herbert G. May and Bruce M. Metzger, editors., *The Oxford Annotated Bible with Apocrypha: Revised Standard Version* (NY: Oxford University Press, 1965): "The sun, the moon, and the stars are not divine powers that control man's destiny, as was believed in antiquity, but are only *lights.*"

3. The lunar division resulted in the designation of the seventh, fourteenth, twenty-first, and twenty-eighth days of the month as unlucky. This division was recalculated every month, however, so that it had not yet been regularized into a recurring cycle of seven days, See Roland de Vaux, *Ancient Israel*, volume 1, *Social Institutions* (NY: McGraw-Hill, 1965), pages 186–188.

4. The pre-Jewish origins (if any) of the sabbath are a matter of dispute. The Babylonian observance of "unlucky" day noted above is often contrasted to the positive meaning of the sabbath in Judaism. But as a *social* institution it would have functioned like the sabbath: an unlucky day is one on which no one would want to undertake business; cessation of labor was prescribed for religious reasons on the Jewish sabbath. Studies of parallels to the Jewish word for sabbath in other near-Eastern languages have generally been inconclusive and do not shed much light on the Jewish institution.

5. Schmemann, *For the Life of the World,: Sacraments and Orthodoxy*, revised edition, (Crestwood, NY: St. Vladimir's Seminary Press, 1973; first edition 1963) pages 14–16. Schmemann had opened his discussion here with Feuerbach's dictum, "Man is what he eats." Schmemann's rejection of "religion" is nearly as absolute as Barth's, but (like Louis Bouyer, whose work in this field he sometimes quotes) he does make cautious use of the discipline which we know as comparative religion.

6. This introductory material is a slight adaptation of the introductory material to chapter 6 of my dissertation, "An Architecture of Time."

7. Louis Bouyer, *Rite and Man: Natural Sacredness and Christian Liturgy*, translated by M. Joseph Costelloe (Notre Dame, IN: University of Notre Dame Press, 1963), page 88.

8. Bouyer, *Rite and Man*, page 90.

9. Lucien Deiss, *Springtime of the Liturgy: Liturgical Texts of the First Four Centuries*, translated by Matthew J. O'Connell (Collegeville, MN: Liturgical Press, 1979), pages 6–7.

10. Deiss, *Springtime of the Liturgy*, pages 7–8, citing Finkelstein, "The birkat ha-mazon," *Jewish Quarterly Review* 19 (1929), pages 243–259.

11. Text as given in Deiss, *The Springtime of the Liturgy*, page 6.

12. Annie Jaubert, *The Date of the Last Supper*, translated by Isaac Rafferty (Staten Island, NY: Alba House, Paulist Publications, 1965).

13. Her reconciliation of the synoptic and Johannine traditions about the relationship between the last supper and the passover seems to harmonize the conflicting data too neatly to be accepted without suspicion, for example.

132   CHAPTER TWO

14. Roland de Vaux, *Ancient Israel*, Volume 1, *Social Institutions* (NY: McGraw Hill; 1965; London: Darton, Longman, & Todd, 1961), page 188 (emphasis added).

15. Justin Martyr, *First Apology* 67, cited by Deiss, *Springtime of the Liturgy*, page 94.

16. Cited in Thomas K. Carroll and Thomas Halton, *Liturgical Practice in the Fathers*, Message of the Fathers of the Church 21 (Wilmington, DE: Michael Glazier, 1988), page 36; translated from volume 172 in the edition in the French series Sources chrétiennes, page 186.

17. In biblical and early Christian usage, "Pentecost" designates both the fifty-day festal season after the feast of *pascha* and the day which concludes the season. The *season* of Pentecost is thus the fifty-day season between what we now call Easter and the day of Pentecost, *not* the season *after* Pentecost.

18. Ignatius of Antioch, *Letter to the Magnesians*, as cited by Carroll and Halton, *Liturgical Practice of the Fathers*, pages 21–22; translated from the edition in Sources chrétiennes 10, page 87.

19. Origen, *Homilies on Numbers*, 23:4, as cited by Jean Daniélou, *The Bible and the Liturgy* (Notre Dame, IN: University of Notre Dame Press, 1956), page 239. Carroll and Halton also give this passage In *Liturgical Practice in the Fathers*, pages 69–70, but a typographical error ("from" for the "for" I have italicized in the text) disastrously alters its meaning.

20. *Didache* 8:1.

21. *Didascalia* 5:13.

22. Cf. BCP 1979, page 17, under the title, "Days of Special Obligation," to be "observed by special acts of discipline and self-denial:" "Good Friday and all other Fridays of the year, in commemoration of the Lord's crucifixion, except for Fridays in the Christmas and Easter seasons, and any Feasts of our Lord which occur on a Friday."

23. Justin Martyr's description of the service of the Lord's Day, *First Apology*, chapter 67, supplemented by material in italics taken from his description of the baptismal eucharist, chapter 65. The translation is taken from Deiss, *Springtime of the Liturgy*, pages 93–94 (chapter 67), and 92 (chapter 65). Clearly the bread would need to be broken before distribution, but Justin does not find this practical action significant enough to mention. Probably one of the deacons, who were in charge of keeping order in the assembly, would have concluded the service with a dismissal—a diaconal function in later rites.

24. Like every interpreter of the eucharist, I am indebted to Gregory Dix, *The Shape of the Eucharist*, Seabury edition with Additional Notes by Paul Marshall (NY: Seabury Press, 1982; first and second editions, London: A and C, Black, 1945) for this account of the development of the shape of the eucharist. The outline draws on his work and the more nuanced recent account of Robert Taft in *Beyond East and West* (Washington, DC: Pastoral Press, 1984), chapters 10 and 11, "The Structural Analysis of Liturgical Units: An Essay in Methodology" and "How Liturgies Grow: The Evolution of the Byzantine Divine Liturgy."

25. See Jean-Jacques von Allmen, *Worship: Its Theology and Practice*, translated by W. Fletcher Fleet (London: Lutterworth, 1965), pages 54–56.

26. von Allmen, *Worship*, chapter 2. See the reference to Peter Brunner, on whom he is drawing, on page 43.

27. Alexander Schmemann, *The Eucharist: Sacrament of the Kingdom* (Crestwood, NY: St. Vladimir's Seminary Press, 1988), chapter 1, pages 11–26.

28. On the entrance procession and stational liturgy, see John F. Baldovin, *The Urban Character of Christian Worship: The Origins, Development, and Meaning of Stational Liturgy*, Orientalia Christiana Analecta 228 (Rome: Pont. Institutum Studiorum Orientalium, 1987).

29. *The Hymnal 1982* (NY: Church Hymnal Corporation, 1985), Hymn 312 (translated by Charles William Humphreys, alterations by Percy Dearmer).

30. Schmemann, *The Eucharist*, pages 68–69.

31. *Summa Theologica* 3a 73:3

32. See the careful study by Robert Taft, *The Great Entrance: A History of the Transfer of Gifts and other Pre-anaphoral Rites of the Liturgy of St. John Chrysostom*, which explores the development of the preparation of the gift in the Byzantine rite.

33. See Joseph Jungmann, *The Mass of the Roman Rite: Its Origins and Development*, 2 volumes (reprint edition, Westminster, MD: Christian Classics, 1986), volume 1, pages 71–72 for a description of the offertory procession in the stational services in Rome in the seventh century; volume 2, pages 1–26 for an extended discussion of the offertory procession.

34. I am here following Alexander Schmemann's account in *For the Life of the World*, pages 16–18.

35. The key central sections of the Roman Canon were already fixed by the time of Ambrose in the fourth century, for he cites a long portion of that prayer in a form not substantially different from what we know today. For an extended discussion of the Roman canon, see Jungmann, *The Mass of the Roman Rite*, volume 2, pages 101–274. Jungmann is inclined to believe that the intercessory portions of the canon are an early addition and interrupt the theological sequence of the prayer—a conviction which is by no means shared by all contemporary liturgical scholars. In any case, the problem with the Roman canon is that the theme of sacrificial offering has become so predominant that it has largely obscured the function of the prayer as articulating the church's thanksgiving, its eucharist. Yet it was by giving thanks that Christ "consecrated" the bread and wine at the last supper; a canon which no longer emphasizes this note of thanksgiving deviates from the rite as the New Testament understood it.

36. Justin Martyr, *Dialogue* , 41, as cited in H. Boone Porter, *The Day of Light: The Biblical and Liturgical Meaning of Sunday* (Washington, DC: Pastoral Press, 1987), page 51.

37. Irenaeus, *Against all Heresies* 4:17.5, cited in Porter, *Day of Light*, page 53.

38. Irenaeus, *Against all Heresies* 4:18.5,6, cited in Porter, *Day of Light* page 53.

39. This is my free translation of the paragraph which begins, *Supra quae propitio ac sereno vultu*. The phrase *de tuis donis ac datis* comes from the preceding paragraph and parallels the expression in the Byzantine anaphoras, τα σα εκ των σων σοι προσφεροντες. . . .

40. For a revealing discussion of the meaning of fasting and of communion as the conclusion of the fast, see Alexander Schmemann, "Fast and Liturgy: Notes in Liturgical Theology," in *St. Vladimir's Seminary Quarterly* 3:1 (1959), pages 2–9.

41. Various programs of votive commemorations on specific days of the week developed. These commemorations were articulated in votive propers for a daily eucharist. For these developments in the West, see J. A. Jungmann, *Public Worship*, translated by Clifford Howell (London: Challoner Publications, 1957), pages 230–238, "The Christian Week." Similar developments occurred in the Byzantine rite, but they affected only the hymnological material of the daily office, because a daily celebration of the eucharist was alien to the theology of the Byzantine rite.

42. For a discussion of this piety and its impact, see Alexander Schmemann, *Introduction to Liturgical Theology*, translated by Asheleigh E. Moorhouse, third edition (Crestwood, NY: St. Vladimir's Seminary Press, 1986; first edition, 1966), pages 91–110).

43. In the East, it was already beginning by the time of Justinian in the sixth century, who vainly sought to forbid the practice in a novella cited by Meletius Michael Solovey, *The*

Byzantine Divine Liturgy: History and Commentary (Washington, DC: Catholic University Press, 1970), on page 256: "I order all bishops and priests to pronounce the anaphora not silently but aloud, in order that the faithful might hear it and be inspired with piety and glorify God. Therefore, it is necessary that the bishops and the priests offer aloud the holy sacrifice and the other prayers to our Lord Jesus Christ who is with the Father and the Holy Spirit."

44. The early form of the litany seems to be preserved in the *Deprecatio Gelasii*, later reduced to the final *Kyries*. For the text of the *Deprecatio*, see Joseph Jungmann, *The Mass of the Roman Rite*, volume 1, pages 336–337. How the morning hymn *Gloria in excelsis* entered into the festive form of the Roman rite is unclear.

45. See Joseph Jungmann, *The Mass of the Roman Rite*, volume 1, pages 388–390 for the *laudes*. They followed the collect and thus concluded the entrance procession of the Roman rite and preceded the primitive opening of the rite with the liturgy of the word on special occasions. The *polychronion* can still be found in some printed texts of the Byzantine rite.

46. On this issue, see Alexander Schmemann's article, "Sacrament and Symbol," Appendix 2 in his book, *For the Life of the World*.

47. The texts are taken form Adrien Nocent, *The Liturgical Year*, volume 4, *Sundays in Ordinary Time*, translated by Matthew J. O'Connell (Collegeville, MN: Liturgical Press, 1977), page 48. This is a relatively free translation, but the contrast is clear.

48. See the treatment of these themes in the introduction by Paul Meyendorff to his translation, *St. Germanus of Constantinople on the Divine Liturgy*, Crestwood, NY: St. Vladimir's Seminary Press, 1984).

49. For a thoughtful treatment of Aquinas' eucharistic doctrine, see William R. Crockett, *Eucharist: Symbol of Transformation* (NY: Pueblo, 1989), pages 113–131. He emphasizes that for Aquinas, "substance" does not mean "material substance."

50. Once the consecration is understood to occur with the recitation of the words of Christ, the subsequent offering of the gifts in the paragraph, *unde et memores*, will easily be understood in this way.

51. Kenneth Stevenson provides a careful study of the development of the theology of the eucharistic sacrifice in his book, *Eucharist and Offering* (New York: Pueblo, 1986). For this period, see particularly chapter 5.

52. For a very thoughtful examination of the shift in the meaning of both communion and fasting, see Alexander Schmemann, *Great Lent: Journey to the Pascha* (Crestwood, NY:

136   CHAPTER TWO

St. Vladimir's Seminary Press, 1973), pages 45–52; and "Fast and Liturgy: Notes in Liturgical Theology," *St. Vladimir's Seminary Quarterly* 3:1 (1959), pages 2–9.

53. BCP 1549, page 230.

54. BCP 1549, page 229. Cranmer apparently expected that a daily eucharist might be continued in some churches, for he speaks (rubric, page 216) of "Cathedral churches or other places, where there is dailie Communion." Rubrics of the various prayer books always specify a minimum number of communicants—thus safeguarding the corporate nature of the eucharist.

55. W. Jardine Grisbrooke, *Anglican Liturgies of the Seventeenth and Eighteenth Centuries*, Alcuin Club Collections 40 (London: SPCK, 1958), xii–xiii.

56. BCP 1552, page 393. I have added the bold-faced emphasis. The key here is the understanding of "real and essential" and "natural." Recent authors have on the whole argued that the 1552 rite made explicit what Cranmer intended to be implicit in 1549, but had phrased in such as way as not to offend the more conservative. The same teaching is found in Cranmer's original article on the Lord's Supper in the 42 Articles of 1553.

57. See Crockett, *Eucharist: Symbol of Transformation*, pages 148–150, for Calvin's doctrine; pages 164–173 for Cranmer.

58. Cranmer, *Defense of the True and Catholic Doctrine of the Sacrament* (1550), in *Works*, ed. Jenkyns, volume 3, page 413–414, as cited by Gregory Dix, *The Shape of the Liturgy*, pages 650–651. The emphasis is Dix's. The problem here is that the language of "sign, token, and figure" means something quite different in the sixteenth century than it did in the first four centuries. Cranmer's doctrine is an inadequate way of articulating the eucharistic presence because the meaning of the words has shifted.

59. Kenneth Stevenson, summarizing the first sense in which the eucharist is a sacrifice for Cranmer according to F. E. Brightman and Geoffrey Cuming, in *Eucharist and Offering*, page 144.

60. Kenneth Stevenson, ibid., summarizing the second and third senses in which Brightman understood the eucharist to be a sacrifice for Cranmer, which he and Cuming consider to be a single sense, the thankful self-oblation of the people in response to Christ's sacrifice. For the offertory rubric below, see BCP 1549, page 219; for texts from the eucharistic prayer, see pages 222–223.

61. In 1552 a petition for the acceptance of alms was incorporated into the Prayer for the Whole State of Christ's Church.

62. Augustine, *City of God* 10:5, 6. But Augustine links the sacramental presence of Christ and the sacrifice in a way that Cranmer does not.

63. John Johnson, *The Unbloody Sacrifice*, I-II-I, page 230, as cited in Grisbrooke, *Anglican Liturgies of the Seventeenth and Eighteenth Centuries*, page 78.

64. Johnson, *The Unbloody Sacrifice*, I-II-I, page 238, cited in Grisbrooke, *Anglican Liturgies*, page 81.

65. See the references from *The Unbloody Sacrifice* excerpted in Grisbrooke, *Anglican Liturgies*, pages 84–86.

66. Johnson, *The Unbloody Sacrifice*, I-II-I, pages 71–72, cited in Grisbrooke, *Anglican Liturgies*, pages 74–75.

67. Johnson, *The Unbloody Sacrifice*, I-II-I, page 60, cited in Grisbrooke, *Anglican Liturgies*, page 75.

68. Johnson, *The Primitive Communicant*, page 115, cited in Grisbrooke, *Anglican Liturgies*, page 83.

69. Note that the eucharistic prayer itself remains constant in the English prayer book after 1552. Such changes as were made in the eucharistic rite do not affect the text of the eucharistic prayer itself.

70. Grisbrooke, *Anglican Liturgies*, page 71.

71. See the text and related commentary in Grisbrooke, *Anglican Liturgies*.

72. The rubric also requires that they be "offered" at this point—a custom derived more from Western usage than from Eastern rites, which knew of no offering or "lesser oblation" at this point in the rite.

73. BCP 1979, *Concerning the Service of the Church*, page 13.

74. BCP 1979, page 859.

Chapter Three

Redeeming the Year: The Easter and Incarnation Cycles and Baptism

The Year as a Unit of Time and the Problem of the Calendar

Besides the day, the natural cycle that makes its influence most directly felt on the rhythms of human life is that of the solar year—the period of time required for the earth's orbit around the sun. The impact of that cycle on the crops and herds by which settled communities and semi-nomadic peoples sustain themselves means that all societies, but particularly those in temperate climates, seek to correlate the rhythms of their own existence to those of the solar year. The nodal points of this cycle are the summer and winter solstices (the longest and shortest days of the year) and the spring and fall equinoxes (the times when day and night are equal in length).

But such societies have also usually worked with the month as a unit of time. Days are dated not from the first of the year, but from the first day of each month. The problem is that the solar year, consisting of 365 days and a fraction of a day, does not break down into twelve lunar months without remainder. Today, we work with months that are made up of varying numbers of days (and are no longer strictly lunar), with leap years, and with rules for when to omit leap years. All of this is necessary to keep our annual cycles synchronized with the solar year. That is a very complicated system which attained its final form after the Reformation, was implemented by the various Western nations over the course of several centuries, and has yet to be adopted by some of the non-Western churches for their religious calendars.

No such uniform observance existed in late antiquity. Even within Judaism, various systems of intercalation were employed to adjust a year of lunar months to the solar year. It has become increasingly apparent to us in the light of recent research that even within first-century Judaism no complete consensus existed. The Jewish calendar with which we are familiar was that of Pharisaic and Sadducean Judaism of that era. But sectarian Judaism sometimes worked with an older sacral calendar, as we noted earlier. Thomas Talley describes the salient features of this calendar, apparently used by the Essenes, as follows:

CHAPTER THREE

The year has only 364 days and we are still in the dark as to how it might have been intercalated without destroying its most characteristic feature: so fundamental an emphasis on the week as to make every date in every month fall every year on the same day of the week. The 364 days are divided into four completely symmetrical quarters of 91 days each, each quarter divided into two months of 30 days each and a third month of 31 days. The first day of the first month, however, does not fall on the first day of the week, but on the fourth day, the day of the creation of the heavenly lights, according to Genesis 1:14–19. So the first days of the first, fourth, seventh, and tenth months are all Wednesdays. Those of the second, fifth, eighth, and eleventh months are Fridays. Those of the third, sixth, ninth, and twelfth months are Sundays. Passover, the fifteenth day of the first month, falls always on a Wednesday, placing the Passover celebration in the night from Tuesday to Wednesday. The Feast of Weeks, kept on the fifteenth day of the third month at Qumran, fell always on Sunday. The Day of Atonement, the tenth day of the seventh month, was always a Friday, and the feast of Tabernacles, the fifteenth day of that month, a Wednesday. Thus, all of the major cultically significant days assigned to a fixed month fell on Sunday, Wednesday, or Friday.[1]

There are further complications with which we will deal in this chapter, however. The focus of the Christian faith is the resurrection of Jesus. The gospels are unanimous in their testimony that Jesus was crucified on Friday—the day of preparation (παρασκευη in the Greek) for the sabbath, and that he appeared on Sunday, the first day of the week (μια των σαββατων in the gospel accounts), risen from the dead. These events stood in some relation to the feast of the Passover for which he had gone up to Jerusalem. The gospels do not agree on what this relation is, however. For the synoptics, the crucifixion occurred sometime after Jesus had eaten the passover meal with his disciples. According to John, however, Jesus was crucified as the lambs were being sacrificed for the passover meal.

From the first, as we noted in the last chapter, Christians made the day of Christ's resurrection their weekly feast day. If they were to organize the year around any commemoration, it would likewise be his resurrection. But by whose calendar would the reckoning be made? Was his resurrection to be dated according to the dominant Jewish calendar, by the sacral one which we have noted above, or by the calendar which predominated in the culture in which a particular church found itself? If the calendar used was one which was not regulated to make the same date fall on the same day of the week each year, should the commemoration be made on the following Sunday to coordinate it with the day of the week on which he rose? How should the celebration be related to the Jewish passover? Should it always fall afterwards? Should it represent simply the Christian transformation of the Jewish *pasch*, on the date set by Jewish authorities for that observance? Was the issue important enough that all communities need to reckon the observance in the same way?

In actual fact, it would appear that not all Christian communities initially kept a yearly celebration. The resurrection was celebrated each week, and some communities apparently found that entirely sufficient. Others did not, however. Those who did keep an annual observance reckoned its date in many different ways. It would appear that many Christians coordinated the date of the celebration in various ways with the date which different Jewish authorities set for the Jewish passover. Others apparently kept the Christian passover on the fixed date for the Jewish passover in an Asian solar calendar, which appointed April 6 as the date for the observance every year. Hippolytus in his paschal tables attempted to fix the actual date of the crucifixion, which he set as March 25, and some Christians apparently used this in reckoning the date of their annual celebration. Christians in remote areas apparently managed as best they could in setting the date each year. What is known to us as the quartodeciman controversy[2] would appear, Thomas Talley argues, to encompass two different issues in its various stages: in the first stage, whether local communities (Rome in this case) were bound to keep a yearly feast in addition to the weekly one at all; in the second stage, whether the yearly feast was to fall on the fourteenth of Nisan, whatever day of the week it fell, or was always to be observed on a Sunday. This was one issue which the Council of Nicaea sought to resolve in the fourth century, and the determination was that the feast was to fall on Sunday following the first full moon after the spring equinox—the Alexandrian tradition. Even then there seem to have been compromises. In Gregory of Tours we find two curious entries in a list of vigils established by Martin, bishop of Tours 371–397, in the churches of his see city:

> On the Resurrection of our Lord Jesus Christ, March 27, in St. Martin's church.
>
> At Easter, in the cathedral.[3]

The church at Tours apparently adopted the Nicene determination for a moveable feast, but also observed a doublet of this feast on a fixed date. In fact, issues involved in choosing the proper date for the celebration appear several times in Gregory's narrative. Publishing the date for Easter each year was a responsibility which bishops took seriously because it was a calculation that many people found difficult to make.

The Year, the Pilgrimage Feasts, and their Rites in Judaism

In Palestine (with different agricultural seasons than ours) the spring equinox saw the beginning of the harvest and new births in the flocks.[4] The ancient Jewish festivals were related to these events. The feast of unleavened bread marked the beginning of the grain harvest, and the feast of weeks marked its conclusion; the feast of booths or tabernacles marked the time of vintage and fruit harvest. These were feasts of settled agricultural communities (and probably Canaanite in origin). The feast of Passover (later fused with the feast of unleavened bread) seems to have been the spring feast of nomadic herdsmen, marking the birthing season for the flocks.

These feasts, then, all had their origins in the rhythms of nature. But Israel had been delivered from bondage in Egypt during the celebration of Passover (the feast that Moses had sought permission from the Pharaoh to go out into the wilderness to celebrate, according to Exodus 3:19; 5:1), and so, when Israel adopted this feast and linked it with the feast of unleavened bread, the focus shifted from the celebration of God's bounty in nature to the celebration of God's grace in redemption.[5] Passover became the annual *anamnesis* of the deliverance from Egypt; in a similar way, Pentecost (the feast of weeks) became the *anamnesis* of the covenant into which Israel entered at Sinai. And the feast of booths was eventually understood as the *anamnesis* of Israel's sojourn in the wilderness.

The characteristic rite for feasts, as we have already noted, is the festive meal—a meal understood as one which is shared by God as host and provisioner. Such a meal in religious language is a sacrifice of food, drink, and meat.[6] When we use the word "sacrifice," we almost invariably think of the slaughter of animals or the taking of life. This, however, was not the main focus of the rite, but a necessary preliminary in preparing the meal. While Jewish households celebrated the sabbath with a weekly festive meal in their homes, for the pilgrimage feasts the whole Jewish people, so far as possible, gathered in Jerusalem, so that the feasts took on a communal as well as a familial character.

Alexander Schmemann argues forcefully that to understand the theological meaning of the cycles of time and the feasts which are their nodal points we must begin with the "natural cycles":

> For man of the past a feast was not something accidental and "additional": it was his way of putting *meaning* into his life, of liberating it from the animal rhythms of work and rest. A feast was not a simple "break" in the otherwise meaningless and hard life of work, but a justification of that work, its fruit, its—so to speak—sacramental transformation into joy and, therefore, into freedom. A feast was thus always deeply and organically related to time, to the natural cycles of time, to the whole framework of man's life in the world. And, whether we like it or not, whether we want it or not, Christianity *accepted* and made its own this fundamentally human phenomenon of feast, as it accepted and made its own the whole man and all his needs. But, as in everything else, Christians accepted the feast not only by giving it a new meaning, by transforming its "content," but by taking it, along with the whole of "natural" man, through death and resurrection.[7]

The "form" in which the church accepted the feast was part of its heritage from Judaism. The church accepted two of the great pilgrimage feasts of Judaism—passover and the feast of weeks

(Pascha and Pentecost). They were the beginning and the end of a fifty-day festal season which we call Easter Season but which the early church knew as Pentecost (using the name for the season as well as for its concluding feast)

It did so, Schmemann argues, because "they were, even before Christ, the announcement, the anticipation of time and of life in time, of which the Church was the manifestation and the fulfillment."[8] To put it another way, he argues:

> They were . . . the "material" of a *sacrament of time* to be performed by the Church. We know that both feasts originated as the annual celebration of spring and of the first fruits of nature. In this respect they were the very expression of feast as man's *joy about life*. They celebrated the world coming back to life again after the death of winter, becoming again the food and life of man. And it is very significant that this most "natural," all-embracing and universal feast—that of life itself—became the starting point, and indeed the foundation of the long transformation of the idea and experience of feast. It is equally significant that in this transformation each new stage did not abolish and simply replace the previous one, but fulfilled it at an ever deeper and greater meaning until the whole process was consummated in Christ Himself. The mystery of *natural* time, the bondage to winter and release in spring, was fulfilled in the the mystery of time as *history*—the bondage to Egypt and the release into the Promised Land. And the mystery of historical time was transformed into the mystery of eschatological time, of its understanding as *passover*—the "passage" into the ultimate joy of salvation and redemption, as movement toward the fulfillment of the Kingdom. And when Christ "our Passover" (1 Cor 5:7) performed His *passage* to the Father, He assumed and fulfilled all these meanings—the whole movement of time in all its dimensions; and on the "last and great day of Pentecost" He inaugurated the new time, the new "eon" of the Spirit.[9]

CHAPTER THREE

This leads us from our brief consideration of the Jewish year into an exploration of how Christianity transformed these Jewish observances in developing its own liturgical year.

The Year, the Pascha, and Baptism in the Early Christian Centuries

From the beginning the dominant rhythm of the church's liturgical life was, as we have seen, the weekly cycle, which found its focus in the celebration of Christ's resurrection in the eucharist on the Lord's Day, the first day of the week. Christians also seem to have observed the discipline of daily prayer from the beginning, and the pattern of daily prayer developed into the rhythm of the daily office, which celebrated Christ as the rising sun of righteousness and the light that knows no setting. These cycles have been normative for the church's liturgical life throughout the ages because they are rooted in apostolic practice.

But we cannot make the same claims for the liturgical year. We have already seen that there is good reason to believe that some of the early Christian communities kept no annual observances. The cultural context of individual communities was no doubt the determining factor in this matter. In a Jewish milieu, Christians who remained in close contact with the rhythms of Jewish life would undoubtedly reinterpret Jewish observances from the perspective of their new messianic faith. This was true above all of those observances closely related to the principal events in the life of Jesus and of the early church. Jesus died at passover season. On the feast of Pentecost (that is, the feast of weeks) that same year, according to Acts, the church experienced the empowerment of the Holy Spirit.

Already in the New Testament these facts found theological interpretation. Christ was understood as the true paschal sacrifice (1 Corinthians 5:7) and his death was understood as "his exodus which he was to accomplish in Jerusalem" (Luke 9:31). The passover meal which celebrated the events of the exodus provided the context for understanding the church's sacramental meal which celebrated Christ's exodus. In the typological interpretation characteristic of biblical thought and of early Christian theology all of this was worked out, then, as follows: Christ's death is the *reality* which the paschal sacrifice *foreshadows* and of which the Christian eucharist is the *type*. Christ's death and resurrection are the *reality* which Israel's exodus from Egypt foreshadows and of which the church's passage as the new Israel from sin and death to righteousness and new life is the *type*.

In Greek and Latin the word *pascha* (which transliterated the Aramaic word for passover) was understood in two ways. One etymology (found in the paschal homily of Melito of Sardis in the second century)[10] derived *pascha* from the Greek word πασχειν, "to suffer." Latin-speaking Christians made the same link with the Latin word for suffering, *passio*. This is, of course, a false etymology, but it worked very well for an understanding of Jesus as the paschal sacrifice. The second way of understanding *pascha* was closer to its Aramaic and Hebrew roots. This understanding is expressed in the way we usually render the word in English—"pass-over." In actual fact the Hebrew word refers to the testimony of Exodus that the angel of death "passed over" the houses of the people of Israel in Egypt but slew the first-born in Egyptian households. But in a wider sense Jews often referred to the whole cluster of events in Israel's exodus from Egypt as the passover. Greek and Latin-speaking Christians took "passover" in a broader sense (not

CHAPTER THREE

warranted by the Hebrew word) as a reference to Israel's "passover" through the waters of the Reed Sea from bondage in Egypt to freedom in the land of promise. This understanding grounded the Christian typological interpretation which linked this event with Christ's "passover" from death to life and with the passover of the church in him. This was the way in which the meaning of the feast of the Passover was already being interpreted by New Testament authors.

In a similar way the covenant of Israel at Sinai and the gift of the law, celebrated by some Jews in Jesus' day at the feasts of weeks or Pentecost, provided the theological ground for the Christian understanding of the gift of the Spirit which Acts records and the new covenant established by that gift of the Spirit. This theological reinterpretation is, once again, already at work in the literature of the New Testament.

But the theological interpretation of these feasts does not necessarily entail their Christian observance. We have no solid evidence that Christians ever observed the feast of Tabernacles or Booths, the third great pilgrimage feast, even though a theological reinterpretation of that feast seems to be articulated in John's gospel;[11] and there is no evidence whatsoever that Christians ever developed an observance of the Day of Atonement, even though the Jewish ritual for that day provides a basis for the interpretation of Christ's priesthood and death in Hebrews. It was the events reported in the New Testament as occurring on Passover and Pentecost which eventually led to Christian observance of these days.

That development was undoubtedly a gradual one and depended on the context of a community's life. Jewish Christians, once they had separated from the community of the Jewish synagogue, were no doubt the first to develop such observances. Gentile communities, particularly those outside Palestine, were much slower in developing such observances in many cases. Rome resisted longest, if Talley and others are reading the quartodeciman controversy correctly. When the church did adopt the feasts, it adopted both Passover and Pentecost. It seems to have adopted them together, as a fifty-day festal season opened by the paschal fast and concluded by the celebration of Pentecost.

The earliest observance of Passover seems to have been the paschal eucharist, preceded by the paschal fast—a Christian adaptation of the Jewish observance. This eucharist (the Christian *seder*) differed from the weekly eucharist principally in the hour of its observance—normally, as we shall see, the paschal eucharist was timed to begin at cockcrow. For Pentecost no distinctive observance developed: the events of Acts 2 simply formed the theme for the Sunday eucharist on the Sunday of Pentecost. By the end of the second century it seems reasonably clear that all churches had adopted the fast and vigil eucharist of the passover or *pasch* (Christians invariably used the Jewish name—a fact disguised by the use of the name Easter in Germanic languages today), followed by a fifty-day festival season culminating on the Sunday of Pentecost. The annual cycle had now become normative for Christianity, though how to establish its date remained a dispute for some time to come.

We have no undisputed evidence for what we have come to think of as the characteristic feature of the Christian celebration of Easter, the baptisms of the paschal vigil, until early in the third century. The theological interpretation of Christian baptism in terms of Christ's death and resurrection and of the gift of the Spirit is quite firmly rooted in the New Testament. But it is equally evident from the New Testament that baptism was administered at whatever time individual conversion to Christ warranted its administration. The restriction to Easter and Pentecost was a gradual development—one which could not have occurred in any case before local communities adopted the feasts.

Once Christian communities were securely rooted, they took more care in the preparation of their converts. By the second century, a period of preliminary instruction (catechesis) and testing (scrutiny) was required before prospective converts were initiated into the community through the baptismal liturgy. As local churches organized their lives, baptismal catechesis and baptismal initiation were gradually woven into the rhythms of community life. Once this took place, the interpretation of baptism in terms of the theology of the Christian passover made the paschal season (often referred to as Pentecost) the time of choice for the administration of baptism, and the paschal feast itself the preeminent baptismal occasion. The relation of the theology of the feast of Pentecost (which closed the paschal season) to the theology of baptism and the account which Acts gives of baptism on that day also made it an appropriate time to administer "make-up" baptisms to those who had been unable to take part in the paschal vigil. By the Council of Nicaea, the church had reached a consensus that, under ordinary circumstances, paschal baptisms were the norm of the church's life. The crowds of converts who were entering the church now that it was becoming the "established" religion of the Roman empire made careful organization of catechesis and initiation a necessity in this era—which has left us the classical catechetical literature and our first fully-articulated liturgies for the process of conversion and initiation. Even in this period, however, the church recognized the legitimacy of baptism at other times in cases of pastoral necessity (with a preference for Sunday in such circumstances, since Sunday also articulated the paschal and pentecostal themes of baptism and so that the newly baptized could complete their initiation with the reception of communion at the community's eucharist). The church had now established the celebration of Passover and Pentecost as normative for the annual cycle; and the baptismal and eucharistic vigil of Easter, with a preceding fast and a festal season which culminated in Pentecost (which might also have a baptismal liturgy) was the normative form which its observance of this annual cycle took. With this development, the foundations of the church's rule of prayer were all in place. Its "architecture of time" had taken on its basic shape. If we wished to describe this liturgical architecture in the language of the New Testament, we might put it like this: in the course of each day, the church's worship finds its focus in the services of praise and prayer which celebrate the risen Christ as the *Light of the World*. In its weekly rhythm, that worship finds its focus in the eucharistic service of word and sacramental meal on the Lord's Day, a service which celebrates the risen Christ as the *Word of Life* and the *Bread of Life*. Within the span of the year, that worship comes to a climax in the paschal season and the paschal feast, where in the celebration of *Christ our Passover* the newly-baptized take part in the church's journey with Christ from death to life. Indeed, the paschal vigil in its full classic form will deploy all the elements of this architecture in its liturgy: it begins with the evening service of light, it continues with the baptismal vigil with its liturgy of the word, its baptisms, and its eucharist, and it concludes at dawn with its celebration of the rising sun of righteousness. In this celebration the church deploys all its liturgical resources in the celebration of its Lord's Resurrection.

The Pasch, the Paschal Fast, and Pentecost

The Christian observance of the year began with the adaptation of the passover or pasch.[12] Almost certainly this first took place in Jewish Christian circles. It was a unitive celebration, encompassing Christ's passover from death to life by way of the cross and indeed the whole meaning of his work. We get a sense of its thematic focus from the paschal homily of Melito of Sardis, which takes the form of a Christian interpretation of the account of the institution of the pasch in Exodus 12. The liturgy probably took the form we find in the early quartodeciman observance. Thomas Talley describes this observance in this way:

> [In the *Epistula Apostolorum*, which Talley dates to the second half of the second century], Passover, surely kept in the night from 14 to 15 Nisan, is the memorial of the death of Jesus. In other second-century documents from Asia Minor, it becomes clear that this death is not seen as merely one incident in an extended Holy Week scenario. Rather, the content of the celebration is the entire work of redemption: the incarnation, the passion, the resurrection and glorification, all focused upon the Cross as locus of Christ's triumph. The observance is described as a watch, a vigil, and is kept past the midnight hour, which terminated the Jewish Passover, extending to cockcrow when it was concluded with "my agape and my commemoration," an expression that must be understood to include the eucharist.[13]

What we have here is a Christian *seder*.[14] Of the paschal fast associated with that *seder* Talley writes:

> The *Mishnah* requires a fast from all food from the time of the offering of the evening sacrifice that preceded the sacrifice of lambs for Passover. While this daily evening sacrifice was normally completed around 3 P.M., on the Preparation of the Passover the hour was advanced somewhat to allow more time for the slaughter and offering of the paschal lambs. This fast was not broken until night-fall, and then only with the eating of the Passover. It was such a fast, however modest in its extent, that would be the germ of the

Christian paschal fast. For Christians, however, that fast was progressively extended. As the Christian Pascha emerged it would not, as memorial of Christ's death, share in the festivity of the Jews. Therefore, the Christian fast was extended through the hours of the rejoicing accompanying Passover, past the midnight conclusion of that festivity. *Epistula Apostolorum* and other texts show that this vigil, and presumably the fast, was extended to cockcrow, the hour for the sacramental consummation of the vigil. The established Quartodeciman practice is generally regarded as having extended the fast through the day of 14 Nisan to cockcrow of 15 Nisan.[15]

Those Christians who always celebrated their pasch on Sunday, keeping the vigil through the preceding night, might do so for two reasons: 1) whatever day the Jewish pasch fell in the dominant Jewish calendar, they kept their pasch on Sunday, the day of the *week* when Jesus rose; 2) they followed a calendar like that of Qumran, where the day of Jesus' resurrection would always fall on a Sunday.[16] In either case, their paschal fast was soon likely to encompass Friday as well, because Friday was observed from a very early date as a weekly fast, a station day. So the early paschal fast soon extended from Friday until the paschal feast after cockcrow on Sunday. Here we have the germ of the later paschal triduum, but at this date it is a unitive observance whose principal liturgical expression is the paschal vigil. Eventually many extended the paschal fast to include all of what we should call Holy Week. The *Didascalia* supplies us with the grounds for this extension among those who worked with the Qumran calendar: by its reckoning, Judas made his pact with the Jewish authorities to betray Jesus on what we would reckon as Monday of Holy Week.[17]

It seems likely that those Christians who observed the paschal fast and the pasch also adapted Pentecost as a festal season. In Judaism Passover and Pentecost were the feasts that marked the beginning and the end of the harvest season, and the whole season—a week of weeks—had a festal character to it. Jewish literature reveals a very complicated controversy about how to reckon the feast of weeks which concluded that season. We need not review that here: the feast of Pentecost itself, so far as we have any evidence, was always observed by Christians on a Sunday. In both Jewish and Christian literature, the name Pentecost is used for both the season and its concluding feast. For Christians it was a season of joy, in which there was to be no fasting (not even on the customary station days) and no kneeling for prayer.[18] Later evidence witnesses to a daily eucharist. The whole season, then, was observed as an extended Sunday. The feast which brought it to a conclusion had its own theme, the theme of the covenant, which took a Christian form as well, but the early focus was not so much on this theme as on the whole season as a time of paschal rejoicing.[19] The paschal fast, the pasch, and the festal season culminating in Pentecost are the germ of later expansion of the Christian liturgical year. The further development of the liturgical year took place as it became the setting for the administration of baptism: hence-forth the liturgical year and the process of baptismal initiation would develop in close relationship to each other.

The Core of the Baptismal Rite

Christian baptism is perhaps best understood as the Messianic transformation of the baptism of John, rather than as the "institution" of a totally new rite. In the gospels, Jesus drew many of his early disciples from John's followers; the Baptist testifies of Jesus, according to the New Testament witness (John 1:33), "this is he who baptizes with the Holy Spirit." In Jesus' messianic anointing with the Spirit at his own baptism, the meaning of the rite is transformed. And his question to his disciples in Mark 10:38, "Are you able to be baptized with the baptism that I am baptized with," relates his baptism to his death—a theme which Paul uses in Romans 6 and which forms the basis for the comparison in the early church between baptism and martyrdom. Our evidence for the liturgical deroulement of baptism before the second century is very slight—a few sentences in the *Didache* and brief descriptions in such authors as Justin Martyr and Irenaeus. The key components were the use of water and the administration of the rite in the name of the Father, and of the Son, and of the Holy Spirit. But even this description is deceptive. Early documents express a preference for "living" water—that is, running water— but they generally make allowance for the use of any water if running water is not available. They express a preference for immersion, but allow for affusion if necessary. If later usage is any evidence, baptism may often have involved bringing the candidates into a pool of water and immersing their heads under a spigot from which water flowed into the pool, or pouring water over their heads while they stood in the pool. We generally take the words of Matthew 28:18, "in the name of the Father, and of the Son, and of the Holy Spirit," as a formula used in administering baptism, but here—as in the case of the last supper—we are probably reading rubrics as liturgical formularies. In the earliest liturgical texts the form of baptism was interrogation about belief in the Father, the Son, and the Holy Spirit, to which the candidates gave their assent, being immersed after each response. The earliest hard evidence for the use of a declarative formula is found in John Chrysostom and Theodore of Mopsuestia at the end of the fourth century. The act of baptism itself soon underwent ritual expansion, which expressed and unfolded its meaning. The interrogative formula also underwent expansion and took on the form of a creed. But baptism started with water and the trinitarian name.

156

Many New Testament texts witness to the administration of baptism as soon as converts were moved to request it. But within a few decades, instruction was seen as prerequisite to baptism. The instruction in the "two ways" which serves this purpose in the *Didache* is primarily moral instruction. It seems to derive ultimately from Jewish sources and is also used in other early Christian literature. Fasting too was mentioned in the *Didache* as a necessary preparation—probably we should understand this in terms of prayer intensified by ascetical effort.

The New Testament is rich in baptismal theology. The gospels record Jesus' own baptism and his reference to his suffering as the baptism which he must undergo. Romans speaks of baptism as death and resurrection with Christ, and Galatians speaks of putting on Christ in baptism. John speaks of baptism as new birth from above. Christians are said to be sealed in their baptism. The gift of the Spirit is associated with baptism in various ways. Baptism incorporates the Christian into the church. Baptism is also linked with the forgiveness of sins. 1 Peter suggests that baptism initiates us into a royal priesthood. Different regions would build their baptismal rites around various motifs from this rich lore of teaching.

Baptisms at the Paschal Vigil

Easter as the normative time for baptism: Baptism is a central element in the paschal vigil as we now know it. Biblical scholars have found allusions linking baptisms to the paschal liturgy in the New Testament (particularly in 1 Peter and in Revelation), and patristic scholars find such allusions in Melito and often assume that baptism was a constitutive part of the quartodeciman vigil. But in both cases we are working with issues of interpretation. Certainly the theology of baptism in Romans 6 makes the pasch an eminently appropriate time for the rite. But we have no hard evidence for baptism as a fixed component of the Easter vigil until the early third century, when this feast was beginning to become the normative time for administering the rite. The classical reference comes from Tertullian's treatise on baptism:

> Easter [*pascha*] affords the most solemn day for baptism; when, withal, the Lord's passion, in which we are baptized, was completed. . . . After that, [the fifty-day season of] Pentecost is the most joyous time for conferring baptism; in this interval the resurrection of the Lord was repeatedly proved among the disciples, and the hope of the second coming of the Lord indirectly pointed to. . . . However, every day is the Lord's; every hour, every time, is apt for baptism; if there is a difference in the solemnity there is no distinction in the grace.[20]

This text, from about 200, shows us several things: Easter is the time of preference for administering baptism; the whole season between Easter and Pentecost is considered an appropriate time; and no time is to be considered inappropriate for baptism if circumstances warrant its administration. The actual day of Pentecost soon became fixed as the make-up time for those who could not be present for the Easter baptisms. In the fifth century Pope Leo the Great would be adamant about restricting baptism to these two times except in pastoral emergencies.[21] Other churches baptized regularly on other feasts—Christmas and Epiphany and also saints' days. Indeed, Epiphany always remained a major baptismal feast in Eastern texts because it celebrated the baptism of Jesus. But until infant baptism as soon as possible after birth overthrew the whole institution of baptismal feasts, Easter and Pentecost remained the two normative times in Western practice. In the basic liturgical formularies of all rites, the sacramentaries in the West and euchologies in the East, baptism does not have its own section, but is found in the propers for the Easter vigil. We shall now turn to the vigil in its baptismal form and then look at its larger context in the development of the liturgical year.

The Classic Form of the Vigil: Different regions incorporated baptisms into the paschal vigil in somewhat different ways, but the rites as they have come down to us all take the same basic shape.[22] Our earliest witness to a baptismal vigil is the *Apostolic Tradition* of Hippolytus from the early third century That document does not, in fact, designate Easter as the context for this vigil. It may well have been used at other times. Nevertheless, Hippolytus affirms elsewhere the tradition of baptism at Easter,[23] so that we may reasonably assume that that rite would be used at Easter as well as any other time that baptism was administered. It is in the fourth century that the Easter vigil assumed its classic shape, and most of our evidence comes late in that century—the catecheses of Ambrose, of Cyril of Jerusalem, and of John Chrysostom and Theodore of Mopsuestia in Antioch, the liturgical provisions of the *Apostolic Constitutions*, and the pilgrim diary of Egeria, which describes the liturgy in Jerusalem about the end of the fourth century.[24] The rite attested by these witnesses stands in recognizable continuity with that of Hippolytus a century and a half earlier. The essential components of the vigil itself are these:

The Vigil Service of Light and Readings

1. A light ritual which replaces vespers (at Rome) or is an expanded form of vespers and which opens the service.

2. A vigil of readings, in the course of which baptism is administered to the candidates.

The Prebaptismal Rites and the Baptism

1. A procession to the baptistry by the candidates and those who will take part in the administration of baptism.

2. The blessing of the font (and originally of the oil or oils).

3. The removal of old clothing by the candidates.

4. Renunciation of Satan and profession of a baptismal creed (normally in the interrogative form).

5. Often, a prebaptismal anointing.

6. Threefold immersion while the threefold profession is made.

The Postbaptismal Rites

1. Often, a postbaptismal anointing.

2. The assumption by the baptized of new clothes and (sometimes) the reception of candles.

3. At times in the West, a second baptismal anointing and/or the laying on of hands and consignation by the bishop.

The Procession into Church and the Paschal Eucharist

Parts of this rite might be split off. In Antioch and Constantinople, the renunciations and affirmations took the form of a separate rite on Good Friday.[25] This may have made the administration of baptism to large numbers during the vigil easier. However, it separated baptism from its earlier form, the interrogative creed, which was here replaced by the passive formula, "The servant of God is baptized in the Name of the Father, and of the Son, and of the Holy Spirit." The reduction of the form of baptism to such a formula only happens considerably later in the West.

The *lucernarium* or light ritual with which the vigil opened took different form in different regions. In the East, it generally was an adaptation of the thanksgiving for the evening light which was a part of vespers, though at Jerusalem it took on a special form because the light was brought from the tomb of Christ. In Rome it developed into the diaconal *praeconium paschale*, which is known to us as the *Exsultet*. Here the thanksgiving for light probably replaced vespers, but vespers in the Roman tradition was monasticized at so early a time that we really have almost no idea of what shape a popular evening service took. The *praeconium paschale* as we know it is a magnificent text which develops the many-faceted theology of the Christian pasch in terms of its Jewish antecedent.

The lessons of the vigil were drawn from the Old Testament and formed in older usages an extended series: they needed to fill the time from the opening of the service until the celebration of the eucharist at cockcrow and did so by reading significant types of the paschal redemption which was celebrated in this vigil. The readings were interspersed with appropriate psalmody and canticles; in Roman usage, each had a prayer associated with it. The first three readings of the Jerusalem series (which appear in many other rites as well) show the close links with the Jewish pascha. They are the story of creation from Genesis (Genesis 1:1–3:24), the binding or sacrifice of Isaac (Genesis 22:1–18), and the institution of the passover (Exodus 12:1–24). Their link with the Jewish pasch can be seen in a text from the *Targum Onkelos* which Thomas Talley cites:

> Four nights are there written in the book of Memorial before the Lord of the world. Night the first, when he was revealed in creating the world; the second, when He was revealed to Abraham; the third, when He was revealed in Mizraim [Egypt], His hand killing all the firstborn of Mizraim, and His right hand saving the firstborn of Israel; the fourth, when He will yet be revealed to liberate the people of the house of Israel from among the nations. And all of these are called Nights to be observed; for so explained Mosheh, and said thereof, It is to be observed on account of the liberation which is from the Lord, to lead forth the people of the sons of Israel from the land of Mizraim. This is that Night of preservation from the destroying angel for

> all the sons of Israel who were in Mizraim, and of redemp-
> tion of the generations from their captivity.[26]

For Jewish Christians, of course, the night of their final redemption from captivity had come, and they awaited a fifth night,
when their Messiah would come to consummate the redemption
achieved on that fourth night.

Additional readings in the series were drawn from similar literature, which typologically foreshadowed the redemption
achieved in Christ and appropriated by the church in baptism.
Invariably these included two types of paschal redemption: the
passage of Egypt through the waters of the Reed Sea (Exodus
14–15) and the deliverance of the three children from the fur-
nace in Babylon (Daniel 3). Each of these last two readings had
its attached canticle, which became important components not
only of the Easter vigil, but also of the Sunday morning vigil of
the resurrection which became its weekly analogue.

Although actual administration of baptism followed the
lessons of the vigil in the classic Roman usage as it has come
down to us, the rubrics of Eastern rites no doubt signal earlier
usage: while the faithful were occupied with the vigil in the
church, the administrants of baptism and the candidates withdrew to the baptistry for the rites of initiation. In the classic
period, baptism was administered apart from the congregation
because candidates stripped before entering the baptismal pool.

The service proceeds with the blessing of the water and
the oil(s) to be used in the process of initiation (some rites later
transferred the blessing of some or all of the oils to an earlier
occasion). The blessing of the font is a major euchological text
in all the classical rites, and takes on a shape similar to that of
the Great Thanksgiving at the eucharist. It was also recited to
a melodic formula like that of the Great Thanksgiving (the
tonus praefationis in Roman usage). It is rich in baptismal

theology and gives perhaps the fullest interpretation of the church's understanding of the meaning of baptism.

The procedures which follow vary in sequence from age to age and rite to rite. They are obviously so ordered as to allow for the most efficient administration of baptism. In the classical period when multitudes would be baptized each Easter, this procedure involved the coordinated liturgical actions of great numbers of assisting ministers under the supervision of the bishop. Eastern usage, first attested in Antioch in the writings of John Chrysostom, split off the renunciations and baptismal affirmations into a separate service held at the hour of Christ's death on Good Friday. As already noted, this separation of these elements from the rite weakened the eloquence of the baptismal action itself, but it undoubtedly greatly reduced the amount of time required for the baptism of great numbers on Easter eve.

Before we go on to follow the rest of the rite, we should take note of the rite of anointing.[27] This was a multivalent activity in antiquity and its meaning varies significantly from rite to rite and (within the same rite) from age to age. It is always associated with the work of the Holy Spirit. But that work may take quite different forms. In Palestine and in Western usage it is frequently associated in prebaptismal usage with exorcism: it serves as a tangible sign of the strength which the Spirit gives the convert in the struggle against the forces of evil. In this usage the prebaptismal anointing at baptism may be the last in a series of such anointings. The oil used is known as the oil of exorcism or the oil of catechumens. In Syria (and probably Cappadocia and Armenia) the prebaptismal anointing is associated with the bestowal of the Spirit which conforms the convert to the royal priesthood of Christ; Christ's own messianic anointing at his baptism is the paradigm here. The anointing sometimes overshadows the baptism itself in the richness of its theological meaning. In their anointing, the candidates put on Christ. This meaning is elsewhere associated with the postbaptismal anointing (and with the laying on of hands). Postbaptismal anointing can also be associated with the bestowal of particular gifts of the Spirit (developed along the lines of Isaiah 11). In the twofold postbaptismal anointing of the Roman rite, the first of the anointings is associated with the bestowal of the Spirit in the work of baptismal rebirth, the second with the bestowal of the Spirit's gifts. A related theme is the seal of the Spirit, which is sometimes understood as a sign of Christ's inalienable claim on the baptized, like the seal of circumcision in the old covenant. This seal may be associated with anointing (before or after baptism), with consignation with the cross, and with the laying on of hands. At times all three ritual acts are done simultaneously (as in the final anointing of the Roman tradition). Oil used for this anointing is customarily known as chrism (in the West) or myrrh (in the Byzantine rite). At times, the multiple meanings of anointing are associated with a single oil (the "oil of gladness" in the Byzantine rite seems to have served for all purposes at one time). The perfumed oil of chrism or myrrh was said to impart the "fragrance of Christ."

The multivalence of the act of anointing means that no one answer can be given to the question what it means. The answer will depend on the context. We must also claim, I think, that anointing is a rite which helps articulate the meaning of the baptismal action itself. It has no separate meaning; it articulates the meaning of what happens in baptism. To claim a separate significance for it is to make the meaning of baptism different in different contexts; it is to deny the creedal affirmation of one baptism. We should do well in our interpretation to heed the warning of Georges Kretschmar: "The unity of baptism . . . does not lie in the execution of a given ritual but in Christ's saving work, bestowed upon the baptized by baptism by virtue of the Lord's institution and promise—from faith to faith.''[28]

Hippolytus presents what is probably the most logical sequence for the actions of the baptismal rite. Men, women, and children were segregated for the sake of modesty. Candidates put off their clothes (their old humanity) and renounce Satan. They are then anointed with the oil of exorcism, strengthening them for the final fight against the powers of evil. Renunciations were often made facing the West, the region of darkness. Then they are taken down into the font. In what developed into an interrogative form of the creed, they are asked to affirm their belief in the Father, the Son, and the Holy Spirit. After each assent, they are immersed in the water. Then they are anointed by a presbyter with the oil of chrism, empowered by the Spirit which has effected their new birth. Once anointed, they are clothed in clean white garments; they have "put on Christ." Next they are led to the bishop (in the assembly of the faithful in the *Apostolic Tradition*, but more commonly somewhere in the baptismal complex) and anointed by him as he lays his hand on them, signs them with the cross, and prays for the sevenfold gift of the Spirit, thus "sealing" them as new Christians. Often at this point they are given tapers as a sign of their "enlightenment" in Christ for their processional entry into the waiting assembly of the faithful.

The differences between various rites lie largely in the sequence of these actions. As we have already noted, the renunciations and affirmations might be split off into an earlier rite, and a declarative formula used in administering baptism. The number of anointings, what parts of the body were anointed, and what significance was given to each anointing varied from rite to rite and from one period to the next within a rite. In some rites the final anointing could be delegated to a presbyter; in others it could not. In Milan, the bishop washed the feet of the candidates. But despite the differences, the shape of the rite remained remarkably constant.

One text which articulates the meaning of baptism is, as we have noted, the blessing of the font. But the most important text was the creed itself, which articulated the meaning of the relationship Christians enter with God through baptism. Boone Porter puts this very well:

> The Creed . . . constitutes the baptismal formula not because it is a legal shibboleth, but because it actually expresses what Baptism means. Here we do become children of the "Father of lights . . . (who) begat us anew with the word of truth" (James 1:17, 18). Here by faith we are made members of Christ and have a new birth by the Spirit through him who was born for us by the same Spirit. Here we die and enter through Christ into a new and unending life. Or, to express these same things in a third way, here the Holy Ghost makes us members of the Holy Church and inheritors of Heaven and (as later generations added) we are given forgiveness of sins and admission to the Communion of saints. . . .
>
> Baptism and confirmation were not administered in order to give certain special benefits or to meet the needs of some special stage in the individual's life. They were intended to communicate rather the wholeness of that life and abundance which God intends for us to have. Here one was remade as "his workmanship, created in Christ Jesus (Ephesians 2:10). Here one experienced the Easter of one's own life: rising from the font early in the morning, receiving that assurance of forgiveness which the risen Lord entrusted to his apostles with the power of the Holy Ghost, and then at last knowing Christ himself in the Breaking of Bread. Here was one's own Pentecost: Baptism by water and by the Spirit, and admission into "the apostles' teaching and fellowship, and in the breaking of bread, and in prayers" (Acts 2:42). Here one knew these things, not

merely as abstract ideas nor as remote historical events, but as immediate realities which in fact totally changed the whole course of one's life and provided a whole new basis for one's future existence. Here one did find a new heart and a new soul to replace the pagan self that had been drowned. In the fellowship of the faithful, one did find the new humanity of the glorious Body of Christ.[29]

All of this was articulated in the baptismal formula and in the liturgical actions of the rite.

The candidates and minsters then reentered the waiting assembly of the faithful. The refrain used in the Byzantine rite for the psalm of entry is apt: "As many as have been baptized into Christ have put on Christ. Alleluia!" While at one time the service may have continued, as seems to be the case in the *Apostolic Tradition*, with the prayers and the exchange of the peace (actions which the newly-baptized were now allowed to take part in for the first time), it seems unlikely that the Easter vigil would continue without a eucharistic liturgy of the word which proclaimed the gospel of the resurrection. At this eucharist the newly-baptized (by themselves or through their sponsors) now made their offering of bread and wine for the first time and shared in the life of their risen Lord at their first Easter communion. Sometimes special food and drink were also given to highlight the occasion (such as a cup of milk and honey). As the eucharist concluded the church celebrated at its morning office of lauds the resurrection of its Lord by the light of the rising sun.

The baptismal rite of the eucharistic vigil was not performed in isolation from the liturgical life of the church for the rest of the year. It was firmly anchored in the context of this life, and the shape of the rest of the year developed in large measure after the fourth century to provide the proper context for a process which reached its climax at this vigil. Henceforth, to understand the meaning of Easter was to understand the meaning of baptism, and to understand the meaning of the liturgical year was to understand the process which reached its goal in the Easter vigil.

The Catechumenate as the Remote Preparation for Baptism: Although the New Testament gives witness to baptisms administered immediately upon conversion, it soon seemed wiser to require a period of preparation in which converts could be formed in both conduct and faith as followers of Christ. This preparation would differ according to the background of the convert. Pagan converts would not bring to Christianity the presuppositions which the Christian faith inherited from Judaism: they would need to acquire some sense of God's dealing with Israel as well as instruction in the specific character of Christian belief in Jesus as Messiah.

In addition, as Christians faced persecution and infiltration by strange beliefs, the church needed assurance that the new converts would not be a fifth column within the church. The result was that interested persons were accepted for baptismal instruction only on the recommendation of sponsors who vouched for their *bona fides*. They were then enrolled as catechumens ("learners") or *audientes* ("hearers") upon application to the bishop. An initial exorcism and a signing with the cross marked their admission as catechumens; in the West they might also be given salt for wisdom. For an extended period of time they underwent probation, in a process that included special instruction (catechesis) and attendance at the Sunday liturgy of the word, intensive prayer and exorcism to break the power of evil on their lives (often with such gestures as the laying on of hands, exsufflation, and anointing), and periodic scrutiny of their conduct. The church interceded for them at its regular services (though the intercessions have disappeared from the daily office except in Lent, they still remain in the eucharistic formularies of the Byzantine rite). Hippolytus sets three years as the normal time for this first stage of the catechumenate, but allows for adjusting the period to the progress of the catechumen. Because of the indefinite length of this stage, it never found liturgical expression in the rhythm of the year. By the time of the classical rites of the fourth century, it is likely that it was in many ways a formality. As the crowds flocked into the church, it was hard to give the individual attention to them that the process called for. Admission as a catechumen was gradually becoming a means of expressing a nominal adherence to the gospel without taking on the more serious obligations of the baptized.

By the end of the classical period of baptismal rites, the majority of catechumens would be coming from Christian families. Parents presented their young children for admission as catechumens, but often discouraged their baptism until the passions of youth were over and they were settled into adult maturity. Augustine, whom his mother enrolled as a catechumen but did not present for baptism, is perhaps the most famous example of this widespread phenomenon. In any case, after the fifth century the second stage of the catechumenate, actual candidacy for baptism when it was next to be administered was the only portion of the prebaptismal period to which the church gave serious attention.

Candidacy for Baptism and the Development of Lent: The second stage of the catechumenate, unlike the first, was closely linked to the rhythms of the church's year. In origin, Lent is not so much a time of preparation for Easter as a time of preparation for baptisms at the Easter vigil. The length of this preparation may have varied from region to region. It appears that Rome first knew only a three-week preparation (perhaps because it stuck stubbornly to beginning its year on the old date of March 1 rather than January 1: an early

Easter would then leave only three weeks open in the new year before the feast). The present Byzantine rite and the oldest euchologies of that rite only begin candidacy in mid-Lent. But sometime in the fourth-century the church reached a consensus that a fast of forty days' duration was the appropriate period of preparation. The probable biblical precedent which led to this consensus was the forty-day postbaptismal fast of Jesus in the gospels. The earliest forty-day fast to be observed by the church was apparently the one customary in Egypt after the feast of the Christ's baptism, observed there on January 6. At the conclusion of this fast baptism was administered to those who had been prepared during these forty days.[30]

This forty-day fast seems originally to have remained independent of the paschal fast after it was detached from Epiphany and attached to Easter. Rome originally reckoned it as a consecutive period: the first Sunday of Lent, the old beginning of Lent in Rome, was exactly forty days before the inception of the paschal fast on Good Friday. Later, when the reckoning included only fast days (thus excluding Sundays in Western usage), the three days of the paschal fast *were* included and four days were added before the first Sunday, giving us the present beginning of Lent on Ash Wednesday. In the East the fast was reckoned in various ways also. Eastern Christians reckoned only five fast days a week (excluding both Saturday and Sunday) and so needed an eight-week Lent. This might include or exclude the week-long paschal fast of the East.

Ultimately of more interest to us than its origin was the way in which this forty-day fast, however reckoned, was observed. Its observance from the first seems to have been closely associated with baptism. The forty-day fast was a fast of those to be baptized—and eventually the faithful associated themselves with candidates for baptism in this fast. Customarily candidates for baptism were enrolled on the first day of Lent.[31]

To the exorcism, prayer, and consignation associated with admission as a catechumen, this rite of admission added the actual recording of names in a register—often called "the book of life." Candidates were known by various names—*competentes* (those "asking for" baptism), the elect (that is, those "chosen" for baptism), and *photizomenoi* (those "to be enlightened" through the reception of the light of Christ in baptism).

The days of Lent were spent in instruction, frequent prayer, fasting, and exorcism. Scrutinies were held periodically to test whether candidates were suited for baptism. The characteristic of Lent most evident to us, however, is the instruction of candidates for baptism, usually held daily under the bishop's supervision. Those responsible for catechesis worked with various outlines for the course of instruction. An extremely widespread custom in the West was the use of the first part of John's gospel for Sunday readings in Lent and the identification of the great Johannine signs as types of baptismal initiation. The series uses five successive pericopes in many Italian lectionaries, where the Sundays are named for the appointed gospels:

1. The Samaritan Woman   *John 4:5–42*
2. Jesus and Abraham   *John 8:31–59*
3. The Man born Blind   *John 9: 1–38*
4. Lazarus   *John 11:1–45*
5. The Anointing at Bethany   *John 11:58–12:11*[32]

In the earliest lectionaries we know, Rome had only three Sundays open: the first Sunday, as everywhere at the time, was devoted to the account of the forty-day fast of Jesus; the second Sunday was displaced by a vigil mass in the night between Saturday and Sunday which concluded the fast of the first month (a local Roman custom); and the last Sunday of Lent was observed in Rome as the Sunday of the Passion. So Rome used the gospels of the Samaritan woman, the man born blind, and Lazarus (though these were later transferred to Lenten weekdays). Rome also employed the first part of John's gospel for weekday readings in the latter part of Lent.

Another very widespread custom was the use of Genesis for catechetical instruction in Lent. This usage is preserved in the readings incorporated into the present Byzantine office, which also includes a course of readings from Isaiah and another from Proverbs. Of these, Alexander Schmemann writes:

> The "continuous reading" of *Genesis*, *Isaiah*, and *Proverbs* has its origin at the time when Lent was still the main pre-baptismal season of the Church and Lenten services were predominantly *catechetical* in their character, i.e., dedicated to the indoctrination of the catechumen. Each of the three books corresponds to one of the three basic aspects of the Old Testament: the history of God's activity in Creation, prophecy, and the ethical or moral teachings. The Book of *Genesis* gives, as it were, the "framework" of the Church's faith. It contains the story of Creation, of the Fall, and finally that of the promise and the beginning of salvation through God's Covenant with his chosen people. It conveys the three fundamental dimensions of the Church's belief in God as Creator, Judge, and Savior. It reveals the roots of the Christian understanding of man as created in the "image and likeness of God," as falling away from God, and as remaining the object of divine love, care, and ultimately salvation. It discloses the meaning of history as the *history of salvation* leading to and fulfilled in Christ. It announces the mystery of the Church through the images and reality of the People of God, Covenant, Ark, etc. *Isaiah* is the greatest of all prophets and the reading of his book during Lent is meant to reveal once more the great mystery of salvation through the sufferings and sacrifice of Christ. Finally, the Book of *Proverbs* is the *epitome* of the ethical teachings of the Old Testament, of the moral law and wisdom—without whose acceptance man cannot un-

derstand his alienation from God and is unable therefore
even to hear the good news of forgiveness through love and
grace.[33]

These readings represent one direction which the church's approach to catechesis took. The many series of homilies on
Genesis which survive in literature of this period provide evidence of how widespread this approach was.[34]

Lent was also the time when candidates for baptism
received instruction on the creed. Toward the end of the period
the text of the creed would be given out to them; they were then
expected to learn it by heart and recite it back before their
baptism. These ceremonies are known as the *traditio symboli*
and the *redditio symboli*. Different churches set different times
for these rites. Palm Sunday was appointed in many places for
the *redditio symboli*. The Antiochene rite for Good Friday
would seem to combine the *redditio* with the renunciations and
creedal affirmations which were once part of the baptismal rite
itself. In any case, instruction on the creed in preparation for
handing it over to the candidates was a universal part of Lenten
catechesis, and many such expositions survive in literature from
the period, including a *Procatechesis* and a series of eighteen
catecheses by Cyril of Jerusalem, a series by Theodore of Mopsuestia, a series by Ambrose of Milan, and several sermons of
Augustine. The Lord's Prayer was often expounded, handed
over, and recited back in a similar fashion. We find in the
Roman rite a handing over of the gospels constructed along the
same lines. This can never have been more than a token rite: it
consisted of reading the opening passages of each gospel, but
there is no indication that the candidates were ever expected to
recite them back. By the time this *traditio* had been added,
Lenten catechesis had degenerated. In the Gelasian sacramentary, these and other rites of the catechumenate are known as

"scrutinies;" the original meaning of scrutiny as an examination of the candidates' progress in faith and conduct had been forgotten.[35]

Holy Week and Preparations for the Baptismal Vigil: In the final week before the paschal baptisms necessary preparations were made for the rites of initiation. In Hippolytus this included a prebaptismal bath on Thursday and a final exorcism sometime on Saturday before the beginning of the vigil. Often the creed would be given back sometime this week as well. As crowds of people applied for baptism in the fourth century, preliminary rites of the baptismal liturgy itself were sometimes split off and performed early in the week. In Antioch, as we have seen, this included even the baptismal renunciations and interrogations, which formed the rite of *apotaxis* and *syntaxis* assigned to a service at the hour of Christ's death on Good Friday. In most rites the blessing of the oil(s) was also split off and made part of a chrismal eucharist on Maundy Thursday. With thousands to be baptized in many cities, the church reserved only the essential actions for the vigil liturgy itself.

Easter Week and Sacramental Catechesis: In the fourth century, instruction on the meaning of the sacraments was not generally given during Lent, but was reserved for post-baptismal catechesis. The series of mystagogic catecheses which we have from Cyril of Jerusalem, Theodore of Mopsuestia, and Ambrose of Milan were all delivered during Easter week. Only John Chrysostom seems to have given sacramental exegesis beforehand. In part, this practice came from the custom of reserving information about the sacraments to the faithful, just as only the faithful were allowed to attend the sacramental meal. In part, no doubt, it also arose out of the sound paedagogical instinct to wait until the candidates had experienced the baptismal and eucharistic rites before exploring their meaning. After the catechesis of Easter week the initiation of the candidates came to a formal close on the first Sunday after Easter. All during that week they had worn the new garments they had received in baptism; often they were also instructed not to wash off the oil with which they had been anointed. Final prayers for them on the Sunday after Easter marked the resumption of their ordinary lives; this was the occasion when they could wash off the chrism and put on ordinary garments. In the West, the "putting off" of baptismal garments gave the Sunday its name (*in albis deponendis*); in the Byzantine rite, chrism was washed off in a special rite.

The Baptismal Process for Children: In the early centuries, the church directed its catechesis to adult converts. The baptism of "households" may well have encompassed the children of the household, but we have no sure way of knowing how the church addressed itself to children born to Christian parents. Our earliest explicit testimony about the baptism of children comes from the end of the second century.[36] By that time we discover provisions for the baptism of children in the *Apostolic Tradition*; on the other hand, we find Tertullian arguing against the baptism of children as a custom which he knows but does not favor. By the time of Origen, the baptism of children was so established a practice that he took it to be an apostolic tradition. The *legitimacy* of the baptism of children seems to have been established at a relatively early stage of the church's history. But the *prevalence* of the baptism of children—and finally of the baptism of infants shortly after their birth—seems to have been established at different periods in different regions of the church. The earliest explicit testimony comes from North Africa.

The issue on a popular level was one of postbaptismal sin. In the beginning, the church was doubtful that it was possible to forgive serious sin once one had received baptismal forgiveness. In ages of persecution, parents hesitated to put their children in the position where they might be forced to choose between apostasy and martyrdom. Even after persecution ceased parents often thought it wise for their children to postpone baptism until the passions of youth had cooled. However, from the time of Cyprian, at least, North Africa urged baptism within eight days of birth. Augustine's doctrine of original sin made baptism as soon as possible after birth a norm which found popular acceptance, and this rule spread widely through the West.

We are less certain about the East, although the Western custom eventually prevailed there as well. But Gregory of Nazianzus in the late fourth century thought it better to wait until the child was capable of minimal instruction. Miguel Arranz reads the evidence of the euchological tradition as suggesting that the rites of the eighth day and the fortieth day (which obviously use the circumcision of Christ and his presentation in the temple as analogues) served to register children as catechumens, and their actual baptism was not administered until after they were old enough to receive some instruction.[37] At the very least we need to note that the rites of both the eighth and fortieth days in their original form presupposed that children will be unbaptized when the rites are administered. How long this custom of delaying baptism of children prevailed in the East we do not know; Symeon of Thessalonika is still urging it in the fifteenth century, but here, as elsewhere, he seems to be fighting a rear-guard action in favor of traditional customs which had fallen out of use. The fourth century was the time that large areas of the empire were Christianized; after this most candidates for baptism would come from Christian families, and the whole logic of the Lenten catechesis was altered. The rites were designed for adults; they now served largely for the initiation of young children—a purpose for which they were not designed. The initiatory process was becoming dysfunctional.

Public Penance as a Baptism of Tears

The church, Ambrose wrote, "possesses both water and tears: the water of baptism, the tears of penance."[38] Lent served eventually not only as a time of preparation of baptism, but also as a time for public penance in preparation for restoration to the communion of the church through the rite of reconciliation, administered in Rome on Maundy Thursday. The early church's ministry of reconciliation did not take the form that has become customary in the West in the discipline of auricular confession (found in the *Book of Common Prayer 1979* under the title, "The Reconciliation of a Penitent"). As we noted above, the church in the early centuries was slow to accept the idea that there could be forgiveness for serious sins committed after baptism. Under the pressure of the problem of how to deal with the lapsed, the church at first allowed for reconciliation after penance once in a lifetime. In succeeding centuries both the length of penance required and the restriction to a single reconciliation were relaxed. But public penance was no easy matter. Penitents were treated like the unbaptized—excluded from the sacraments, segregated at times to a special section of the church, instructed to pray kneeling at all times, given penitential garb, and assigned ascetical tasks.

In Rome, penitents were admitted at the beginning of Lent (perhaps at first on Monday in the first week of Lent, later on Ash Wednesday). Our present Ash Wednesday rite derives ultimately from this rite of admission—though when Rome itself finally accepted the imposition of ashes it was as a general rite of penitence for this day. Throughout Lent, prayers would be offered for penitents as well as catechumens. Some of the later weekday Roman propers for Lent seem to have been selected with penitents, rather than catechumens in mind. After petitioning for forgiveness on Maundy Thursday, penitents were reconciled by the laying on of hands so that they could celebrate the paschal triduum with the church. Properly speaking, Lent as a season of penitence should be understood in the light of baptism. The effect of reconciliation is to restore penitents to their baptismal status in the church. Unfortunately, as we shall see later in this chapter, penitence became the dominant note of Lent once the catechumenate had declined, and Lent acquired a quite different tone than it had had when it was a season to prepare catechumens to make their passover with Christ.

The Refraction of the Pasch and the Further Development of Holy Week

The pasch of the early Christians was a unitive celebration which encompassed the whole of what the early church called the "economy" or "dispensation" (οικονομια) of Christ's saving deeds. The paschal vigil celebrated the full sweep of salvation. Yet the vigil itself had its roots in the commemorative instinct: the quartodeciman debate was ultimately after all a debate about the right time for the annual commemoration of the pasch. The third-century *Didascalia* had already worked out a chronology for the events of Christ's last week in Jerusalem. When Constantine decided to build a great *martyrium* over the supposed site of Christ's tomb and to erect other churches on sites associated with Christ's life, however, the impulse to devise appropriate celebrations at these sites was given new impetus, and Jerusalem's bishops exploited the opportunity through the creation of the pilgrimage liturgy of Jerusalem.[39]

The most notable result is the creation of commemorative liturgies in Holy Week. The week now opened with a procession into the city commemorating Christ's triumphal entry on what we know as Palm Sunday. On Maundy Thursday a eucharist was celebrated in the evening to commemorate the last supper (in stark contrast to the earlier conviction that the paschal vigil was the true Christian *seder*). The supposed discovery of the true cross gave rise to the Good Friday rite of venerating the cross. Pilgrims took these special liturgies back home and soon similar Holy Week rites were known throughout Christendom. Ancient sees like Rome and Constantinople resisted this style of liturgy longest. Rome had already set the Sunday before the paschal fast as the Sunday of the Passion, and only very late in its history did it preface this eucharist with a palm procession. It was also slow to add special features to its Good Friday liturgy of the word. Only in the Middle Ages did the papal liturgy adopt the rite of veneration. In Constantinople this rite never became part of the liturgy of Good Friday: much later the veneration of the cross did enter the Byzantine rite, but as a service for Mid-Lent, not for Holy Week. These commemorative liturgies were very popular, and eventually modified forms of the Jerusalem commemorations spread almost everywhere.

From a critical perspective, this refraction of the pasch fragmented its unity; positively we might say that it allowed the Christian to enter more fully into the meaning of every aspect of Christ's redeeming work. The refraction affected Easter season as well as Holy Week. Originally the whole season celebrated the fullness of redemption. The commemorative instinct, however, eventually led to observance of the Ascension forty days after Easter and to celebration of the day of Pentecost not as the closing feast of Easter season, but as the celebration of the gift of the Holy Spirit.[40] In addition, the feast of Pentecost became the standard time for initiation of those who had been unable to take part in the Easter baptisms, acquiring in its new commemorative focus its own distinctive justification as a baptismal feast.

In the celebration of the paschal cycle, the focus had now shifted from the pasch itself to the component parts of Christ's work of salvation. The end result of all these developments might be set out like this:

1. Lent as a season of preparation for baptism
   and a season of preparation for the reconciliation of penitents;

2. Holy Week as the ancient time of the paschal fast
   with the addition of necessary preliminaries to baptism,
   with the reconciliation of penitents,
   and with the addition of special commemorative rites;

3. The Paschal Triduum of the Good Friday, the Great Sabbath, and Easter
   as the original paschal fast, vigil, and feast,
   expanded first with the addition of baptism to the vigil,
   then with the commemorative rites of Good Friday,
   and finally understood as a triduum of Thursday, Friday, and Easter Eve

4. Easter week as the time for sacramental catechesis of the newly-baptized

5. Pentecost as a fifty-day paschal season.
   with Ascension and Pentecost as later commemorative feasts.
   and with Pentecost as a second baptismal feast

The Cult of the Saints:
The Paschal Triumph of Christ displayed in his Members

The refraction of the paschal victory of Christ in those who bore witness (*martyria*) to him by their deaths in the face of persecution led very early in the church's history to the development of a chronologically distinct but theologically related annual cycle—the cycle of annual commemoration of the deaths of these martyrs in the place of their martyrdom. Christ's victory became real to a persecuted church in the steadfast witness that these men and women bore to Christ in their deaths. Local churches celebrated the anniversaries of their martyrs with intense pride each year—customarily gathering at their graves for a vigil and a eucharist which reproduced on a smaller scale the annual celebration of the pasch of Christ. At times such occasions were even thought appropriate for baptism. The martyr's baptism in blood provided a warrant for the baptism of neophytes in water. An early and very moving witness to such a cult is the written account from the church in Smyrna of the martyrdom of their bishop Polycarp. Eventually others who suffered under persecution but had not been required to seal their witness with their lives were accorded a similar cult as confessors. After the peace of the church in the fourth century ascetics attracted a similar cult: their ascetical lives were a witness to a worldly church of the cost of discipleship when the age of persecution was past. Each church kept its calendar of such saints, as well as of its bishops, for annual commemoration.

The language used in relation to these commemorations is suggestive. They were originally referred to as "birthdays," *nataliciae*. The earliest account that has come down to us speaks of the annual celebration of Polycarp's death in 155 or 156 as the "birthday" of his martyrdom—την της μαρτυριας ἡμεραν γενεθλιαν. The martyr's death is the day of his birth into eternity, into life in its fullness. The later form of calendar entry as the *depositio*, "burial," suggests a weakening of the passionate eschatological faith of early Christians once the church had become integrated into society and was no longer a church of the martyrs.[41] One name for the early accounts of martyrdom, *passiones*, suggests the theological link between the passion of Christ and the passion of the martyrs—a link which is more suggestive when we remember that *passio* was thought of by early Latin-speaking Christians as the Latin form of *pascha*.

Christmas and Epiphany

The Origins of Christmas and Epiphany: The attentive reader of the early paschal homily of Melito will be struck by the fact that it develops a Christology in a way which for us would be more customary for a Christmas homily than an Easter one. But for the early church the pascha was, as we have repeatedly noted, a unitive celebration—its focus was the whole of Christ's "economy" (οικονομια).[42] That means that it encompassed not only his death and resurrection but his birth. In this way it was heir to the sectarian Jewish traditions whose calendar has already come to our notice. In these traditions, commemorations of birth and death were made on the same day.[43] For this reason, Christians went about setting the day of Jesus' birth not by means of historical research, as we would, but by a theological identification of the day of his birth with the day of his death.

Theological developments, however, eventually led to a

shift in the way in which the church adapted this Jewish custom. The church celebrated the incarnation of Christ on the day of his pascha. At first this meant it considered the pascha the day of his birth. But for the mature Christology of the church, it was not the birth of Christ which marked the day of his incarnation, but his conception. This perspective is set forth laconically in a tractate contained in a collection of Latin homilies spuriously attributed to John Chrysostom, *De solstitia et aequinoctia conceptionis et nativitatis domini nostri iesu christi et iohannis baptistae*:

> Therefore, our Lord was conceived on the eighth day of the kalends of April in the month of March, which is the day of the passion of the Lord and of his conception. For on the day he was conceived, on the same day he suffered.[44]

The pascha no longer marks the date of Christ's birth; it is now understood as the date of his conception. This has left its mark in our liturgical calendars, where the two fixed dates computed for the passion, March 25 (in the Western tradition) and April 6 (in the Asian tradition) remained as dates for the feast of the Annunciation, even after the church had altered its way of calculating Easter and made it a moveable feast.

The origins of the liturgical celebration of Christmas and Epiphany remain shrouded in mist. The first record we have of the celebration of Christmas is the entry in the chronograph of 354 under the date of December 25: *natus Christus in Betleem Judaeae*. Suggestively, the same chronographer notes for this day in the civil calendar: *N(atalis) Invicti (Solis)*, "the birth of the Unconquered Sun." Historians of the liturgy often followed the hint implicit in the parallel inscriptions in the two lists and understood the Christian feast as a conscious Christian counterpart of the pagan observance of the solstice as the birth of the sun. The understanding of Christ as the "sun of righteousness" (Malachi 4:1) was traditional in the church. Was it the conversion of Constantine from the syncretistic monotheism of the cult of the sun to his own form of Christian faith that led to this observance on December 25? For Constantine, no doubt, the shift in his vocational understanding from his status as the earthly counterpart of the Apollo to his status as the earthly counterpart of the sovereign logos represented a movement of natural fulfilment. The issue is probably not so simple in the adoption of December 25 as the day of Christ's birth, however.

Christians here are working with two traditions brought into accidental (or providential) agreement: the Jewish custom of keeping the day of death as the anniversary of birth, and the solstice festival of the birth of the sun—a festival instituted by the emperor Aurelian. This concurrence of the the date of Christ's birth as reckoned theologically and the popular solstice festival instituted by Aurelian was no doubt irresistible for the church. How early the day received liturgical commemoration is uncertain, however. Talley cites the argument that the Donatist acceptance of Christmas and their rejection of Epiphany makes it probable that the observance in North Africa of December 25 as the feast of Christ's birth antedates the Donatist schism of 311. By this reckoning, the institution of the feast may still represent a Christian attempt to appropriate a popular festival and give it a Christian meaning, but the initiative is not to be attributed to Constantine since the feast antedates his ascendancy.

Similar arcane reckonings led to the association in the East of Christ's birth and his baptism with January 6—a date which also had connections with solstice celebrations. When West and East later exchanged birth festivals, the East shifted its major commemoration of the birth to the Western date of December 25 and kept January 6 primarily as a feast of Christ's

CHAPTER THREE

baptism. By the late fourth century, Eastern Christians marked this day as they did Pascha and Pentecost with a baptismal eucharist at a vigil celebration. Thus Byzantine Christianity had three major baptismal feasts, while under the pressure of the see of Rome the West restricted baptism to the earlier feasts of Easter and Pentecost. The observance of Epiphany in the East gave it a more balanced baptismal theology than the West, which had tended to focus first on the paschal character of baptism, then on the forgiveness of sins, but to neglect other baptismal themes. Epiphany baptisms provide us with Christ's baptism as a theological paradigm and ground the interpretation of baptism as a messianic anointing which conforms us to Christ's royal priesthood. This theme was characteristic of Syrian Christianity, even though Syrian churches, like others, had first made the paschal vigil the ordinary context for baptism.

Advent: The association of Easter with baptism had led to the organization of the liturgical year around this feast, with a set of preparatory seasons (Lent and Holy Week) and a concluding festal season. In the West Christmas eventually became a second axis for the organization of the year, with a preparatory season of Advent and a twelve-day festal season between Christmas and Epiphany. The origins of Advent are ambiguous. Its eschatological themes are not directly related to the nativity and may antedate the feast.[45] Elsewhere in the West—in Spain and Gaul, for example—Sundays before Christmas were more closely linked to the theme of the nativity and used appropriate pericopes from the first chapters of the gospels of Matthew and Luke. Advent, Christmas, and Epiphany in the tradition that developed work with the tension between the advent of Christ in the flesh and his final advent in glory.

In some areas of the West there was a period of ascetical preparation for the nativity: a fast of forty days before Epiphany reckoned by counting five fast days a week and so beginning on St. Martin's Day, November 11, and known as St. Martin's Lent. The liturgical and ascetical preparations for Christmas and Epiphany seem to have developed independently, and neither was associated with the preparation of catechumens for baptism. Even in the East, where Epiphany became a baptismal festival, whatever catechesis was done did not take liturgical shape. The East, in fact, never developed Christmas and Epiphany into a second axis of the year. Like other major feasts in that tradition, they have forefeasts and afterfeasts and a preparatory fast, but they never developed into liturgical *seasons*.[46] For the East, the whole year finds its focus in Easter as its single axis. Easter thus stands out in the Byzantine rite in a way that makes it far more prominent that it is in the West, and outside Lent and Easter season, the strong liturgical emphasis on the paschal character of Sunday keeps all time focussed on the resurrection of Christ.

Even in the West, however, it was centuries before Christmas would rival Easter as a focus for popular piety. We find in Augustine's letters to Januarius a discussion of the feasts of pascha (the *triduum* of Christ's crucifixion, burial, and resurrection) and Pentecost as *sacramenta*. In a long and often obscure discussion, he argues that these feasts are *sacramenta* because they celebrate redemptive events in the life of Christ which we can appropriate by faith as we pass over with him from death to life and receive the gift of the Spirit, whereas feasts like Christmas are only *memoriae* because we cannot appropriate Christ's birth as our own.[47]

By the time of Pope Leo in the fifth century, however, such a sharp distinction was no longer being made. For Leo all feasts which celebrate the *mysteria* or *sacramenta* of Christ's life have a sacramental character, for in some way we can appropriate in faith the *virtus* of each of them, so that "what is done

in the limbs coincides with what is done in the head himself."[48]
"What was visible of our redeemer passed over into the sacraments (*in sacramenta transivit*),"[49] he says in a sermon for the
feast of the Ascension. His homilies for each feast are devoted
in part to exploring how we may appropriate the *virtus* proper
to that feast. Unlike Augustine, he believes that we *can* appropriate the *virtus* of Christ's nativity: we can do so because the
church's rites enable us to put off the old humanity of Adam
and to put on the new humanity of Christ, and in so doing to
make the humility of Christ displayed in his birth our own.[50]
But even for Leo, whose tome testifies to the theological importance for him of the incarnation, Easter is "the season, when all
the *sacramenta* of the divine mercy meet together."[51] In the
celebration of Easter, the church encounters Christ in the fulness of his saving work. The nativity is one refraction of that
all-encompassing mystery.

   ***The Refraction of the Nativity in the Course of
the Year:*** Just as the pascha of Christ was refracted into feasts
celebrating its components, so Christmas acquired its own cycle
of feasts celebrating the various events associated with the incarnation. The first of these is the feast of Christ's conception,
which we customarily call Annunciation—a feast whose origins
we have already noted and which antedated Christmas and
Epiphany, if the history of those feasts sketched above is cor-
rect. Similar commemorations include the octave day of Christmas, which according to Luke was the day on which Jesus was
circumcised and received his name; the feast of his Presentation
in the temple, which is fixed forty days after his birth; the
nativity of John the Baptist, six months before Christ's birth
according to Luke's account; and the later feast of the Visitation, which also commemorates an incident in Luke's gospel.
All of these feasts are theologically and even chronologically

dependent on the date of Christmas. We might also think of the Marian feasts as loosely linked to the incarnation cycle; they depend largely on the apocryphal *Protevangelion* of James.

The Elaboration of the Yearly Cycle

The Easter Cycle: With the decline of adult baptisms and the growing predominance of infant baptism administered soon after birth, Lent and the Easter vigil lost their original rationale. Though infants born during Lent often had their baptisms postponed until the vigil, Lenten catechesis and the rites of the catechumenate could hardly prepare them for baptism in the way that it had prepared adults. Even if catechumens were adults, the rich provision of readings in the Roman rite would benefit them little by the early middle ages: the liturgy was in Latin, which was no longer the vernacular of Western Europeans. Such catechesis as survived now came after baptism. Public penance had also fallen largely out of use, and the penitential themes of Lent now transformed it into a largely penitential season for the whole church. The focus of Lent had shifted radically.

The commemorative instinct took over once Holy Week began. The expressive rites of Palm Sunday, Maundy Thursday, and Good Friday were exploited to make the gospel narrative come alive for people who could no longer understand the readings which narrated them, since they were read in an alien language. The Easter vigil, once the climax of the whole cycle, came to be anticipated earlier and earlier in the day.[52] The allegorical instinct took over and gave expressive but extrinsic meaning to many rites whose original rationale was no longer

CHAPTER THREE

understood (such as stripping the altar on Good Friday). The same instinct also gave rise to new rites of dubious theological merit—such as the burial of a consecrated wafer in the "Easter sepulchre" on Good Friday or the release of doves through the "Holy Ghost hole" in the chancel on Pentecost. The early pasch had been completely fragmented. And Good Friday became a more characteristic focus of Western piety than Easter. The paschal sacrifice was more real than the paschal victory—a fact displayed in the crucifixes that were the most common form of the cross in the middle ages.

The Incarnation Cycle: If one focus of mediaeval piety was Good Friday, the other was Christmas. In the West the liturgical year now had two pivotal celebrations, each with its own cycle of feasts and seasons. But the piety of the incarnation colored the whole year. The original Western scheme for the daily office was worked out, as we have seen, as a commemoration of the passion. These commemorations survived in the Middle Ages in the hours of the cross, a kind of votive office. But a new series of commemorations with the incarnation as its focus was incorporated into an even more popular form of the office—the little office of our Lady or the hours of the Virgin. Substitutes for the office for those who were not literate such as the Angelus also focussed on the incarnation. Votive eucharists of the Virgin became a characteristic observance for Saturdays. By now, then, the Christmas creche rivalled the crucifix in Christian devotion.

The Sanctoral Cycle: The Christological focus of the year (and even of the week) was obscured in this period by the calendar of the saints. The early church had understood the saints primarily as witnesses to the paschal triumph of Christ through their death (martyrs), their suffering (confessors), or their ascetical lives (monastics and virgins). But the emphasis began to shift by the end of late antiquity, and the saints were honored as patrons and intercessors, from whose relics miraculous power emanated. Popular piety sought to appropriate this power in the cult of the saints.[53] The early church had a strong sense of the solidarity of the living and the dead in the communion of the saints and considered it appropriate both to pray for the departed and to ask their prayers. Augustine distinguishes the saints and the rest of the departed: we ask the prayers of the saints, but we offer prayers for the rest of the departed. As Augustine put it, the martyrs "have departed this world in such perfection that instead of being our 'clients' they are our advocates."[54] He has moved beyond the paschal piety of the early cult of Polycarp. When nearly every day of the year was marked by the commemoration of a saint (no longer restricted to the place of burial), and when many of these feast days took precedence over Sunday itself, the paschal architecture of both liturgical week and liturgical year became increasingly obscured.

The Cult of the Dead: The confidence of the early church in the face of death was on the wane by the fourth century. Despite their radically variant outlooks, Pelagius and Augustine agreed on one thing: few would be saved. The Western doctrine of purgatory has early roots, but the idea that the offering of the eucharist assists the departed in their purgatorial suffering is a Western doctrine that radically alters the original meaning of the eucharist in this context. Early celebrations of the eucharist at burials were paschal in tone: they were celebrations of the realization of Christ's triumph over death in the departed Christian as a member of Christ's body, and communion at such a eucharist was a tangible expression of a fellowship within that body that death might alter but could not destroy. In the mediaeval West, the eucharist was offered for the dead to assist them in their purgatorial suffering. So dominant a practice did this become that it colored the whole liturgical life of the middle ages in the West.[55] The fragmentation of

CHAPTER THREE

the paschal cycle, the severed link between baptism and Easter, the growth of the incarnation cycle, the increasing importance of the cult of the saints, and the rise of the cult of the dead—all of these developments served to obscure the paschal focus of the church's architecture of time.

Development of the baptismal rite: We have already noted the almost exclusive prevalence of infant baptism at the close of late antiquity and the insistence that baptism be administered as soon as possible after birth. This had a radical effect on the baptismal liturgy. Eventually it was linked to neither Sunday nor the Western baptismal feasts of Easter and Pentecost, and it no longer served as the rite of entrance into the church as a eucharistic community.[56] Both the conclusion of the baptismal rite and the admission to communion were severed from the baptismal liturgy in much of the West. Both tended to be delayed until the age of reason—whatever that might be. The conclusion of the baptismal rite was split off because it was ordinarily reserved to the bishop in the Roman rite, and once baptism was administered shortly after birth by parish priests immediate "confirmation" by the bishop became an impossibility. This accidentally severed segment of the baptismal rite eventually acquired its own theology: what had once been significant gestures which unfolded the meaning of baptism now was understood to convey a separate grace.

The rite itself was a truncated form of the rites of the catechumenate and the baptismal vigil. But only the most mechanical version of a theology of liturgical efficacy can see much benefit to be gained by putting an infant through the liturgical paces of an initiatory process designed for adults. Moreover, Augustine's form of the doctrine of original sin reduced the meaning of baptism largely to "the forgiveness of sins," requisite to save a child from the fires of hell to which that child is subject through this inherited taint. The rich patristic theology of baptism was narrowed and its ecclesial context became secondary.

Cranmer's Reforms
and the Prayer Book Tradition

The Liturgical Year: Cranmer's reform of the liturgical year followed the basic pattern of the German reformers. In general terms, that means that he kept the temporal cycles for Sunday related to Christmas and Easter and the major feasts of Christ in the course of the year, but reduced the sanctoral cycle to commemorations of major New Testament saints. This had the effect of reducing the architecture of the year to its approximate shape in the fourth and fifth centuries. There were two major differences, however:

1. Lent had no weekday propers and did not regain its catechetical focus but retained a primarily penitential character. Indeed, Cranmer in the exhortation of the Ash Wednesday service expressed the hope of restoring the discipline of public penance.[57]

2. The criterion used for admission to the sanctoral cycle was entirely different. Martyrdom, confession of the faith under persecution, or ascetical witness were the original criteria. The Reformers generally worked with the criterion of restricting commemoration to apostles and evangelists (and John the Baptist); a general commemoration was also kept on All Saints' Day. The older feasts of Christ in the course of the year, which are related to the Christmas cycle but were generally in-

cluded in the sanctoral cycle because they fell on fixed dates, were also retained.[58]

Special liturgies related to the church year (the imposition of ashes, the Palm procession, and the rites for the triduum) were generally suppressed. Since the custom of baptismal feasts (to which we shall turn shortly) was not restored, the liturgical year regained something of its early shape but did not regain its original theological rationale.

The Time of Baptism: Cranmer was well aware of the ancient restriction of baptism to Easter and Pentecost. The preface to the baptismal rite in 1549 acknowledges that

> *It appeareth by auncient wryters, that the Sacramente of Baptisme in the olde tyme was not commonly ministred, but at two tymes in the yeare, at Easter and whytsontyde, at which tymes it was openly mynstred in the presence of all the congregacion. . . .*[59]

Cranmer goes on to argue that this restriction "(now beeyng growen out of use) . . . cannot for many consideracions be wel restored again. . . ."[60] It appears, however, that, while he understood the ecclesial significance of this context for baptism, he either did not know or did not consider important the theological link between Easter and Pentecost and baptism. His emphasis in the section quoted above falls on the words, "in the presence of all the congregation." Of course in the early church the congregation would been have been present to receive the newly baptized into the eucharistic assembly, but not at baptism itself, which was administered to naked initiates in a separate baptistry.

Leo the Great in the fourth century had, in the course of justifying Pentecost as a baptismal day, admitted that Sunday bore the same theological relation to baptism as Easter did.[61] Centuries later missionary bishops meeting in council on the banks of the Danube in 796 still remembered the link:

> We know, moreover, that the holy and revered joy of Easter and the coming of the Holy Ghost which is Pentecost, have been combined in the Lord's Day. And during every week on the First Day, which is the Lord's Day, we celebrate the solemn gladness of the Resurrection and the glory of the ineffable presence of the Holy Ghost. If, therefore, by a happy presumption under this circumstance we do not fear to anticipate the aforesaid times [to administer baptism], neither by any rash venture do we presume, except when death is imminent, to disregard the sacred date of the Lord's Day. . . .[62]

Cranmer, however, argued

> *that it is moste convenient that baptisme shoulde not be ministred but upon Sondayes and other holy dayes. . . . [a]s well for that the congregacion there presente may testifie the receiuyng of them, that be newly baptysed, into the noumbre of Christes Churche, as also because in Baptisme of Infantes, euery manne presente maye be put in remembraunce of his owne profession made to God in his Baptisme.*[63]

He has got the ecclesial context right, but the Reformation motive of edification has replaced the theological rationale. We note that "other holy days" have been added to Sundays as appropriate days, and "remembrance" of one's own baptism has been added as a justification.

In actual fact, the baptismal feasts of the early church became the principal occasions for the celebration of the eucharist in England after the Reformation. Cranmer's hopes for a weekly general communion of the congregation were not realized. Morning Prayer, Litany, and Antecommunion became the ordinary Sunday service for most people. But the requirement of receiving communion three times a year was generally fulfilled by eucharistic celebrations on Christmas or Epiphany, Easter, and Pentecost.[64] Quarterly communion often became a rule, with the fourth occasion falling sometime in the fall and not related to the liturgical year. The eucharistic shape of the week had disappeared in practice, if not in theory. The baptismal shape of the year had vanished in both theory and practice. In practice, the ancient baptismal days had become eucharistic days.

The Baptismal Rite: In drafting his baptismal rite for the 1549 book, Cranmer drew on the Latin rite then in use in England (basically the truncated rites for the catechumenate and baptism run together as a continuous service) and German church orders (especially the *Consultation* of Hermann von Wied, largely the work of Martin Bucer). The service was a relatively conservative work in which the prebaptismal portion of the service remains relatively distinct from the actual rite of baptism and is performed at the door of the church. It was appointed to be inserted into the service of Sundays and holy days after the second lesson of Morning or Evening Prayer. The following outline, adapted from Marion Hatchett, shows the general shape of the rite:[65]

Baptism
in the *Book of Common Prayer 1549*

The Prebaptismal Rites at the Door of the Church

Exhortation
Prayer

Naming and Signation
Prayer and Exorcism

Gospel and Exhortation
Lord's Prayer and Apostles' Creed
Prayer

The Baptismal Rite at the Font

Entrance with prayer

Blessing of font (once a month)
    Invocation of Spirit upon font
    Prayers for those to be baptized
    Prayer for fruitful reception of baptism

Charge to the godparents
Renunciations
Creedal Affirmations
Threefold immersion with baptismal formula

Clothing (in "chrisom" or christening gown) with formula
Chrismation with formula

Exhortation to godparents

The theological emphases of the rite are the forgiveness of sins and incorporation into the church. This represents a considerable narrowing of the rich baptismal theology of the early church—a narrowing which had been characteristic of the West since the Augustinian doctrine of original sin had become the principal theological key to the meaning of baptism. In 1552 Cranmer made changes which were to be characteristic of subsequent Anglican rites. The entire rite now took place at the font and the prebaptismal elements were integrated into the baptismal rite itself. The exorcism disappeared and the prebaptismal signation and formula replaced the postbaptismal chrismation. The use of the "chrisom" (christening gown) also disappeared from the service. The prayers at the font now became part of every service, but the invocation of the Spirit disappeared: what remained was a prayer for the fruitful reception of baptism.[66] Much the same thing had happened in the eucharistic rite of 1552: the invocation of the Spirit there had been transformed into a prayer for fruitful communion. Marion Hatchett has argued persuasively that the formula for signation, now placed after baptism, articulates the mediaeval understanding of "confirmation," and that Cranmer intended to reintegrate the parts of the ancient baptismal rite.[67] Changes in subsequent editions of the prayer book generally represented a simplification of this rite, avoiding duplication of material already used elsewhere in Morning or Evening Prayer. In the American tradition, this unfortunately led to the loss of the interrogative form of the creed for the baptismal affirmations: the original *form* of baptism had disappeared. In the seventeenth century, an adaptation of the rite was provided for the baptism of adults—originally as a separate service, then (in the American tradition) through adaptations printed in the rite for infants.

Other Initiatory Rites: A rite for the "churching of women" (as it was subtitled in 1552) was also included in the prayer book by Cranmer. In its origin, this was a rite which made a child a catechumen (as we saw in service for the fortieth day after birth in the Byzantine rite). It had long since become a rite whose focus was on the mother, not the child, and had become a post-baptismal rite in most cases.

The 1549 service entitled "Confirmation" was an English adaptation of the Roman rite and very simple in form. It consisted of preces and a prayer based on Isaiah 11, a consignation with the laying on of hands with an appropriate formula, an exchange of the peace, and a concluding prayer and blessing. The principal difference between this and the Roman form was the omission of chrismation. This new rite of "confirmation" was to be administered to children by the bishop after they had learned the brief catechism prefixed to it. In accordance with the Reformation understanding of confirmation, it served as a conclusion of catechesis and an admission to communion. In 1552 the opening prayer was revised (probably to make it clear that the Spirit had been given in baptism), the formula for administration was redrafted, and the consignation was omitted. In 1662 an opening exhortation was added, and the service was associated with the renewal of baptismal vows and promises. American books replaced the introductory exhortation with a lesson from Acts 8 (whose relation to "confirmation" is, in fact, very problematic). "Confirmation" served a real purpose in Cranmer's work. Nevertheless, it is quite inappropriate to understand that purpose in terms of the original function of the postbaptismal rites from which it is ultimately derived.

The Year and Baptism in the Book of Common Prayer 1979

The Liturgical Year

The Baptismal Feasts: *The Book of Common Prayer 1979* restores the liturgical year to very much the shape that it took in the fourth and fifth centuries. It does so by reinstituting the baptismal feasts as a focus of the year. It is like the Byzantine Rite in that it treats not only Easter and the day of Pentecost but also Epiphany (that is, the Feast of the Baptism of Christ on the Sunday after Epiphany) as baptismal occasions; it is characteristically Western in retaining a Christmas/Epiphany cycle of seasons as a second axis of the year. To these three baptismal feasts, it adds a fourth—All Saints' Day or Sunday—as an occasion for baptism. It also designates the bishop's visitation as an appropriate occasion. The operative rubric is found on page 312:

> Holy Baptism is especially appropriate at the Easter Vigil, on the Day of Pentecost, on All Saints' Day or the Sunday after All Saints' Day, and on the Feast of the Baptism of our Lord (the First Sunday after the Epiphany). It is recommended that, as far as possible, Baptisms be reserved for these occasions or when a bishop is present.

The rubrics (page 298) still permit, however, Cranmer's 1549 usage (though the context is the eucharist, not Morning or Evening Prayer):

> Holy Baptism is appropriately administered within the Eucharist as the chief service on a Sunday or other feast.

Similar emphasis on the baptismal feasts is found in the reforms of other churches (see, for example, *The Lutheran Book of Worship*); surprisingly, perhaps, current Roman Catholic formularies place great emphasis on the baptismal vigil of Easter but make no mention of the other baptismal feasts.

The Seasons: Other revisions remove later growths which obscured the seasonal shape of the year. The Sundays of Pre-Lent have been removed; they were a late Roman extension of Lent. Sundays after Epiphany and Pentecost are designated as Sundays *after* those feasts; they are really Sundays "in ordinary time," as they are named in Roman Catholic usage. The Sundays before Advent and Lent have propers which make them appropriate introductions to those seasons (focussing respectively on the sovereignty of Christ and the transfiguration). The Sundays after Epiphany and Pentecost are feasts in their own right (the

Baptism of Christ and Trinity Sunday). Rogation days and ember days have been made votive propers, to be used when appropriate rather than at a fixed time.[68] The integrity of Easter season has been restored by dropping the division into Eastertide and Ascensiontide. Octaves have been removed except for the primitive provisions for Easter week.

Lent has regained its initiatory focus. In Year A, the Sunday lessons are the ancient Johannine signs. Weekday eucharistic propers are provided for Lent and Easter seasons in *Lesser Feasts and Fasts*. The prayer book itself has a whole section of "Proper Liturgies for Special Days," which provides careful contemporary versions of the traditional services for Ash Wednesday, Palm Sunday, and the paschal *triduum*. The focus of the whole year is the restored liturgy for the Great Vigil of Easter.

The Catechumenate and Parallels: In addition to these provisions, *The Book of Occasional Services* has also restored a contemporary form of the catechumenate in preparation for adult baptism in four stages:

1. The Precatechumenal Period, a time of inquiry and exploration;

2. The Catechumenate, beginning with the Admission of Catechumens and including prayers for use by catechists during the period of catechesis;

3. Candidacy for Baptism, beginning with Enrollment and including special prayers for the eucharist during this time;

4. Sacramental catechesis and introduction into the fulness of the church's life during the post-baptismal period.

To meet the needs of the contemporary church, *The Book of Occasional Services* also provides parallel processes and rites for those preparing for the Reaffirmation of the Baptismal Covenant and for the parents and sponsors of infants and young children before baptism (utilizing the thanksgiving for the birth or adoption of a child, derived from the "churching," in the way the Byzantine rite once used it). All of these provisions have proved effective tools for evangelism; the provision for parents and sponsors also has strongly emphasized the ecclesial character of baptism and provides a safeguard against indiscriminate baptism. When implemented, these also integrate the initiatory process once again into the architecture of the liturgical year in a very effective way.

Penitential Themes: By restoring the initiatory themes of Lent, the 1979 book does not eliminate the penitential themes of Lent, but puts them back into their proper perspective as a reminder of "the need which all Christians have continually to renew their faith and repentance."[69] Repentance is understood as a turning to Christ, not a turning in on ourselves in our wretchedness. Similar themes appear in the form for the Reconciliation of a Penitent:

> Holy God, heavenly Father, you formed me from the dust in your image and likeness, and redeemed me from sin and death by the cross of your Son Jesus Christ. Through the water of baptism you clothed me with the shining garment of his righteousness, and established me among your children in your kingdom. But I have squandered the inheritance of your saints, and have wandered far in a land that is waste. . . .
>
> Therefore . . . I turn to you in sorrow and repentance. Receive me again into the arms of your mercy, and restore me to the blessed company of your faithful people; through him in whom you have saved the world, your Son our Savior Jesus Christ. Amen.

> Now there is rejoicing in heaven; for you were lost, and are found; you were dead, and are now alive in Christ Jesus our Lord. Go (*or* abide) in peace. The Lord has put away all your sins.[70]

This presents a very strong understanding of penitence as the power of baptism in our lives.

Restoration of the Primacy of Sunday: Although Cranmer in 1549 radically pruned the sanctoral cycle, its feasts could still displace Sunday in many cases. The 1979 revisions privilege Sunday absolutely, allowing only a major feast of Christ to take precedence over the propers for a Sunday. This represents a restoration of the Christological and paschal focus of the temporal cycle and prevents the proper of the year from disrupting the weekly cycle.

Lesser Feasts: We have already noted the restoration of the weekday propers for Lent and Easter season. Provision is also made for optional commemoration of "lesser feasts," so that the sanctoral cycle is no longer restricted to New Testament saints. A rubric for Easter season grounds these commemorations in their original paschal rationale:

> . . . the triumphs of the saints are a continuation and manifestation of the Paschal victory of Christ. . . .[71]

Here the medieval stress on the merits and intercession of the saints and the Reformation stress on the saints as examples of "virtuous and godly living" have been replaced with the original paschal focus.

The Rites of Initiation

The *Book of Common Prayer 1979* represents a thorough rethinking of the rites of initiation—with results similar to contemporary reforms in many other churches. We have already seen the shift in context: baptism is set in the context of the eucharist, and the rite is intended to be reserved insofar as possible to the four baptismal feasts set out in the rubrics. This in itself represents a considerable enrichment of baptismal theology. Epiphany baptisms articulate the theology of the first paragraph of the creed: we are God's sons and daughters by adoption and grace, recreated by the Creator of heaven and earth in the likeness of Christ, and reborn in the image of God's only Son whose messianic vocation was revealed at his baptism. Easter baptisms set out the theology of the second article of the creed: we die with Christ to sin and rise with him to newness of life and by so doing share in his destiny. Baptisms at Pentecost and All Saints' give expression to the third paragraph of the creed: in baptism we are empowered by the Spirit and incorporated into the church as the communion of saints; it is in the power of this Spirit that we experience the forgiveness of sins and are sealed for the life everlasting. Baptism as the forgiveness of sins is not repudiated but set in its larger context. The theology of Sunday also relates to these baptismal themes in a different key. Baptism on occasions when the bishop is present gives expression to the truth that we are incorporated into a community which transcends the local parish.

The rite itself is incorporated into the eucharist after the sermon. It might be outlined as follows. Headings from the text are in boldfaced type; headings which I have provided are in regular type. Optional components are in brackets. Rubrical material is in italics.

Baptism in
The Book of Common Prayer 1979

Liturgy of the Word with Gathering Rite Proper to Baptism

Presentation and Examination of Candidates
　　Presentation of Adults and Older Children
　　　　Expression of desire for baptism
　　Presentation of Infants and Younger Children
　　　　and Commitment of Sponsors
　　Renunciations and Turning to Christ
　　[Presentation of Candidates for Various Forms of Reaffirmation]
　　　　Reaffirmation of Renunciations and Renewal of Commitment
　　Commitment of Congregation to Candidates

The Baptismal Covenant
　　Threefold Creedal Affirmations
　　Commitments to a Christian Life
　　Prayers for the Candidates

[Procession to font, with a psalm such as Psalm 42 or a hymn or anthem]

Thanksgiving over the Water
[Consecration of the Chrism by the Bishop]

The Baptism
　　Immersion or affusion with traditional formula

　　[Procession to chancel, with a psalm such as Psalm 23 or a hymn or anthem]
　　[Presentation of baptismal candle]
　　Prayer for gifts of the Spirit (Isaiah 11) over the baptized
　　Laying on of hands and consignation (optional use of chrism)

Welcome by the congregation
The Peace (unless Reaffirmation follows)

Reaffirmation of the Baptismal Covenant
Prayer over the candidates
Laying on of hands by bishop with formulas
  For Confirmation
  For Reception (laying on of hands optional)
  For Reaffirmation (laying on of hands optional)
Peace

Celebration of the Holy Communion
starting with the Prayers of the People or the Offertory
[*Candidates or sponsors may present bread and wine.*]

This is a new rite, not merely a revision of prior prayer book rites, although it uses materials from them. The baptismal rite itself starts with the presentation of candidates and the renunciations, carefully cast in contemporary language. Then the whole congregation is asked for its commitment to the candidates and joins in the baptismal covenant, which takes the form once again of an interrogative creed, followed by commitments to a Christian life. After this, the baptismal party may go in procession to the font, using the traditional psalm or other appropriate music. The Thanksgiving over the Water articulates classic baptismal types and themes: creation, the exodus, the baptism of Jesus, death and resurrection with Christ, rebirth by the Holy Spirit, cleansing from sin. The consecration of chrism, if the bishop is presiding, articulates the themes of the royal priesthood into which we are incorporated in baptism.

The baptism itself follows the traditional form, and is followed by the components associated with what Roman Catholics call confirmation—a prayer for the gifts of the Spirit and sealing (with the laying on of hands, signing, and optional chrismation). A baptismal candle may be given. The baptismal party may move to the chancel for these postbaptismal rites, using the traditional Psalm 23 or other music. The congregation then welcomes the newly-baptized and the peace is exchanged. The ecclesial elements (important to Cranmer and intended by the rubrics of earlier books but ignored in "private" baptisms) are here strongly reinforced. This rite is meant as "full initiation by water and the Holy Spirit into Christ's Body the Church," as an opening rubric explicitly states (page 298). What is still called "Confirmation" in this book has a new set of formularies and is *not* a part of initiation. If the intentions of this rite are followed, *baptism itself* admits to communion at any age; the rite of initiation is completed in the reception of communion by the newly-baptized.

The formularies for Reaffirmation of the Baptismal Covenant (confirmation of those who have never made a mature reaffirmation of the covenant, reception for those who have made it in another communion, and reaffirmation for those renewing their commitment after a lapse or renewing it before the bishop after adult baptism) are incorporated in this rite. This is not a rite understood to bestow the Spirit, but a rite understood to impart "strength from the Holy Spirit through prayer and the laying on of hands by a bishop" upon expression of "a mature commitment."[72] Although the laying on of hands is not rubrically required for reception or reaffirmation, the canons stipulate that it is required to confer "confirmed" status in the church. Someone baptized as an adult is considered confirmed if the bishop has presided at the rite and done the consignation (the reaffirmation prayers are *not* intended to be added); if an adult has been baptized by a presbyter, reaffirmation is the appropriate formula for the episcopal rite.

The recovery of the the initiatory shape of the architec-

CHAPTER THREE

ture of the year and the carefully rethought initiatory rites, with their far richer baptismal theology, find their most dramatic expression in the restoration of the Easter vigil. These two inter-related reforms are perhaps the most significant contributions of the *Book of Common Prayer 1979* to the life of the Episcopal Church. With these reforms both the week and the year, in their distinctive ways, find their true focus in the passover of Christ. What is still lacking is a similar recovery of the liturgical architec-ture of the day in the Daily Office, which is greatly enriched in this book but has not as effectively exploited the celebration of Christ as the risen sun of righteousness at dawn.

Notes to Chapter Three

1. Thomas Talley, *The Origins of the Liturgical Year* (NY: Pueblo, 1986), pages 28–29.

2. The name is derived from the Latin *quartodecimanus*, "fourteenth," for the fourteenth day of Nisan, the Jewish date of the passover. On all of this see Talley, *the Origins of the Liturgical Year*, pages 1–30. Talley pays careful attention to the complicated calendric questions under discussion in these paragraphs.

3. Gregory of Tours, *The History of the Franks*, translated by Lewis Tharpe (NY: Penguin Books, 1974), 10:31, page 596.

4. In the description of the pilgrimage feasts which follows, I am relying on de Vaux, *Ancient Israel*, volume 2, *Religious Institutions*, chapter 17, "The Ancient Feasts of Israel," pages 482–506.

5. We should remember that these feasts were probably pre-Israelite (hence pagan) in origin. Israel took them over and gave them a new meaning by historicizing them.

6. On sacrifice as a meal which establishes communion between God and humans, see chapter 2 above.

7. Schmemann, *For the Life of the World*, page 54.

8. Schmemann, *For the Life of the World*, page 56.

9. Schmemann, *For the Life of the World*, pages 56–57.

10. Melito of Sardis, *On Pascha and Fragments*, translator and editor, Stuart George Hall (Oxford: Clarendon Press, 1979), page 2, line 10.

11. See the commentary on that gospel by Raymond Brown in the Anchor Bible Series. Brown uses the heading, "Jesus and the Principal Feasts of Judaism," for his commentary on John 5–12.

12. This section relies on Part I of Thomas Talley, *The Origins of the Liturgical Year*—a section which he entitles "Pascha, the Center of the Liturgical Year." His work on the whole sets out the present *status quaestionis*.

13. Talley, *The Origins of the Liturgical Year*, page 6.

14. Our tendency to treat the Maundy Thursday eucharist as the Christian *seder* derives from considerably later usage. We have no evidence for a Maundy Thursday commemoration of the last supper until the fourth century, when the historicizing tendency of contemporary Christians fragmented the unity of the original paschal observance of the church.

15. Talley, *The Origins of the Liturgical Year*, page 27.

16. For those who followed the dominant Jewish calendar, the *pasch* might fall on a Sunday, for the day on which the *pasch* fell changed from year to year. For those who followed the fixed calendar of Qumran, the Jewish *pasch* always fell on a Wednesday, the crucifixion on Friday, and the resurrection on Sunday.

17. Jaubert reproduces relevant parts of the *Didascalia* in *The Date of the Last Supper*. The relevant text here is from 17:2, found on page 73 in Jaubert.

18. Our earliest reference to a distinctly Christian season of Pentecost only dates from about 200 and is found in a work attributed to Irenaeus. The work itself, a treatise on the pasch, is lost; it is cited in fifth-century work by an unknown Syrian author, *Quaestiones et responsiones ad orthodoxos*. Tertullian, writing at about the same time, makes several references to the season. The *Epistula Apostolorum*, cited above, refers allusively to Pentecost, but the reference is not to an indisputably Christian observance of the season (though it seems likely that this community would have known such an observance).

208

19. The observance of Pentecost as a feast of the covenant is attested for sectarian Judaism of the first century. Rabbinic Judaism also developed the feast as a commemoration of the covenant at Sinai, but it is not clear how early this took place. Our sources are later than the first century, although the account of Pentecost in Acts seems to develop the theme of covenant and may be an indirect testimony to it.

20. Tertullian, *Treatise on Baptism* 19, translated by S. Thelwall, in *Baptism: Ancient Liturgies and Patristic Texts*, editor, A. Hamann (NY: Alba House, 1967), pages 47–48. I have added the words in brackets: in this context, Pentecost obviously refers to what we should call Easter season, not to the feast of Pentecost. The translator has for some reason rendered the two Latin superlatives ("most solemn" and "most joyful") as comparatives ("more . . ."). I have restored the superlatives, which make more sense in the context.

21. Letter 16 to the bishops of Sicily, which can be found in translation in volume 12 of *A Select Library of Nicene and Post-Nicene Fathers*, second series (New York, 1895), pages 26–30.

22. The best survey on the initiatory rites in English is probably to be found in R. Cabié, "Christian Initiation," in Aimé Georges Martimort, editor, *The Church at Prayer*, volume 3, *The Sacraments*, new edition, translated by Matthew J. O'Connell (Collegeville, MN: Liturgical Press, 1988), pages 11–100. He should be consulted especially for Western rites. For the Byzantine Rite, the definitive study at the present time is the series of ten articles by Miguel Arranz with a critical text of the euchology and commentaries, published in *Orientalia Christiana Periodica* 48–55 (1982–1989) under the title "Les sacrements de l'ancien euchologe constantinopolitain." For the rites of the vigil itself in the traditions of Jerusalem and Constantinople, see Gabriel Bertonière, *The Historical Development of the Easter Vigil and Related Services in the Greek Church*, Orientalia Christiana Analecta 193 (Rome: Pont. Institutum Studiorum Orientalium, 1972.) Also useful are Alexander Schmemann, *Of Water and the Holy Spirit: A Liturgical Study of Baptism*, revised edition (Crestwood, NY: St. Vladimir's Seminary Press, 1974), and the short article by Kenneth W.Stevenson, "The Byzantine Liturgy of Baptism," in *Studia Liturgica* 17 (1987), pages 176–190. For the Syrian traditions, a good resource is Sebastian Brock, *The Holy Spirit in the Syrian Baptismal Tradition*, Syrian Church Series 5 (Poona, India: Anita Printers, 1979). For the Armenian rite, see Gabriele Winkler, *Das armenische Initiationsrituale: Entwicklungsgeschichtliche und liturgievergleichende Untersuchung der Quellen des 3. bis 10. Jahrhunderts*, Orientalia Christiana Analecta 217 (Rome: Pont. Institutum Studiorum Orientalium, 1982). An English source for her insights is her article, "The Original Meaning of the Prebaptismal Anointing and its Implications" in *Worship* 52 (1978), pages 22–45.

23. Talley, *The Origins of the Liturgical Year*, page 73, note 70, cites *Commentarium in Danielem* 1.16.1–3 as evidence for this.

24. A convenient source for the those homilies relating directly to the baptismal rites is Edward Yarnold, *The Awe-Inspiring Rites of Initiation: Baptismal Homilies of the Fourth Century* (Middlegreen, Slough, UK: St. Paul Publications, 1971). A good collection of the liturgical texts is that of E. C. Whitaker, *Documents of the Baptismal Liturgy*, Alcuin Club Collections 42 (London:SPCK, 1970). For Egeria, see *Egeria: Diary of a Pilgrimage*, Ancient Christian Writers 38, translated and edited by George F. Gingras (NY: Newman Press, 1970).

25. See the eleventh instruction of Chrysostom in *St. John Chrysostom: Baptismal Instructions*, translated by Paul W. Harkins (NY: Newman Press, 1963), where he makes reference to the rite (pages 166–169). The homily found in the Byzantine euchologies as a part of this ceremony may ultimately derive from Chrysostom. The text can be found in E. C. Whitaker, *Documents of the Baptismal Liturgy*, page 60–63. See the commentary in Miguel Arranz, "Les sacrements de l'ancien euchologe constantinopolitain," *Orientalia Christiana Periodica* 50 (1984), pages 372–397.

26. J. W. Etheridge, *The Targums of Onkelos and Jonathan ben Uzziel on the Pentateuch, with the Fragments of the Jerusalem Targum* (New York, 1968), pages 483–484, as cited by Talley, *The Origins of the Liturgical Year*, page 49.

27. See the general bibliography on baptism given above for treatment of such anointings. Gabriele Winkler gives particular attention to this complex issue in her article, "The Original Meaning of the Prebaptismal Anointing and its Implications."

28. Georges Kretschmar, "Recent Research on Christian Initiation," *Studia Liturgica* 12 (1977), pages 87–106.

29. H. Boone Porter, *The Day of Light*, pages 68–69.

30. Thomas Talley argues persuasively that the origin of Lent is this forty-day fast *after the baptism of Jesus*. In Egypt, Epiphany was kept as the feast of the baptism of Jesus, and at the conclusion of the fast which followed, baptism was administered. This was associated in a curious way with "the baptism of the apostles"—which a tradition held to have taken place at the home of Lazarus before the entry into Jerusalem on Palm Sunday. So in Egypt baptism was once administered at the end of the fast after the baptism of Jesus and before the beginning of the week-long paschal fast. In the fourth century, the two fasts were joined after the forty-day fast was detached from Epiphany. A remnant of this Egyptian custom is still found in the Byzantine euchologies, which designate Lazarus Saturday, the day before Palm Sunday and the paschal fast of holy week which follows, as a baptismal day.

31. In Milan, candidates were summoned to enroll on Epiphany; perhaps this was a remnant of a time when the forty-day fast began on Epiphany there also. As we have already

210

noted, the Byzantine euchologies presently seem to presume enrollment in mid-Lent—after this, prayers for candidates for baptism are added to those for the catechumens.

32. See the lists given in Adrien Nocent, *The Liturgical Year*, volume 2, *Lent*, translated by Matthew J. O'Connell, Collegeville, MN: Liturgical Press, 1977), pages 227 (Aquileia and Benevenuto), 228–229 (Milan); compare also the Gallican uses on page 232 and the Spanish uses on pages 233–234. Antoine Chavasse has investigated the Roman Lenten lectionary and summarizes his findings in "La structure de carême et les lectures des messes quadrigesimales dans la liturgie romaine," in *La Maison-Dieu* 31 (1952), pages 75–120. His very skillful attempt to show how the Johannine pericopes were shifted in various revisions is weakened, I think, by the fact that he gives inadequate weight to the strength of the tradition of a series of five Sunday pericopes elsewhere. Either Rome once had these five too (which weakens the argument for a three-week Lent) or the series came to Rome from elsewhere and was reduced to fit the shorter Lenten season at Rome. Oscar Cullmann gives a good account of the way these lessons relate to baptism in *Early Christian Worship*, translated by Steward Todd and James B. Torrance, Studies in Biblical Theology 10 (London: SCM, 1953).

33. Schmemann, *Great Lent: Journey to the Pascha*, (Crestwood, NY: St. Vladimir's Seminary Press, 1973), pages 40–41.

34. We have, for example, homilies by Chrysostom on Genesis which were preached to catechumens in Antioch, and a similar series by Ambrose in Milan.

35. These *traditiones* are set for a weekday in the fourth week of Lent in *Ordo Romanus XI*, which probably dates to the sixth century. In earlier usage, they were probably appointed for the third, fourth, and fifth Sundays of Lent. Texts for these rites are found as items 34–36 in the Gelasian Sacramentary, where they are called *praefationes*. English translations may be found in Whitaker, *Documents of the Baptismal Liturgy*, pages 162–169 (Gelasian), 189–191 (*Ordo XI*).

36. For a short summary of the data on this issue, see R. Cabié, "Christian Initiation," in Martimort, editor, *The Church at Prayer*, volume 3, pages 62–63.

37. See Miguel Arranz, "Les sacrements de l'ancien Euchologe constantinopolitain (3)," *Orientalia Christiana Periodica* 49 (1983), pages 284–302, "Admission dans l'église des enfants des familles chrétiennes ('premier catéchumenat')."

38. Ambrose, *Letter* 41:12. A summary of the pertinent data on penance may be found in P. M. Gy, "Penance and Reconciliation," in Martimort, editor, *The Church at Prayer*, volume 3, *The Sacraments*, pages 101–112; see also John Gunstone,*The Liturgy of Penance*, Studies in Christian Worship 7 (London: Faith Press, 1966).

39. For this stage of the development, see the very readable summary in J. Gordon Davies, *Holy Week: A Short History*, Ecumenical Studies in Worship 11 (Richmond, VA: John Knox Press, n.d.), chapter 2, "Holy Week in the Fourth Century," pages 23–38. Davies probably makes too sharp a contrast between the relatively historicized celebration of the fourth century and the more "eschatological" observance of the second-century pasch.

40. A good summary of these developments is found in John Gunstone, *The Feast of Pentecost*, Studies in Christian Worship 8 (London: Faith Press, 1967).

41. The word *depositio* was also used for the date that relics were placed in a new location after they had been "translated"—i.e., moved. But early lists of the *depositiones* of martyrs and bishops refer to the initial burial of their bodies.

42. In this account of Christmas and Epiphany, I am following Talley, *Origins of the Liturgical Year*, Part 2, which he entitles "The Day of His Coming. Talley's argument is very complex; I have not attempted here to set out the course of his argument for the development of Epiphany.

43. See Talley, *The Origins of the Liturgical Year*, page 130.

44. Lines 78–84 in the edition published by Bernard Botte in *Les origines de la Noël et de l'Épiphanie*, Textes et études liturgiques 1 (Louvain, 1932), cited by Talley, *The Origins of the Liturgical Year*, page 94

45. Rome may originally have had as many of six Sundays of Advent. Adrien Nocent provides a summary of lectionary provisions in various Western rites in *The Liturgical Year*, volume 1, *Advent, Christmas, Epiphany*, translated by Matthew J. O'Connell (Collegeville, MN: Liturgical Press, 1977), pages 167–177.

46. The Syrian rites, however, developed the year along quite different lines, as a whole series of seasons which were (theoretically) seven weeks in length.

47. Letter 55 to Januarius (PL 33:205–223). Louis Bouyer, *Liturgical Piety* (Notre Dame, IN: University of Notre Dame Press, 1955) gives an exposition of both Augustine's and Leo's thought on the Easter and Christmas cycles, pages 185–214.

48. Letter 16:3: (PL 54:698).

49. Sermon 74:2 (PL 54:398).

50. See Germain Hudon, *La perfection chrétienne d'après St. Léon le grand* (Paris: Éditions du Cerf, 1958), Lex Orandi 26., pages 190–200, esp. pages 193–196 (for the new humanity) and 198–200 (for the *virtus* of humility).

51. Sermons 46:1 and 49:4 in the Migne edition (PL 54:292, 303).

52. I am dealing here with Western Christendom. But the baptismal vigil of the Byzantine rite also came to be anticipated on Saturday—a fact disguised by the creation of a new vigil, created out of a special form of the morning office, *orthros*, and the second eucharist of Easter.

53. See Peter Brown, *The Cult of the Saints: Its Rise and Function in Latin Christianity*, Haskell Lectures on History of Religions, n.s. 2, (Chicago: University of Chicago Press, 1981), for an account of this phenomenon.

54. Schmemann, *Introduction to Liturgical Theology*, 190, citing Augustine, Sermon 285:5 (PL 38:1295), "ut non sint suscepti nostri sed advocati."

55. This development never occurred in the East, which even abandoned the custom of the burial eucharist. The Byzantine rite knows no such thing as a "votive" eucharist for special intentions.

56. See J. D. C. Fischer, *Christian Initiation: Baptism in the Medieval West: A Study in the Disintegration of the Primitive Rite of Initiation*, Alcuin Club Collections 47 (London: SPCK, 1965). It was in the thirteenth and fourteenth centuries that these changes became encoded in the church's legislation. Before this date, the legislation attempted to reserve baptism for the ancient feasts (probably with growing lack of success); after this date they insisted on baptism as soon as possible after birth.

57. BCP 1549, page 280: the restoration of the discipline of public penance "is muche to bee wyshed."

58. These include the feasts of the Circumcision, the Presentation, and the Annunciation.

59. BCP 1549, page 236.

60. BCP 1549, page 236.

61. Letter 16 in volume 12 of *A Select Library of Nicene and Post-Nicene Fathers*, second series (New York, 1895), pages 26–30.

62. Monumenta Germaniae Historica, Legum sectio II, Concilia, Tom. II, *Concilia aevi karolini I*, Albert Werminghoff, editor (Hanover and Leipzig, 1906), item 20, pages 172–176, as cited by H. Boone Porter, *The Day of Light*, page 71.

63. BCP 1549. page 236.

64. This requirement dates from 1552. The rubric is found in the BCP 1552, page 392.

65. Marion Hatchett, *Commentary on the American Prayer Book*, page 262.

66. In 1662 an invocation of the Spirit was reincorporated into this prayer, transforming it into a consecration of the water.

67. Marion Hatchett, *Commentary on the American Book of Common Prayer*, page 264. He argues at length for this interpretation in his unpublished 1967 S.T.M. thesis for General Seminary, "Thomas Cranmer and the Rites of Christian Initiation."

68. In the BCP 1928 the ember days were listed under the "table of fasts" and the rogation days as "days of solemn supplication" (page li), with notes about when ember and rogation days fell in relation to the moveable feasts. In the BCP 1979 both ember and rogation days are listed under the heading "Days of Optional Observance." Ember days are no longer fast days. Both ember days and rogation days are *optional* observances on the traditional days, to which the notes on page 18 make reference, but the rubrics with the collects for their propers (Various Occasions 15 on pages 205 and 256 and Various Occasions 19 on pages 207 and 258) designate them for observance "for use on the traditional days or at other times."

69. BCP 1979, page 265 (Ash Wednesday exhortation).

70. BCP 1979, pages 450–451 (portions of the confession and dismissal from Form 2 of the rite).

71. *The Proper for the Lesser Feasts and Fasts together with The Fixed Holy Days*, fourth edition (NY: Church Hymnal Corporation, 1988), page 56.

72. BCP 1979, page 860 (the catechism).

CHAPTER THREE

Conclusion

The Temporal Refractions of the Mystery of Christ

Christic as the Mysterium Salutis

For Christians, Christ is the mystery of salvation, the *mysterium salutis*. The religions of personal salvation in late antiquity were commonly known as "the mysteries." But this is not where we should begin in our exploration of what Christians mean when they speak of Christ as the mystery of salvation.[1] To understand what this expression means, we need to begin with the Book of Daniel in the Old Testament. In Daniel 2:27 and 47 God is described as the "revealer of mysteries." The key words here are "reveal" (Greek ἀποκαλύπτειν) and "mysteries" (Aramaic *raze*, Greek μυστηρια). The mysteries here are the *hidden purposes of God*, which God *reveals* to the prophet. We find this concept picked up in the New Testament in the Pauline (and deutero-Pauline) literature. Here Christ is understood as the *embodiment, realization, and manifestation* of the saving purposes of God revealed to the prophetic insight of the church but hidden from a world estranged from God. Thus we read in 1 Timothy 3:16:

> Great indeed is the mystery of our religion (το της ευσεβειας μυστηριον, *pietatis sacramentum*):
>
> He was manifested in the flesh,
> vindicated in the Spirit,
>   seen by angels,
> preached among the nations,
> believed on in the world,
> taken up in glory.

Here Christ is the "mystery of our religion." It is Colossians and Ephesians which develop this line of thought most fully, however. There Christ *is* the mystery of salvation in whom God's saving purposes are "summed up" or "recapitulated" and "fulfilled" (ἀνακεφαλαιωσθαι: Ephesians 1:10) and the world is "reconciled" to God (ἀποκαταλλαξαι: Colossians 1:20). This is the wisdom which is the mystery of God's will, which "he has made known to us . . . according to his good pleasure that he set forth in Christ, as a plan for the fullness of time, to gather up all things in him, things in heaven and on earth" (Ephesians 1:8). Colossians 1:26 describes it as "the mystery that has been hidden throughout the ages and generations but has now been revealed to [God's] saints."

This is where classic patristic literature starts when it speaks of Christ as the "mystery of salvation." In that literature "mystery" acquires a broad range of meanings. It is a starting point for the sacramental theology of the period, for in Latin *sacramentum* was used as an equivalent of the Greek μυστηριον (which was also employed frequently in the Latinized form *mysterium*: *sacramentum* and *mysterium* are treated as interchangeable synonyms in patristic Latin). It is Pope Leo the Great (ca. 400–461) who most fully develops this line of thought in the Latin church in a theology which speaks even today to the liturgical life of the church.

Leo is a towering figure in Christian antiquity. As the structures of civil authority were collapsing before barbarian invaders in the twilight of the Roman empire in the West, Leo's courage and administrative ability assured the survival of the church as a stable refuge in a chaotic world and as a guardian of the heritage of Latin civilization. His theological acumen is evident in what we know as the *Tome of Leo*, a letter which set out the language which formed the basis for the definition of the union of the divine and human natures in Christ adopted by the Council of Chalcedon in 451. The collection of his homilies for the feasts and fasts of the liturgical year testify to his eloquence as a preacher. Some of the formularies in what is often known as the Leonine sacramentary may be his compositions, though this collection of texts, compiled at a later time, is the work of many hands. His surviving letters witness to how widely he made his influence felt in his day. The homilies and letters of Leo articulate a theology of Christ as the mystery or sacrament of our salvation which provides the starting point for a far more adequate theology of the sacraments than the mediaeval version of that theology which we have inherited. The theology as Leo articulates it is better described as a liturgical theology than as a sacramental theology, for it encompassed the whole of Christian worship, not just that particular category of rites for which later ages reserved the name "sacrament."

In Leo's time, both *mysterium* and *sacramentum* have a far broader range of meanings than they would have in later times. Maria Bernhard de Soos, in his careful study of the terminology employed by Leo in his homilies and letters, gives the following range of meanings for the terms *mysterium* and *sacramentum* in Leo's writings:

> *a.* reality hidden under another, secret, mystery (aspect of obscurity); *b.* mysterious truth, mystery of faith, body of doctrine, faith, religion; *c.* reality signified by another, figure, symbol, type; *d.* mystery of salvation, source of grace, secret instrument (aspect of efficacity), device; *e.* hidden plan, mysterious design, divine economy, sacred work, work of salvation; *f.* historical mystery, detail of the particular works of Christ which realize the plan of salvation; *g.* liturgical mystery, feast, celebration of the historical mysteries; *h.* cultic mysteries[2]

This list gives us a good sense of the broad range of what was understood to be sacramental in the patristic era.

When the the early church spoke of Christ as the "mystery of salvation," the reference could be Christological (to his person) or soteriological (to his work). Further, when the reference was soteriological, the mystery could be viewed either from the perspective of the initiation of Christ's work (as the mystery of the incarnation) or from the perspective of its consummation (as the paschal mystery). The terms "mystery of the incarnation" and "paschal mystery" could also refer to the whole economy of salvation in Christ, as well as to the particular saving acts which we now think of as the incarnation and the *pascha*. We find all of these usages in the works of Leo. He often works from the perspective of the incarnation. His tome testifies to the importance of that doctrine to him. It is the perspective of the paschal mystery, however, which holds pride of place for him. In his sermons, he can speak of "the paschal feast, in which all the *sacramenta* of our religion meet together (*concurrent*)" and of "the season, when all the *sacramenta* of the divine mercy meet together."[3] In the celebration of Easter, the church encounters Christ in the fulness of his saving work.

Day, Week, and Year as Refractions of the Mysterium Salutis

The temporal cycles of Christian worship as an architecture of time are best understood as media through which the mystery of Christ is *refracted*. In *Liturgy for Living* , Charles Price and Louis Weil write:

> Time has a crystalline character. Crystals are a mineral formation which have a unique character. No matter how small or how large the crystal, it always has the same shape, the same number of facets. We are coming to a similar understanding of time itself, as a result of our experience of Christian worship. Every time is a time to observe, celebrate, and participate in the great mystery of Christ.[4]

The mystery of Christ is the paschal mystery. Christ's *pascha* is refracted by what we have called the nodal points of each cycle: in the course of the day, sunrise and sunset refract the dazzling brightness of the risen Christ as the Light of the World; in the course of the week, the Lord's Day refracts the compelling presence of the risen Christ as the Lord of Time; in the annual cycle, Easter refracts the saving power of the risen Lord as our *pascha*, our Passover.

These are the primary refractions of the mystery of Christ in the temporal cycles of the church's worship. In each cycle the paschal mystery was soon further refracted into its most important aspects, the cross and the resurrection, and each aspect acquired separate commemoration. In the year the paschal fast (which developed into Holy Week and then into Lent) is the counterpart of Friday as the weekly fast, and each came to be understood as a commemoration of the cross. Similarly, the paschal feast (the fifty days of Pentecost which we now customarily call Easter Season) is the counterpart of the Lord's Day, and each came to be understood as a commemoration of the resurrection. Even the day, which opens with the celebration of the risen Christ as the sun rises, eventually developed the hours of the passion to commemorate the various events on Christ's way of the cross. Here the paschal focus has been retained, but as the celebrations become more strongly commemorative, their unitive character begins to be lost.

The original architecture of the church's liturgy was entirely paschal in its focus, and at first it remained so as the liturgy began to take on more historicized form. But in the process of refraction Christians began to speak of the *mysteries* of Christ as well as the *mystery* of Christ. The *mystery* of Christ is the whole economy; the *mysteries* of Christ are the acts by which Christ achieves our salvation within this economy. Pope Leo can speak of the *sacramenta* or *mysteria* of Christ's nativity, epiphany, transfiguration, cross, resurrection, and ascension in his sermons.[5] "In all [Christ's] actions mysteries of sacraments shone forth (*sacramentorum mysteria coruscasse*)," he wrote to the bishops of Sicily.[6] As the emphasis shifted from the mystery of Christ to the mysteries of Christ, the church's architecture of time underwent considerable change.

CONCLUSION

One refraction of the mystery eventually became so significant that it acquired an independent status of its own. We have already noted that the *pascha* originally was understood to encompass the incarnation of Christ as well as his death and resurrection. The increasingly sophisticated Christology of the church in its struggle with heresy, however, moved from thinking of the birth of Christ as the moment of the incarnation and celebrating that birth on the day of his death, in Jewish fashion, to thinking of the conception as the moment of his incarnation. So the pascha came to be understood as the day of his conception, not of his birth. The old fixed dates for the pascha (March 25 and April 6) remained the days when the church celebrated Christ's incarnation—that is, his conception, whose feast is the Annunciation to Mary—even after the church had reached consensus on making the *pascha* a moveable feast.

Once this shift from locating the moment of the incarnation at the birth of Christ to locating it as his conception had occurred, it was simply a matter of time until Christ's nativity would receive its own commemoration nine months later in the course of the year—our feast of Christmas and Epiphany. The prehistory of these feasts is obscure, but once they became part of the church's calendar they became the axis for another annual cycle of feasts (in Byzantine usage) or of seasons (in Western usage). With this development, the church's architecture of time had gained the contours which we know today. This was primarily refracted in the annual cycle. The mysteries of the incarnation were never refracted in the weekly cycle in any systematic way. In the West these mysteries were, however, refracted for a time in the commemorations of the daily cycle in the office which we know as the little hours of the blessed Virgin Mary.

The Liturgical Embodiment of the Mysterium Salutis

Leo the Great, as we saw, spoke of Christ as the mystery or the sacrament of salvation out of the conviction that in the person of Christ God's saving purposes take concrete, tangible form. He likewise spoke of deeds of Christ in which these saving purposes were worked out as mysteries or sacraments: they are the "mysteries of Christ" in an expression which we still use today. Christ is for him the *Ursakrament*, the primordial sacrament or mystery, to use a term coined to express this conviction in contemporary theological discourse. But with the ascension of Christ, the modality of this presence of God's saving purposes takes on another form.

Prophets such as Hosea used marriage, in which man and woman become one flesh, as a figure for the union of God with Israel as God's people. In Ephesians the same metaphor is picked up and marriage becomes a figure for the μυστηριον (*sacramentum* in Latin translations) of the union between Christ and his church (Ephesians 5:32). In the patristic era, the church came to be understood as a mystery and a sacrament on the basis of this text. Humanity itself is the sphere in which Christ's redemptive work is to have its fruition, and the church is the sphere in which that redemption is being realized even now. One of the Christmas collects found in the so-called Veronese Sacramentary (no. 1239) illustrates the way in which Christ and the church are sacramentally linked by Christ's assumption of our humanity:

222   CONCLUSION

O God, who wonderfully created, and yet more wonderfully restored, the dignity of human nature (*humanae substantiae*): Grant that we may share the divine life (*divinitatis*) of him who humbled himself to share our humanity, your Son Jesus Christ. . . .[7]

And as the language of mystery and sacrament can encompass both the person of Christ and the work of Christ, so it can encompass both the church and its redemptive actions. This is what is meant when the church is spoken of as the sacrament of Christ. In the words of Edward Schillebeeckx,[8] "The earthly church is the visible realization" of the saving purposes of God in history. As Christ is the sacrament of God, so the church is the sacrament of Christ.

This broad perspective on what is meant by the church as sacrament finds articulation in a collect which is found in the Gelasian Sacramentary (no. 432) for the Easter vigil:

O God of unchangeable power and eternal light: Look favorably on your whole Church, that wonderful and sacred mystery (*sacramentum*); by the effectual working of your providence, carry out in tranquillity the plan of salvation (*opus salutis humanae*); let the whole world see and know that things which were cast down are being raised up, and things which had grown old are being made new, and that all things are being brought to their perfection by him through whom all things were made, your Son Jesus Christ our Lord.[9]

This ancient prayer sums up the theme of the sacramentality of the church and its rites. It is to those rites that we now turn.

We said earlier that with the ascension the modality of the presence of God's saving purposes in human history takes another form. God's saving purposes are now present (however imperfectly) in the church. The transition from the sacramental sphere of Christ as the *mysterium salutis* to that of the Church takes place when the words "mystery" and "sacrament" are used for the annual feasts which celebrate the mysteries of Christ. Here Leo's teaching represents a shift from that of Augustine, as we saw in the last chapter. For Augustine the feasts of *pascha* and Pentecost are *sacramenta* because they celebrate redemptive events in the life of Christ which we can appropriate by faith as we pass over with him from death to life and receive the gift of the Spirit, whereas feasts like Christmas are only *memoriae* because we cannot appropriate Christ's birth as our own. For Leo, as we have seen, all feasts which celebrate the *mysteria* or *sacramenta* of Christ's life have a sacramental character, for in the liturgical celebration of these mysteries we can enter into them in such a way that "what is done in the limbs coincides with what is done in the head himself."[10]

In this way the church came to designate as *sacramenta* or *mysteria* not only the feast days but the rites proper to them (the liturgy of the word, the eucharistic feast, and—on Easter and Pentecost in the West, and also at times on Christmas, Epiphany, and Lazarus Saturday in the East—baptism).[11] Leo links rites tightly to the days to which he considers them appropriate. In a letter to the bishops of Sicily, for example, he decries the Eastern custom there in force of baptizing on Epiphany as well as at Easter and Pentecost: his paschal interpretation of baptism leads him to insist that it should be restricted to Easter and Pentecost except in cases of necessity.[12] In the East, where the theology of baptism as consecration to the royal priesthood forfeited by Adam but fulfilled in Christ was prevalent (and in the Syrian Church predominant), Epiphany as the feast of Christ's baptism seemed entirely appropriate as a day for the administration of baptism.[13] The key here is the relation of particular rites to particular feasts which celebrate particular mysteries of Christ. In terms of baptism, this relation began to

224

be attenuated once parents were urged to present their children for baptism as soon as possible after birth—something which happened as early as the time of Cyprian in North Africa.

Eventually the term *sacramentum* or *mysterium* was extended to any rite of the church which was thought to have transformative significance. In the West, Leo could, in a letter to bishops in Africa, speak of ordination as a *sacramentum*.[14] Augustine apparently speaks of the rites by which catechumens were admitted as a *sacramentum*.[15] In the East, a theological tradition which goes at least as far back as Pseudo-Dionysius lists the rites of monastic profession among the sacraments of the church.[16] In other words, neither the Roman Catholic distinction between a sacrament and a sacramental nor the Reformation distinction between sacraments of the gospel and other sacramental rites holds for this period. In fact, neither the Latin sacramentaries nor the Greek *euchologia* make distinctions between sacramental and non-sacramental rites: this is a distinction imposed on the actual rites, not implicit in them.

From this perspective, the liturgical rites of the church, its "regular services" in the language of the *Book of Common Prayer*, are "sacramental" refractions of the mystery of Christ appropriate to the nodal points of each of the cycles in the church's rule of prayer, its architecture of time. This is most clearly visible in the eucharist as the characteristic rite for the Lord's Day and baptism as the characteristic rite for Easter (and other baptismal feasts). It is also implicit in the celebration of light at sunrise and sunset in the daily cycle.[17] The theology of the daily office has historically received the least systematic treatment of the regular services of the church in the West, however, because the office was understood more and more as a matter of monastic and clerical obligation rather than as an integral part of the church's corporate worship. Nevertheless, the theological foundations for a sacramental theology of daily worship are laid in Leo's thought, and developing such a theology is an important task if this part of the church's worship is to regain its rightful place in the church's life.

In the era of Leo, then, there was no real distinction between sacramental theology and liturgical theology. The life and worship of the church and of the Christian was "sacramental" to Leo because it flowed out of Christ as the *mysterium salutis* and out of his redemptive acts as *mysteria* or *sacramenta*. Leo grounded the church's life in the mystery of the incarnation, but he gave pride of place to the paschal mystery in which the incarnation reached its goal. The liturgical context of the sacraments and the theological link to the place where they fit in the church's architecture of time received careful attention in his works.

Linguistic usage soon shifted, however, and *sacramenta* came to be reserved for certain rites as "means of grace," while *mysterium* came to be used for the rest of the spectrum of the meanings which these two words had in Leo's vocabulary. When this happened, the links between the *sacramenta* of the church and the *mysteria* of Christ became more tenuous, faded from the church's consciousness, and no longer received adequate theological articulation. The church's "sacraments" began to be understood apart from their liturgical context. Much of the language of later sacramental theology seems to have been forged in North African controversies—with Novatians, Donatists, and Pelagians in particular. In these controversies the church became concerned with what constitutes a "valid" and "efficacious" sacrament and developed the categories of institution, form, matter, minister, and intention with which later Western sacramental theology worked. Sacramental theology thus developed a pronounced legal and juridical character and often lost touch with the actual liturgical context of the rites. It strove for precise definition. Sacraments came to be

226

understood as "certain sure witnesses, and effectual signs of grace, and God's good will towards us, by the which he doth work invisibly in us, and doth not only quicken, but also strengthen and confirm our Faith in him."[18] The concern for precise definition led to a narrowing of which rites were accounted sacramental; Peter Lombard's list of seven, accepted by Thomas Aquinas, prevailed in the West during the Middle Ages. At the Reformation, precision about which rites were "ordained of Christ our Lord in the Gospel"[19] led churches of the Reformation to narrow the list further to two (Baptism and the Eucharist) or three (Luther was ambiguous about Reconciliation), or to distinguish between sacraments of the gospel and "other sacramental rites."[20] Careful theologians did not forget the relation of the sacraments to the paschal mystery: Thomas Aquinas, for example, grounds the sacraments in Christ's Passion or his death.[21] Nevertheless, the tight link between the mystery of Christ, the appropriate day for the celebration of that mystery, and the rites by which that mystery is realized in our life and the life of the church was lost, and the actual liturgical rite with its text and ceremonial context played an increasingly smaller part in the formulation of definitions.

Thoughtful liturgical scholars and theologians in recent decades have come to regret this "overdefinition" and its consequences in the way the church understands its worship. In a strong critique of these developments, Louis Bouyer writes:

> What is called the "institution of sacraments," when conceived too narrowly, includes in its definition the seeds of their destruction. . . . The Fathers did not in the least imagine that the rite of eating or of washing was a profane action, bare of any religious significance before Christ's intervention, but upon which He bestowed a particular meaning by a purely arbitrary decision. . . . The words of institution simply gave a new meaning to rites already

charged with meaning. And the new meaning was not forced upon the natural meaning but rather amplified and enriched it. . . .

. . . Rituals are never artificial compositions, the work of theologians who first think in the abstract and then try to the best of their ability to make their creations accessible to a common herd that is little accustomed to their lofty speculations. Quite the contrary, it is everywhere evident that the rites are first and the theological constructions so subordinate to them that they regularly flow from them.[22]

The close study of early Christian authors, such as that done by Dom Odo Casel, Louis Bouyer, Jean Daniélou, Maria Bernhard de Soos, Germain Hudon, and many others, has helped the West to recover the sacramental perspective of the early church in recent decades. Such careful work, which shows the integration of theology, liturgy, and ethics in early Christian thought, safeguards liturgical scholarship against the danger of isolation from a broad concern with the life of the church and against a lapse into mere historicism or aestheticism. It also allows us to discover once again in the church's rule of prayer and the regular services of the church something of the authentic lineaments of the liturgy as an architecture of time.

The Liturgical Shaping of our Lives

Christians are those who have been captivated by the compelling love of God which has taken flesh and blood in Jesus Christ. Drawn irresistibly by that love into relationship with God, they seek to let that relationship shape their lives. Liturgy as a rule of prayer which is worked out as an architecture of time is a framework designed to let the rhythms of time shape our lives through our encounter with the crucified and risen Christ who is the mystery of our salvation. In this way the mystery is woven into the very texture of what we might call, following Ludwig Wittgenstein, the Christian *Lebensform* or form of life.

In the Christian life, the rule of faith, the rule of right living, and the rule of prayer are inextricably related and are but different articulations of one rule, for they have one norm. And that norm, we should note, is inscribed not on a page but in a life. The authentic Word of God is embodied not in printer's ink but in human flesh. The authoritative witness to Christ is likewise embodied not in printer's ink but in the lives of the faithful who walk with him the way of the cross. Doctrinal truth, liturgical truth, and ethical truth are to be sought not so much in words as in embodied patterns of actions inseparably linked with words. Sunday observance and the Sunday eucharist, for example, are liturgical actions which are earlier witnesses to the central truth of the cross and resurrection of Jesus Christ than the written text of the letters of Paul and the canonical gospels. There was a time when the apostolic church had no canonical scriptures of its own; there was never a time when the apostolic church did not bear witness to Christ by the observance of the Lord's Day and the Lord's Supper. Even the pattern of Christian doctrine is in its definitive form only the verbal echo of the lived reality of the relationship with the triune God into which we enter through baptism. The appropriate response to the story of Jesus is baptism in the name of the Father and of the Son and of the Holy Spirit—which does not merely mean being baptized in water while these words are recited, but rather being plunged into the death of Jesus that we may emerge as those who dare to address God as Father because we have been made God's sons and daughters by adoption and

The Temporal Refractions   229

grace, being conformed to the likeness of the Son in his death and resurrection, and being sealed with the Spirit as God's own for ever. The confession of our faith which we know as the creed was not devised as a doctrinal statement but as a liturgical formula, which articulates the relationship into which we have entered through baptism. The pattern of Christian doctrine is nothing more than the explication of the meaning of the pattern of that relationship. We are also coming to understand the pattern of Christian ethics from a similar perspective: ethical formation does not consist of learning some process of ethical reflection or of committing to memory some ethical code, but of conformity to Christ in his crucifixion and resurrection—that is, in the formation of Christian character so that the pattern of our lives is conformed to the pattern of Christ's life. Liturgy forms us as Christians. The Word of the church's doctrine and the Word of the church's worship and the Word of the the church's ethics are one Word, who was made flesh and died and was raised from the dead by the mighty hand of God—"Christ in you, the hope of glory."

The ultimate touchstone of Christian faith and practice for all who bear the name of Christ by virtue of their baptism is the cross of Christ. All of us must in the end make our own the words of Paul, who determined to know nothing among the Christians of Corinth "save Christ Jesus, and him crucified." It is to him and to his *pascha* by the way of the cross that the church's architecture of time bears such persuasive witness. The embodiment of that theology in the church's worship, our rule of prayer, is the most effective means God has given us to keep our rule of faith and our rule of right living true to him who is the way, the truth, and the life, so that we may pass over with him into God's kingdom, where God has stored up for us such good things as pass human understanding.

Notes to the Conclusion

1. This *was*, however, the place where the recovery of the theology of Christ as the *mysterium salutis* began. Dom Odo Casel, the pioneer in this recovery, started from the meaning of musthrion in the Greek mysteries. See his work, *The Mystery of Christian Worship and Other Writings* (Westminster, MD: Newman, 1962), page 56. Most of Casel's critics argue that the church did not "borrow" the language of these cults in any extensive way until the fourth century, and that the real roots of Christian liturgy are in Jewish practice. Jungmann concludes in *The Early Liturgy to the Time of Gregory the Great*, trans. Francis A. Brunner, (Notre Dame, IN: University of Notre Dame Press, 1959), page 159, "It was not until . . . about the fourth century . . . that there can be any question of an influx into the liturgy of customs and institutions connected with the ancient mysteries . . . " A careful treatment of the complex history of the understanding of worship as the mystery of salvation is found in the article of Irénée Henri Dalmais, "Theology of Liturgical Celebration," in Aimé Georges Martimort, editor, *The Church at Prayer*, volume 1, *Principles of the Liturgy*, pages 227–280, here pages 253–272.

2. Maria Bernhard de Soos, *Le mystère liturgique d'après Saint Léon le grand* (Münster Westfallen: Aschendorffsche Verlagsbuchhandlung, 1958), Liturgie wissenschaftliche Quellen und Forschungen 34, page 143 (my translation). This is the list of meanings for *sacramentum*. The list for *mysterium* has the same items, although there is a slight variation in the definitions for individual items. It does not, however, appear that de Soos intended to distinguish between the items on the two lists. The treatment of the two terms in Leo which follows is based on de Soos and on Germain Hudon, *La perfection chrétienne d'après St. Léon le grand* (Paris: Éditions du Cerf, 1958), Lex Orandi 26.

3. Sermons 46:1 and 49:4 in the Migne edition (PL 54:292, 303).

4. Charles Price and Louis Weil, *Liturgy for Living* (Minneapolis: Seabury Press, 1979), The Church's Teaching Series, pages 220–221.

5. See Hudon, *La perfection chrétienne d'après St. Léon le grand*, pages 152–154.

6. Letter 16:2 (PL 54:697–698).

7. The Latin text is found in *Sacramentarium Veronese*, ed. Leo Cunibert Mohlberg (Rome: Casa Herder, 1956), Rerum Ecclesiasticarum Documenta: Series Maior: Fontes I, page 157. Some of the *libelli* which make up this so-called sacramentary may go back to the time of Leo, but attribution of any text is a matter of guess-work based on style and vocabulary. The translation here is from the BCP 1979, where it is used for the second Sunday after Christmas and also with the lesson from Genesis 1 at the vigil of Easter.

8. E. Schillebeeckx, *Christ, the Sacrament of the Encounter with God* (NY: Sheed and Ward, 1963), page 47. As he develops the theme, Christ is the sacrament of God and the church is the sacrament of the risen Christ.

9. The Latin text is found in *Liber Sacramentorum Romanae Aeclesiae Ordinis Anni Circuli*, ed. Leo Cunibert Mohlberg, (Rome: Casa Editrice Herder, 1960), Rerum Ecclesiasticarum Documenta: Series Maior: Fontes IV, page 70.. The translation here is from the BCP 1979, where it is used at the vigil of Easter, in the solemn intercessions of the Good Friday liturgy, and in the rites of ordination.

10. Letter 16:3: (PL 54:698).

11. The days in the Byzantine rite are those on which the baptismal *troparion*, "As many as have been baptized into Christ," replaces the *trisagion* for the first entrance at the eucharist. It would seem that this *troparion* was used whenever this procession originated in the baptistry. It was also used during the Easter octave because of special observances in the baptistry during this period. See Juan Mateos, *La célébration de la parole dans la rite byzantine: Étude historique* (Rome: Pont. Institutum Studiorum Orientalium, 1971), Orientalia Christiana Analecta 191, page 125. Despite the use of the baptismal *troparion* at Christmas, however, we have no other textual evidence that baptisms were ever administered at Christmas in the Byzantine rite.

12. Letter 16:1–4 (PL 54:696–700).

13. Syrian baptismal themes receive careful treatment in Sebastian Brock, *The Holy Spirit in the Syrian Baptismal Tradition.*

14. Letter 12 (PL 54:645–656). See especially chapter 2 (PL 54:647–649). Here the word *sacramentum* still has some sense of a rite appropriate to a certain time (the Lord's Day), because ordination is a tangible expression of the mystery which is proper to the Lord's Day.

15. *De catechizandis rudibus*, chapter 26, section 50 (PL 40:344–345). From the sense of the passage, this would seem to hold true even if one does not accept the editor's emendation of *sacramentum salis* for *sacramentum sane*.

16. See Colm Luibheid, trans. (with foreword, notes and translation collaboration by Paul Rorem), *Pseudo-Dionysius: The Complete Works* (NY: Paulist Press, 1987), Classics of Western Spirituality, text and notes on pages 243–247, 269–280. On the two monastic professions as sacraments, see also A Monk of the Eastern Church [Lev Gillet], *Orthodox Spirituality: An Outline of the Orthodox Ascetical and Mystical Tradition*, second edition (Crestwood, NY: St. Vladimir's Seminary Press, 1978), pages 37–38, 47.

17. Cyprian actually calls the hours of prayer "sacraments" in his treatise *On the Lord's Prayer*. When he speaks of the "times and the sacraments" in chapter 35 (which deals with prayer at sunrise and sunset and the meaning of prayer at those times), what he seems to mean is "rites which manifest the meaning of these times."

18. Article 25, BCP 1979, page 872. This Anglican definition represents a fair precis of the Catholic tradition of the West, which obtains for Anglicans and Lutherans as well as for Roman Catholics. The Reformed emphasis differs, however; Reformed Christians have been less willing to speak of "effectual" signs.

19. Article 25, BCP 1979, page 872.

20. A distinction often read into Article 25 (which speaks of "those five commonly called sacraments") and made part of the Catechism of the BCP 1979, pages 860–861.

21. Cf. *Summa Contra Gentiles* IV:56,1 (St. Thomas Aquinas, *On the Truth of the Catholic Faith: Summa Contra Gentiles*, trans. Charles J. O'Neil, *Book 4: Salvation* [Garden City, NY: Image Books, 1957], pages 246–247): "Since, however (as has already been said), the death of Christ is, so to say, the universal cause of salvation, and since a universal cause must be applied singly to each of its effects, it was necessary to show men some remedies through which the benefits of Christ's death could somehow be conjoined to them. It is of this sort, of course, that the sacraments are said to be."

22. Louis Bouyer, *Rite and Man: Natural Sacredness and Christian Liturgy*, translated by M. Joseph Costelloe (Notre Dame, IN: University of Notre Dame Press,1963), pages 64–65.

The Temporal Refractions 233

For Further Reading

There is a vast literature on the issues explored in this study. The works listed below are simply meant as a starting place—a representative sample of the most important works on some of the major topics. Other literature is cited in the endnotes.

Introduction

A good introduction to the concept of Jewish liturgy as an "architecture of time" is found in Abraham Joseph Heschel, *The Sabbath: Its Meaning for Modern Man* (New York: Ferrar, Straus, and Giroux, 1975). Alexander Schmemann develops the idea in a Christian context in *Introduction to Liturgical Theology*, third edition (Crestwood, NY: St. Vladimir's Seminary Press, 1986), though this work is not easy reading. I know of no published work which treats the church's rule of prayer and the regular services of the church in quite the way that I have done here. In recent literature there is frequent talk of the Benedictine origins of the Anglican rule of prayer. Benedictine spirituality did indeed serve as the mediator of this rule of prayer, but Benedict's own rule of prayer is, in fact, simply a monastic form of the early church's rule. My own ideas were developed in my 1991 doctoral dissertation for the graduate faculty of religion at Duke, "An Architecture of Time: A Critical Study of Alexander Schmemann's Liturgical Theology." I have adapted some portions of that dissertation for this present work. Basic patristic texts related to the temporal framework of the liturgy can be found in translation in Thomas K. Carroll and Thomas Halton, editors. *Liturgical Practice of the Fathers*, Message of the Fathers of the Church 21 (Wilmington, DE: Michael Glazier, 1988).Probably the best handbook on the liturgy now available in English is Aimé Georges Martimort, editor, *The Church at Prayer: An Introduction to the Liturgy*, 4 volumes, new edition (Collegeville, MN: Liturgical Press, 1985–1987). A convenient edition of the texts of the first two Books of Common Prayer is found in *The First and Second Prayer Books of Edward VI*, Introduction by E. C. S. Gibson (New York: E. P. Dutton & Sons, 1910). The rites of the American prayer books may be conveniently studied in Paul V. Marshall, *Prayer Book Parallels: The public services of the Church arranged for comparative study* (New York: Church Hymnal, 1990). For an analysis of the *Book of Common Prayer 1979* the reader should consult Marion J. Hatchett, *Commentary on the American Prayer Book* (New York: Seabury Press, 1980).

Redeeming the Day

The understanding of daily worship developed in this chapter is very recent, and most of the early literature was published in French and German. The most important works in English are Robert Taft, *The Liturgy of the Hours in East and West: The Origins of the Office and Its Meaning for Today*

(Collegeville, MN: Liturgical Press, 1985), and Paul F. Bradshaw, *Daily Prayer in the Early Church* (NY: Oxford University Press, 1982). Much useful material is also found in Aimé
Georges Martimort, "The Liturgy of the Hours," in idem, *The
Church at Prayer*, volume 4, *The Liturgy and Time*, new edition, translated by Matthew J. O'Connell (Collegeville, MN:
Liturgical Press, 1985), pages 151–275. George Guiver, *Company of Voices* (NY: Pueblo, 1988) is a very readable history of
the discipline of daily prayer in the church, with much useful
information. This is a relatively recent field of research, and the
reader should be informed that most reconstructions of early
forms of daily worship are hypothetical. Outlines for the office
in various rites which are found in the works cited (and in this
study) often synthesize data from various periods of history.

Redeeming the Week

The most accessible work on Sunday and the week is H.
Boone Porter, *The Day of Light: The Biblical and Liturgical
Meaning of Sunday* (Greenwich, CT: Seabury Press, 1960;
reprint, Washington, DC: Pastoral Press, 1988). The classic
work on the eucharist in this century is Dom Gregory Dix, *The
Shape of the Liturgy*, Seabury edition with Additional Notes by
Paul V. Marshall (New York: Seabury Press, 1982). However
mistaken he was about many details, Dix was right about the
basic shape of the rite, and all revisions of the rite in recent
decades are indebted to his insight. A good discussion of the
current state of the question is found in the last two articles in
Robert Taft, *Beyond East and West: Problems in Liturgical
Understanding* (Washington, DC: Pastoral Press, 1986). A
good source for basic early texts is Lucien Deiss, *Springtime of
the Liturgy: Liturgical Texts of the First Four Centuries* translated by Matthew J. O'Connell (Collegeville, MN: Liturgical

Press, 1979). I have treated the history of the eucharist in Anglicanism at some length in *Eucharistic Celebration 1789–1979* (New York: Church Hymnal, 1988). In my understanding of the theology of the eucharist, I am deeply indebted to two works of Alexander Schmemann, *For the Life of the World: Sacraments and Orthodoxy*, revised edition (Crestwood, NY: St. Vladimir's Seminary Press, 1973), and *The Eucharist: Sacrament of the Kingdom* (Crestwood, NY: St. Vladimir's Seminary Press: 1988). A brief but very capable survey of eucharistic theology can be found in William R. Crockett, *Eucharist: Symbol of Transformation* (NY: Pueblo, 1989).

Redeeming the Year

Thomas Talley, *The Origins of the Liturgical Year* (New York: Pueblo, 1986), is in many ways a revolutionary study of the church's calendar and has redefined many of the questions for us. The older perspective on the questions is reflected in P. Jounel, "The Year, in A. G. Martimort, *The Church at Prayer*, volume 4, *The Liturgy and Time*, pages 31–150. Basic texts of the baptismal liturgy are found in E. C. Whitaker, *Documents of the Baptismal Liturgy*, second edition (Alcuin Club Collections. London: SPCK, 1970). Baptism in the Byzantine rite receives thoughtful treatment in Alexander Schmemann, *Of Water and the Holy Spirit: A Liturgical Study of Baptism*, revised edition (Crestwood, NY: St. Vladimir's Seminary Press, 1974); he treats its setting in the Lenten liturgy in *Great Lent: Journey to the Pascha*, (Crestwood, NY: St. Vladimir's Seminary Press, 1973). The Easter vigil in the Byzantine rite receives careful treatment in Gabriel Bertonière, *The Historical Development of the Easter Vigil and Related Services in the Greek Church*, Orientalia Christiana Analecta 193, (Rome: Pont. Institutum Studiorum Orientalium, 1972).

For the baptismal liturgy in the West, see Aidan Kavanagh, *The Shape of Baptism: The Rite of Christian Initiation*, Studies in the Reformed Rites of the Catholic Church 1 (New York: Pueblo, 1978), and R. Cabié, "Christian Initiation," in Aimé Georges Martimort, editor, *The Church at Prayer*, volume 3, *The Sacraments*, new edition, translated by Matthew J. O'Connell, pages 11–100. The classic mystagogic catecheses of the fourth century on which our understanding of baptism in this era is based can be found in Edward Yarnold, *The Awe-Inspiring Rites of Initiation: Baptismal Homilies of the Fourth Century* (Middlegreen, Slough, UK: St. Paul Publications, 1971). For an understanding of the rites in the *Book of Common Prayer 1979*, the reader should consult Daniel B. Stevick, *Baptismal Moments, Baptismal Meanings* (NY: Church Hymnal Corporation, 1987). Preliminary studies of the current restoration of the catechumenate and parallel rites in the Episcopal Church can be found in the collection of materials by the Department of Evangelism Ministries of the Episcopal Church, *The Catechumenal Process* (NY: Church Hymnal Corporation, 1991), but no adequate commentary on these rites is available.

The Temporal Refractions of the Mystery of Christ

Dom Odo Casel was the pioneer in the exploration of the theology of worship as the theology of the paschal mystery. His most accessible work in English is *The Mystery of Christian Worship and Other Writings* (Westminster, MD: Newman, 1962). In the judgment of later scholars, Casel assimilated the Christian understanding of mystery far too much to the understanding of mystery in the Greco-Roman cults. Louis Bouyer carefully sets out the biblical basis of a liturgical theology of the mystery of salvation in *Liturgical Piety* (Notre Dame, IN: University of Notre Dame Press, 1955). For a recent summary of the issues here, see the article of Irénée Henri Dalmais, "Theology of Liturgical Celebration," in Aimé George Martimort, editor, *The Church at Prayer*, volume 1, *Principles of the Liturgy*, pages 227–280. Edward Schillebeeckx gives the broader dimensions of sacramental theology careful treatment in *Christ the Sacrament of the Encounter with God* (New York: Sheed and Ward, 1963). The most careful study of the thought of Leo the Great, on which I draw extensively, is Maria Bernhard de Soos, *Le mystère liturgique d'après Saint Léon le grand*, Liturgiewissenschaftliche Quellen und Forschungen 34 (Münster, Westfallen: Aschendorffsche Verlagsbuchhandlung, 1958). There is, unfortunately, no similar treatment in English.

Peter E. Fink's article, s.v. "Sacramental Theology" in his *New Dictionary of Sacramental Worship* (Collegeville, MN: Liturgical Press, 1990), argues that the church has moved from scholastic sacramental theology to the sacramental theology of such modern theologians as Schillebeeckx and now beyond sacramental theology to liturgical theology. For him, the final movement recontextualizes the sacraments within the church's liturgy—which is the project which this present book has undertaken.

Index of Names

Note: anonymous works are listed under the name of the work.

Severus of Antioch, 105
Shepherd, Massey, 57
Solovey, Meletius Michael, 135
Stevenson, Kenneth, 136, 137, 209
Stevick, Daniel, 239
Symeon of Thessalonika, 176

Taft, Robert, 56, 57, 102, 133, 134, 236, 237
Talley, Thomas, 140, 143, 150, 153, 161, 184, 207–210, 212, 238
Tertullian, 13, 54, 55, 158, 175, 208, 209
Theodore of Mopsuestia, 86, 156, 159, 173ff.
Thomas Aquinas, 85, 106ff., 115, 136, 227, 233

von Allmen, Jean Jacques, 78, 134

Ware, Kallistos, 22
Watts, Isaac, 125
Weil, Louis, 219, 231
Wesley, Charles, 125
Whitaker, E.C., 209–211, 238
Winkler, Gabriele, 56, 57, 209, 210
Wittgenstein, Ludwig, 229

Yarnold, Edward, 209, 239

Zahany, Tzvee, 54
Zerfass, Rolf, 56
Zwingli, Huldreich, 115